Lecture Notes in Computer Science 2158

Edited by G. Goos, J. Hartmanis, and J. van Leeuwen

Springer
Berlin
Heidelberg
New York
Barcelona
Hong Kong
London
Milan
Paris
Tokyo

Doug Shepherd   Joe Finney
Laurent Mathy   Nicholas Race (Eds.)

Interactive Distributed Multimedia Systems

8th International Workshop, IDMS 2001
Lancaster, UK, September 4-7, 2001
Proceedings

Springer

Series Editors

Gerhard Goos, Karlsruhe University, Germany
Juris Hartmanis, Cornell University, NY, USA
Jan van Leeuwen, Utrecht University, The Netherlands

Volume Editors

Doug Shepherd
Joe Finney
Laurent Mathy
Nicholas Race
Lancaster University, Computing Department
Faculty of Applied Sciences
Lancaster LA1 4YR, UK
E-mail: d.shepherd@lancaster.ac.uk
{joe,laurent,race}@comp.lancs.ac.uk

Cataloging-in-Publication Data applied for

Die Deutsche Bibliothek - CIP-Einheitsaufnahme

Interactive distributed multimedia systems : 8th international workshop ;
proceedings / IDMS 2001, Lancaster, UK, September 4 - 7, 2001.
Doug Shepherd ... (ed.). - Berlin ; Heidelberg ; New York ; Barcelona ;
Hong Kong ; London ; Milan ; Paris ; Tokyo : Springer, 2001
   (Lecture notes in computer science ; Vol. 2158)
   ISBN 3-540-42530-6

CR Subject Classification (1998): H.5.1, C.2, H.4, H.5, H.3

ISSN 0302-9743
ISBN 3-540-42530-6 Springer-Verlag Berlin Heidelberg New York

Springer-Verlag Berlin Heidelberg New York
a member of BertelsmannSpringer Science+Business Media GmbH

http://www.springer.de

© Springer-Verlag Berlin Heidelberg 2001
Printed in Germany

Typesetting: Camera-ready by author, data conversion by Boller Mediendesign
Printed on acid-free paper   SPIN: 10840274   06/3142   5 4 3 2 1 0

Preface

We are very happy to present the proceedings of the 8th International Workshop on Interactive Distributed Multimedia Systems – IDMS 2001, in co-operation with ACM SIGCOMM and SIGMM. These proceedings contain the technical programme for IDMS 2001, held September 4–7, 2001 in Lancaster, UK.

For the technical programme this year we received 48 research papers from both academic and industrial institutions all around the world. After the review process, 15 were accepted as full papers for publication, and a further 8 as short positional papers, intended to provoke debate. The technical programme was complimented by three invited papers: "QoS for Multimedia – What's Going to Make It Pay?" by Derek McAuley, "Enabling the Internet to Provide Multimedia Services" by Markus Hofmann, and "MPEG-21 Standard: Why an Open Multimedia Framework?" by Fernando Pereira.

The organisers are very grateful for the help they received to make IDMS 2001 a successful event. In particular, we would like to thank the PC for their first class reviews of papers, particularly considering the tight reviewing deadlines this year. Also, we would like to acknowledge the support from Agilent, BTexact Technologies, Hewlett Packard, Microsoft Research, Orange, and Sony Electronics – without whom IDMS 2001 would not have been such a memorable event.

We hope that readers will find these proceedings helpful in their future research, and that IDMS will continue to be an active forum for the discussion of distributed multimedia research for years to come.

June 2001

D. Shepherd
J. Finney
L. Mathy
N. Race

Welcome from the Minister of State for Lifelong Learning and Higher Education

To the participants of the 8th International Workshop on Interactive Distributed Multimedia Systems:

I am delighted to welcome you all to the IDMS 2001 workshop in Lancaster, and indeed welcome many of you to the UK. We see throughout the world that conferences are being held to try to educate people in the area of distributed computing as it becomes an increasingly important part of the information society we live in. I am happy to see that the University of Lancaster are part of this drive by hosting this international conference.

I send you my best wishes for a successful workshop and hope that this opportunity to present interesting research results to a broad professional audience gives stimulus for collaboration and further progress in the field.

I wish all participants a pleasant stay in Lancaster.

Margaret Hodge
Minister of State for Lifelong Learning and Higher Education

Welcome to the Computing Department at Lancaster University

I'd like to extend a very warm welcome to all participants to IDMS 2001. We're particularly pleased that IDMS has come to Lancaster this year where the Distributed Multimedia Research Group has played such a prominent role in the distributed multimedia systems research community over the last 10 years.

As a rather envious outsider it has struck me how successful the distributed multimedia systems community has been in tapping the pool of research talent. In recent years at Lancaster, we have enjoyed a very strong flow of students through our Doctoral programme, from our own undergraduate programme and from elsewhere. In large measure, this has been due to the buzz generated by research in distributed multimedia systems and I'm sure this is reflected in other research and development centres.

However, we have seen this phenomenon before, where hot research areas soak up talent and resources. Thankfully, what distinguishes the distributed multimedia systems community is the coexistence of three key factors: it addresses a real economic and societal need; it has attracted the resources and backing needed to make it work; and, crucially, it is delivering. Computer Science needs challenging, high profile and successful areas like this to keep the discipline healthy.

I hope you have a great time at IDMS 2001.

Pete Sawyer
Head of Computing
Lancaster University

Organisation

Programme Chair

Doug Shepherd, Lancaster University, United Kingdom

Programme Committee

Arturo Azcorra, University Carlos III, Madrid, Spain
Gregor v. Bochmann, University of Ottawa, Canada
Jan Bormans, IMEC, Belgium
Berthold Butscher, GMD-FOKUS, Germany
Andrew Campbell, Columbia University, USA
Tim Chown, University of Southampton, United Kingdom
Luca Delgrossi, University of Piacenza, Italy
Michel Diaz, LAAS-CNRS, France
Jordi Domingo-Pascual, Politechnic University of Catalonia, Spain
Wolfgang Effelsberg, University of Mannheim, Germany
Frank Eliassen, University of Oslo, Norway
Serge Fdida, LiP6, France
Joe Finney, Lancaster University, United Kingdom
Vera Goebel, University of Oslo, Norway
Tobias Helbig, Philips Research Laboratories, Germany
David Hutchison, Lancaster University, United Kingdom
Winfried Kalfa, TU Chemnitz, Germany
Guy Leduc, University of Liege, Belgium
Laurent Mathy, Lancaster University, United Kingdom
Ketan Mayer-Patel, University of North Carolina, USA
Jason Nieh, Columbia University, USA
Philippe Owezarski, LAAS-CNRS, France
Fernando Pereira, Instituto Superior Tecnico, Portugal
Thomas Plagemann, University of Oslo, Norway
Timothy Roscoe, Sprint Labs, USA
Hans Scholten, University of Twente, The Netherlands
Patrick Senac, ENSICA, France
Marten van Sinderen, University of Twente, The Netherlands
Greg O'Shea, Microsoft Research Cambridge, United Kingdom
Ralf Steinmetz, TU Darmstadt/GMD, Germany
Fred Stentiford, BTexact Research, United Kingdom
Burkhard Stiller, ETH Zurich, Switzerland
Giorgio Ventre, University Federico II, Napoli, Italy
Lars Wolf, University of Karlsruhe, Germany

Local Organisation

Joe Finney, Lancaster University, United Kingdom
Nicholas Race, Lancaster University, United Kingdom
Laurent Mathy, Lancaster University, United Kingdom
Barbara Hickson, Lancaster University, United Kingdom
Stefan Schmid, Lancaster University, United Kingdom
Daniel Prince, Lancaster University, United Kingdom

Supporting and Sponsoring Organisations (Alphabetically)

ACM SIGCOMM
ACM SIGMM
Agilent
BTexact Technologies
Hewlett Packard
Microsoft Research
Orange
Sony Electronics

Table of Contents

Short Papers

Invited Presentation

Control of Multimedia Networks

QoS for Multimedia – What's Going to Make It Pay?

Derek McAuley

Marconi Research Centre, Cambridge, UK
Derek.Mcauley@marconi.com

Abstract. Delivering the form of QoS we see in the form of Service Level Agreements is a big deal for ISPs; however, this is a long way from the traditional multimedia view of per application instance QoS. Likewise many OS and middleware platforms take one of the two views on QoS: machines are getting faster so who cares, or, we have a real time scheduling class. Are we ever going to drive QoS into the mainstream?

D. Shepherd et al. (Eds.): IDMS 2001, LNCS 2158, pp. 1-1, 2001.
© Springer-Verlag Berlin Heidelberg 2001

New Resource Control Issues in Shared Clusters

Timothy Roscoe[1] and Prashant Shenoy[2]*

[1] Sprint Advanced Technology Labs, 1 Adrian Court, Burlingame, CA 94010, USA.
troscoe@sprintlabs.com
[2] Department of Computer Science, University of Massachusetts,
Amherst, MA 01003, USA.
shenoy@cs.umass.edu

Abstract. We claim that the renting of machine resources on clusters of servers introduces new systems challenges which are different from those hitherto encountered, either in multimedia systems or cluster-based computing. We characterize the requirements for such "public computing platforms" and discuss both how the scenario differs from more traditional multimedia resource control situations, and how some ideas from multimedia systems work can be reapplied in this new context. Finally, we discuss our ongoing work building a prototype public computing platform.

1 Introduction and Motivation

This paper argues that the growth of shared computing platforms poses new problems in the field of resource control that are not addressed by the current state of the art, and consequently there exist important unresolved resource control issues of interest to the multimedia systems community.

The scenario we examine in detail is that of a *public computing platform*. Such a platform consists of a cluster of processing nodes interconnected by a network of switches and provides computational resources to a large number of small third-party *service providers* who pay the provider of the platform for the resources: CPU cycles, network bandwidth, storage space, storage bandwidth, etc. The platform provider offers service providers a platform which can be, for example, highly available, managed, and located in a geographically advantageous location such as a metropolitan area. In return, the platform provider can use economies of scale to offer service hosting at an attractive rate and still generate profit.

Public computing platforms differ from current hosting solutions in that there are many more services than machines: lots of services share a relatively small number of nodes. The challenge for the platform provider is to be able to sell resources like processor cycles and predictable service to many service providers, who may be mutually antagonistic, in a cost-effective manner. Whereas systems for running one, specialized class of application (e.g. web servers, some Application Service Providers) in this manner are already appearing in the marketplace,

---

* Prashant Shenoy was supported in part by NSF grants CCR-9984030, EIA-0080119 and a gift from Sprint Corporation.

D. Shepherd et al. (Eds.): IDMS 2001, LNCS 2158, pp. 2–9, 2001.

the lack of solutions for the more general problem has prevented the range of services offered in this way from being widened.

Two research areas feed directly in to this area: both have much to offer, but do not address areas specific to the support of time- and resource-sensitive applications on public computing platforms.

Resource control in multimedia systems: Resource control has been central question in multimedia systems research for at least the past 10 years or so. Control of resources within a machine is now relatively well-understood: it has been addressed in completely new operating systems (e.g. [1]), modifications to existing operating systems (e.g. [2]), schedulers (e.g., [14]), and abstractions (e.g., [4]).

Many of these advances were motivated by the desire to handle multimedia and other time-sensitive applications. Such mechanisms clearly have a place in a public computing platform designed to handle a diversity of services, not simply for multimedia applications but to provide performance isolation between services owned by providers who are paying for resources. Consequently, public computing platforms enable much of the past and on-going research on resource control for multimedia systems to be applied to *a new and more general setting*. The caveat though is that most of these techniques were developed for single machine environments and do not directly generalize to multi-resource environments (multiprocessors, clusters), for example see [5].

Cluster-based computing platforms: Much work has been performed recently on the use of clustered computing platforms for network services (see [6] for an example and convincing arguments in favor of the approach). This work aims at delivering high-capacity, scalable, highly-available applications, usually web-based.

Typically, a single application is supported, or else the applications are assumed to be mutually trusting—a reasonable assumption in the large enterprise case. Consequently, little attention is paid to resource control, either for real-time guarantees to applications or performance isolation between them [7] ([9] is a notable exception.) Similarly, intra-cluster security is relaxed as a simplifying assumption within the platform [8].

While the arguments for an approach based on clusters of commodity machines carry over into the public computing space, the assumptions about resource control and trust clearly do not: the applications running on such platforms will have diverse requirements and the operators of such applications will be paying money to ensure that those requirements are met. In addition, they may be in competition with each other. Lack of trust between competing applications as well as between applications and the platform provider introduces new challenges in design of cluster control systems.

1.1   What's Different about Public Computing Platforms

This paper argues that the systems problems of public computing platforms are conveniently similar to the two fields above, but have a specificity of their own.

They both present new challenges, but also have properties that help to ground and concretize general classes of solutions.

The most significant property of systems like this that set them apart from traditional multimedia systems and cluster-based servers is that resources are being *sold*. From a cluster architecture point of view this means that performance isolation becomes central: it is essential to provide some kind of quantitative resource guarantees since this is what people are paying for.

From a multimedia systems point of view this property has two effects. Firstly, resource allocation must extend over multiple machines running a large number of services. This amounts to a problem of *placement*: which components of which services are to share a machine?

Secondly, the policies used to drive both this placement and the resource control mechanisms on the individual machines are now driven by a clear business case. Resource control research in the past has been marked by a lack of clear consensus over what is being optimized by the various mechanisms and policies: processor utilization, application predictability, application performance, etc. The notion of graceful degradation is also made more quantitative in this scenario: we can relate degradation of service to a change in platform revenue. This represents a significant advance over current so-called "economic" or "market-driven" resource allocation policies since they can now be explicitly linked to a "real" market. We elaborate on these issues below.

2   Challenges in Designing a Public Computing Platform

2.1   Challenges for the Platform Provider: The Need for Yield Management

The primary goal for the operator of a public computing platform is to maximize revenues obtained from renting platform resources to service providers. A public computing platform services a wide variety of customers; depending on how much each customer pays for resources, not all users are treated equally. This process is known as *yield management*, and adds an important twist to the policy side of the resource control problem. Maximizing yield (revenue) requires that platform resources be overbooked. Overbooking of resources is typically based on an economic cost-benefit analyses, which explicitly links resource allocation not to closed market abstractions (e.g. [10]) but to a "real" commercial operation.

Beyond this, resource policies will take into account such factors as demographics and psychometric models of client behavior in determining allocations and pricing. In other industries where similar challenges exist (for example, the airline industry [11]), much of this is in the domain of business decision-making and operations research models. The challenge for a public computing platform is to allow as much flexibility as possible in business decisions regarding its operation: it must not impose undue restrictions on business policies, but at the same time should facilitate their implementation.

From a systems design point of view this has a number of implications. Firstly, business assessments and policies must be representable in the system, without the system constraining this representation (in other words, without the system taking over too much of the decision-making process). Secondly the system should aid the process of overbooking and reacting to the overloads resulting from overbooking. For instance, service providers that pay more should be better isolated from overloads than others; to achieve this goal, resource control policies should help determine (i) how to map individual applications to nodes in the cluster, (ii) the amount of overbooking on each individual node depending on the yield from that node and the service guarantees that need to be provided to applications, and (iii) how to handle an overload scenario. Thirdly, the system should provide timely feedback into the business domain as the results of the process and the behavior of other commercial parties involved (principally the service providers).

2.2 End-User Challenges: The Need for Appropriate Abstractions

Applications running on a public computing platform will be inherently heterogeneous. One can expect such platforms to run a mix of applications such as streaming audio and video servers, real-time multiplayer game servers, vanilla web servers, and ecommerce applications. These applications have diverse performance requirements. For instance, game servers need good interactive performance and thus low average response times, ecommerce applications need high aggregate throughput (in terms of transactions per second), and streaming media servers require real-time performance guarantees. For each such application (or service), a service provider contracts with the platform provider for the desired performance requirements along various dimensions. Such requirements could include the desired reservation (or share) for each capsule as well as average response times, throughput or deadline guarantees. To effectively service such applications, the platform should support flexible abstractions that enable applications to specify the desired performance guarantees along a variety of dimensions.

We propose the abstraction of a *capsule* to express these requirements. A capsule is defined to be that component of an application that runs on an individual node; each application can have one or more capsules, but not more than one per node. A capsule can have a number of attributes, such as the desired CPU, network and disk reservations, memory requirements, deadline guarantees, etc., that denote the performance requirements of that capsule. It's important to note that capsules are a *post facto* abstraction: for reasons detailed in [12] we try not to mandate a programming model for service authors. Capsules are therefore an abstraction used by the platform for decomposing an existing service into resource principals.

2.3 Implications for System Design

The above research challenges have the following implications on platform design.

Capsule Placement. A typical public computing platform will consist of tens or hundreds of nodes running thousands of third-party applications. Due to the large number of nodes and applications in the system, manual mapping of capsules to nodes in the platform is infeasible. Consequently, an automated capsule placement algorithm is a critical component of any public computing platform. The aim of such an algorithm is clearly to optimize revenue from the platform, and in general this coincides with maximizing resource usage. However, a number critical factors and constrains modify this:

Firstly, the algorithm must run incrementally: services come and go, nodes fail, and are added or upgraded, and all this must occur with minimal disruption to service. This means, for instance, that introducing a new capsule must have minimal impact of the placement of existing capsules, since moving a capsule is costly and may involve violating a resource guarantee.

Secondly, capsule placement should take into account the issue of overbooking of resources to maximize yield; sophisticated statistical admission control algorithms are needed to achieve this objective. Much of the past work on statistical admission control has focussed on a single node server; extending these techniques to clustered environments is non-trivial.

Thirdly, there are technological constraints on capsule placement, for example capsules are generally tied to a particular operating system or execution environment which may not be present on all nodes.

Finally, there are less tangible security and business-related constraints on capsule placement. For example, we might not wish to colocate capsules of rival customers on a single node. On the other hand, we might colocate a number of untrusted clients on a single node if the combined revenue from the clients is low.

To help make this last constraint tractable, and also integrate notions of overbooking, we introduce the twin abstractions of *trustworthiness* and *criticality*, explored in more detail in [13]. These concepts allow us to represent business-level assessments of risk and cost-benefit at the system level.

Trustworthiness is clearly an issue, since third-party applications will generally be untrusted and mutually antagonistic; isolating untrusted applications from one another by mapping them onto different nodes is desirable. Trustworthiness is a function of many factors outside the scope of the system (including legal and commercial considerations), but the placement of capsules must take trust relationships into account.

The complementary notion of criticality is a measure of how important a capsule or an application is to the platform provider. For example, criticality could be a function of how much the service provider is paying for application hosting. Clearly, mapping capsules of *critical* applications and *untrusted* applications to the same node is problematic, since a denial of service attack by the untrusted application can result in revenue losses for the platform provider.

In summary, capsule placement becomes a multi-dimensional constrained optimization problem—one that takes into account the trustworthiness of an application, its criticality and its performance requirements.

Resource Control. A public computing platform should employ resource control mechanisms to enforce performance guarantees provided to applications and their capsules. As argued earlier, these mechanisms should operate in multi-node environments, should isolate applications from one another, enforce resource reservations on a sufficiently fine time-scale, and meet requirements such as deadlines. These issues are well understood within the multimedia community for single node environments. For instance, hierarchical schedulers [14] meet these requirements within a node. However, these techniques do not carry over to multi-resource (multi-node) environments. For instance, it was shown in [5] that uniprocessor proportional-share scheduling algorithms can cause starvation or unbounded unfairness when employed for multiprocessor or multi-node systems. Consequently, novel resource control techniques will need to be developed for these environments.

Failure Handling. Since high availability is critical to a public computing platform, the platform should handle failures in a graceful manner. In contrast to traditional clusters, the commercial nature of a public computing platform has an important effect on how failures are handled: we can classify failures as to whose responsibility it is to handle them, the platform provider or a service provider.

We distinguish three kinds of failures in a public computing platform: (i) platform failures, (ii) application failures, and (iii) capsule failures.

A platform failure occurs when a node fails or some platform-specific software on the node fails. Interestingly, resource exhaustion on a node also constitutes a platform failure—the failure to meet performance guarantees (since resources on each node of the platform may be overbooked to extract statistical multiplexing gains, resource exhaustion results in a violation of performance guarantees). Platform failures must be dealt with by detecting them in a timely manner and recovering from them automatically (for instance, by restarting failed nodes or by offloading capsules from an overloaded node to another).

An application failure occurs when an application running on the platform fails in a manner *detectable* by the platform. Depending on the application and the service contract between the platform provider and the service provider, handling application failures could be the responsibility of the platform provider or the service provider (or both). In the former scenario, application semantics that constitute a failure will need to be specified a priori to the platform provider and the platform will need to incorporate application-specific mechanisms to detect and recover from such failures.

A capsule failure occurs when an application capsule fails in a way *undetectable* to the platform provider, for example an internal deadlock condition in an application. Capsule failures must be assumed to be the responsibility of the service provider and the platform itself does not provide any support for dealing with them.

We have found this factorization of failure types highly useful in designing fault-tolerance mechanisms for a public computing platform.

3   Status of Ongoing Work and Concluding Remarks

We believe that there are compelling reasons to host large numbers of Internet services on a cluster-based platform. In particular, we are interested in the case where there are many more services than machines – this is a different space from current commercial hosting solutions, but one where we feel considerable innovation in applications is possible if the economic barrier to entry is very low.

Facilitating this innovation requires support for highly diverse resource guarantees: current application-level connection scheduling work restricts applications to web-based or similar request-response systems, and consequently restricts the diversity of feasible services (and how cheap it is to offer them). Much research from the field of multimedia systems can be reapplied here – indeed this may be a more compelling case for resource control facilities in the real world than multimedia workstations.

However, both the clustered environment and the business relationships involved in the design of public platforms adds new challenges: (i) heterogeneity of applications, distributed application components, and processing nodes; (ii) place of capsules within the platform; (iii) failure handling in a domain of split responsibility, and (iv) overbooking and yield management.

Our current research focuses on these issues for a public computing platform. Specifically, we are investigating techniques for yield management [13], capsule placement, overbooking and predictable resource allocation in such environments.

Acknowledgments

The authors would like to acknowledge the suggestions of Bryan Lyles in writing this paper.

References

[1] I. Leslie, D. McAuley, R. Black, T. Roscoe, P. Barham, D. Evers, and R. Fairbairns, "The design and implementation of an operating system to support distributed multimedia applications," *IEEE JSAC*, vol. 14, no. 7, pp. 1280–1297, 1996.

[2] V Sundaram, A. Chandra, P. Goyal, P. Shenoy, J Sahni, and H Vin, "Application Performance in the QLinux Multimedia Operating System," in *Proceedings of the Eighth ACM Conference on Multimedia, Los Angeles, CA*, November 2000, pp. 127–136.

[3] J. Nieh and M. S. Lam, "The Design, Implementation and Evaluation of SMART: A Scheduler for Multimedia Applications," in *Proceedings of the Sixteenth ACM Symposium on Operating Systems Principles, Saint-Malo, France*, October 1997.

[4] G. Banga, P. Druschel, and J. C. Mogul, "Resource Containers: a new facility for resource management in server systems," in *Proceedings of the Third Symposium on Operating Systems Design and Implementation*, New Orleans, Louisiana, March 1999, pp. 45–68.

[5] A. Chandra, M. Adler, P. Goyal, and P. Shenoy, "Surplus Fair Scheduling: A Proportional-Share CPU Scheduling Algorithm for Symmetric Multiprocessors," in *Proceedings of the Fourth Symposium on Operating System Design and Implementation (OSDI 2000), San Diego, CA,* October 2000.

[6] A. Fox, S. D. Gribble, Y. Chawathe, E. A. Brewer, and P. Gauthier, "Cluster-Based Scalable Network Services," in *Proceedings of the Sixteenth ACM Symposium on Operating Systems Principles, San Malo, France,* October 1997.

[7] M. Litzkow, M. Livny, and M. Mutka, "Condor - a hunter of idle workstations," in *Proceedings of the 8th International Conference of Distributed Computing Systems,* June 1988, pp. 104–111.

[8] S. D. Gribble, M. Welsh, E. A. Brewer, and D. Culler, "The Multispace: an Evolutionary Platform for Infrastructural Services," in *Proceedings of the 1999 Usenix Annual Technical Conference,* Monterey, California, June 1999.

[9] M. Aron, P. Druschel, and W. Zwaenepoel, "Cluster Reserves: A mechanism for Resource Management in Cluster-based Network Servers," in *Proceedings of the ACM Sigmetrics 2000, Santa Clara, CA,* June 2000.

[10] Neil Stratford and Richard Mortier, "An economic approach to adaptive resource management," in *Proc. 7th IEEE Workshop on Hot Topics in Operating Systems (HotOS VII),* March 1999.

[11] Barry C. Smith, John F. Leimkuhler, and Ross M. Darrow, "Yield management at American Airlines," *Interfaces,* vol. 22, no. 1, pp. 8–31, January-February 1992.

[12] T. Roscoe and B. Lyles, "Distributed Computing without DPEs: Design Considerations for Public Computing Platforms," in *Proceedings of the 9th ACM SIGOPS European Workshop, Kolding, Denmark,* September 17-20 2000.

[13] T. Roscoe, B. Lyles, and R. Isaacs, "The case for supporting risk assessment in systems," Sprint Labs Technical Report, May 2001.

[14] P. Goyal, X. Guo, and H.M. Vin, "A Hierarchical CPU Scheduler for Multimedia Operating Systems," in *Proceedings of the First USENIX Symposium on Operating System Design and Implementation (OSDI'96), Seattle,* October 1996, pp. 107–122.

Transport-Level Protocol Coordination in Cluster-to-Cluster Applications

David E. Ott and Ketan Mayer-Patel

Department of Computer Science
University of North Carolina at Chapel Hill
{ott, kmp}@cs.unc.edu

Abstract. Future Internet applications will increasingly use multiple communications and computing devices in a distributed fashion. In this paper, we identify an emerging and important application class comprised of a set of processes on a cluster of devices communicating to a remote set of processes on another cluster of devices across a common intermediary Internet path. We call applications of this type *cluster-to-cluster (C-to-C) applications*. The networking requirements of C-to-C applications present unique challenges that current transport-level protocols fail to address. In particular, these applications require aggregate measurement of network conditions across all associated flows and coordinated transport-level protocol behavior. A *Coordination Protocol* (CP) is proposed which allows a C-to-C application to coordinate flow behavior in the face of changing network conditions. CP provides cluster endpoints with a consistent view of network conditions, as well as cluster membership and bandwidth usage information. An application may use CP to define and implement a coordination scheme supporting particular flow priorities and other objectives.

1 Introduction

Future Internet applications will increasingly make use of multiple communication and computing devices in a distributed fashion. Examples of these applications include distributed sensor arrays, tele-immersion [9], computer-supported collaborative workspaces (CSCW) [4], ubiquitous computing environments [13], and complex multi-stream, multimedia presentations [16]. In many such applications, no one device or computer produces or manages all of the data streams transmitted. Instead, the endpoints of communication are collections of devices. We call applications of this type *cluster-to-cluster (C-to-C) applications*.

In a C-to-C application, a set of processes distributed on a cluster of devices or computers communicates with another set of processes on a remote cluster of devices or computers. For example, a cluster may be comprised of a collection of capture devices (e.g., video cameras, microphones, etc.), each of which produces a stream of data. The other cluster might be a collection of display devices (e.g., digital light projectors, speakers, head-mounted displays, etc.) and computers that archive data in various ways. Processes are distributed on each device cluster to manage data streams and control the application.

D. Shepherd et al. (Eds.): IDMS 2001, LNCS 2158, pp. 10–22, 2001.

C-to-C applications share two important properties. First, communication between endpoints on the same local cluster takes place with minimal delay and loss. We can make this assertion because the local intranet supporting the cluster can be provisioned to comfortably support application traffic loads. In other words, the local networking environment often will be engineered and implemented with the C-to-C application in mind. Second, while no two flows within the application share the exact same end-to-end path, all flows share a common Internet path between clusters. This shared common path represents the majority of the traversal path between endpoints on different clusters, and the region in which network congestion will most likely affect C-to-C application performance. Although the path between clusters is not guaranteed to be the same for all flows (or even all packets within a flow), in general we can expect that network conditions between clusters will be similar.

Different flows within a C-to-C application may use more than one transport-level protocol to accomplish their communication objectives. Streamed audio and video data, for example, may use UDP or a UDP-based protocol like RTP, while control information is exchanged using TCP to ensure reliability. Application-specific protocols which handle media encoding, flow control, reliability, or congestion control in specialized ways may also be used.

A fundamental problem with current transport-level protocols within the C-to-C application context, however, is that they lack coordination. Application streams share a common intermediary path between clusters, and yet operate in isolation from one another. As a result, flows may compete with one another when network resources become limited, instead of cooperating to use available bandwidth in application-controlled ways. For example, an application may wish to give certain streams priority over others or stipulate that different proportions of available bandwidth be used by specific streams. We are interested in C-to-C applications with rich semantic relationships between flows that can be exploited to improve application performance.

In this position paper, we postulate that the C-to-C application architecture can significantly benefit from network mechanisms that allow transport-level protocol coordination of separate, but semantically related, flows of data. In the following sections of this paper we will:

- Motivate the C-to-C application architecture with a specific example.
- Identify a number of networking challenges posed by such an application.
- Provide a specific proposal for a transport-level coordination mechanism.
- Defend the design decisions made in our proposed mechanism, and discuss related work.

2 A Motivating Example

This section describes a specific application which motivates the need for transport-level protocol coordination and illustrates the networking challenges faced by C-to-C applications. The application is the *Office of the Future*. The Office of the Future was conceived by Fuchs et al., and their experimental prototype of the application is described further in [9].

In the Office of the Future, tens of digital light projectors are used to make almost every surface of an office (walls, desktops, etc.) a display surface. Similarly, tens of video cameras are used to capture the office environment from a number of different angles. At real-time rates, the video streams are used as input to stereo correlation algorithms to extract 3D geometry information. Audio is also captured from a set of microphones. The video streams, geometry information, and audio streams are all transmitted to a remote Office of the Future environment. At the remote environment, the video and audio streams are warped using both local and remote geometry information and stereo views are mapped to the light projectors. Audio is spatialized and sent to a set of speakers. Users within each Office of the Future environment wear shutter glasses that are coordinated with the light projectors.

Fig. 1. The Office of the Future.

The result is an immersive 3D experience in which the walls of one office environment essentially disappear to reveal the remote environment and provide a tele-immersive collaborative space for the participants. Furthermore, synthetic 3D models may be rendered and incorporated into both display environments as part of the shared, collaborative experience. Figure 1 is an artistic illustration of the application.

We see the Office of the Future as a concrete vision of a C-to-C application that progresses far beyond today's relatively simple video applications. The Office of the Future uses scores of media streams which must be manipulated in complex ways. The computational complexity of the application requires the use of several computational resources (possibly including specialized graphics hardware).

The Office of the Future is a good example of a C-to-C application because the endpoints of the application are collections of devices. Two similarly equipped offices must exchange myriad data streams. Any specific data stream is transmitted from a specific device in one environment to one or more specific devices in the remote environment. Within the strict definition of end-to-end used by current protocols, few if any of these streams will share a complete path. If we relax the definition of end-to-end, however, we can see that all of the data streams will span a common shared communication path between the local networking environments of each Office of the Future.

The local network environments are not likely to be the source of congestion, loss, or other dynamic network conditions because these environments are within the control of the local user and can be provisioned to support the Office of the Future application. The shared path between two Office of the Future environments, however, is not under local control and thus will be the source of dynamic network conditions.

Current transport-level protocols fail to address the complex needs of an application like the Office of the Future. For example, this application requires dynamic interstream prioritization. Beyond just video information, the Office of the Future uses a number of other media types including 3D models and spatialized audio. Because these media types are integrated into a single immersive display environment, user interaction with any given media type may have implications for how other media types are encoded, transmitted, and displayed. For example, the orientation and position of the user's head indicates a region of interest within the display. Media streams that are displayed within that region of interest should receive a larger share of available bandwidth and be displayed at higher resolutions and frame rates than media streams that are outside the region of interest. When congestion occurs, lower priority streams should react more strongly than higher priority streams. In this way, appropriate aggregate behavior is achieved and application-level tradeoffs are exploited.

3   Networking Challenges

To generalize the networking challenges faced by complex C-to-C applications like the Office of the Future, we first develop a generic model for C-to-C applications and subsequently characterize the networking requirements associated with this model.

3.1   C-to-C Application Model

We model a generic C-to-C application as two sets of processes executing on two sets of communication or computing devices. Figure 2 illustrates this model.

A *cluster* is comprised of any number of *endpoints* and a single *aggregation point*, or *AP*. Each endpoint represents a process on some *endpoint host* (typically a networked computer) that sends and/or receives data from another

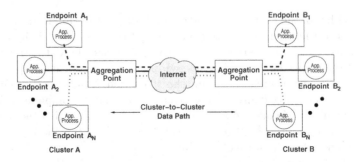

Fig. 2. C-to-C application model.

endpoint belonging to a remote cluster. The AP functions as a gateway node connecting cluster endpoints to the Internet. The common traversal path between aggregation points is known as the *cluster-to-cluster data path*.

Endpoints within the same cluster are connected by an intranet provisioned with enough bandwidth to comfortably support the communication needs of the cluster. In general, latency between endpoints on the same cluster is small compared to latency between endpoints on different clusters. Our overall objective is to coordinate endpoint flows across the cluster-to-cluster data path where available bandwidth is uncertain and constantly changing.

3.2   Networking Requirements

A useful metaphor for visualizing the networking requirements of C-to-C applications is to view the communication between clusters as a rope with frayed ends. The rope represents the aggregate data flows between clusters. Each strand represents one particular transport-level stream. At the ends of the rope, the strands may not share the same path. In the middle of the rope, however, the strands come together to form a single aggregate object. While each strand is a separate entity, they share a common fate and purpose when braided together as a rope.

With this metaphor in mind, we identify several important networking requirements of C-to-C applications:

- **Global measurements of congestion, delay, and loss.** Although each stream of a C-to-C application is an independent transport-level flow of data, it is also semantically related to other streams in the same distributed application. As such, network events such as congestion, delay, and loss should be measured and reported for the flows as an aggregate.
- **Preserved end-to-end semantics.** The specific transport-level protocol (i.e., TCP, UDP, RTP, RAP, etc.) that is used by each flow will be specific to the communication requirements of the data within the flow and the role it plays within the larger application. Thus, each transport-level protocol used should still maintain the appropriate end-to-end semantics and mechanisms. For example, if a data flow contains control information that requires in-order, reliable delivery, then the transport-level protocol used to deliver this

specific flow (e.g., TCP) should provide these services on an end-to-end basis. Thus, although the flow is part of an aggregate set of flows, it should still maintain end-to-end mechanisms as appropriate.

– **A coordinated view of current network conditions.** Even though each flow maintains its own end-to-end semantics, the flows should receive a coordinated view of current network conditions like available bandwidth and global measures of aggregate delay, loss, and congestion. We need to separate the adaptive dynamic behavior of each transport-level protocol, which depends on end-to-end semantics of individual streams, from the mechanisms used to measure current network conditions, which are global across all streams of the application.

– **Interstream relative bandwidth measurements.** Individual streams within the C-to-C application may require knowledge about their bandwidth usage relative to the other streams of the same application. This knowledge can be used to determine the appropriate bandwidth level of a particular stream given application-level knowledge about interstream relationships. For example, an application may want to establish a relationship between two separate flows of data such that one flow consumes twice as much bandwidth as the other.

– **Deployability** Finally, the mechanisms used to provide C-to-C applications with transport-level protocol coordination need to be reasonably deployable.

In the following section, we outline a design for a mechanism that meets these requirements.

4 The Coordination Protocol

Our approach to this problem is to propose a new protocol layer between the network layer (IP) and transport layer (TCP, UDP, etc.) that addresses the need for coordination in C-to-C application contexts. We call this protocol the *Coordination Protocol (CP)*. The coordination function provided by CP is transport protocol independent. At the same time, CP is distinct from network-layer protocols like IP that play a more fundamental role in routing a packet to its destination.

CP works by attaching probe information to packets transmitted from one cluster to another. As the information is acknowledged and returned by packets of the remote cluster, a picture of current network conditions is formed and shared among endpoints within the local cluster. A consistent view of network conditions across flows follows from the fact that the same information is shared among all endpoints.

Figure 3 shows our proposed network architecture. CP will be implemented between the network layer (IP) and the transport layer (TCP/UDP). We call this layer the *coordination layer*. The coordination layer will exist on each device participating in the C-to-C application, as well as on the two aggregation points on either end of the cluster-to-cluster data path.

At the endpoints, CP can be implemented on top of IP in a straightforward manner, much as TCP and UDP are implemented on top of IP. At the aggregation points, CP must be part of the forwarding path. As such, forwarding behavior must be modified to include a CP handling routine before IP forwarding can subsequently take place. We acknowledge this departure from standard IP behavior by labeling the IP layer at the AP's in Figure 3 as IP*.

Transport-level protocols will be built on top of CP in the same manner that TCP is built on top of IP. CP will provide these transport-level protocols with a consistent view of network conditions. These transport-level protocols will in turn use this information, along with various configuration parameters, to determine a data transmission rate and related send characteristics. In Figure 3, we show several possible transport-level protocols (C-TCP, C-UDP, and C-RTP) which are meant to represent coordinated counterparts to existing protocols.

4.1   Basic Operation

Figure 4 shows a CP data packet. CP encapsulates transport-level packets by prepending a small header. In turn IP will encapsulate CP packets and the protocol header will indicate that CP is being used. Each CP header will contain an identifier associating the packet with a particular C-to-C application. The remaining contents vary according to the changing role played by the CP header as it traverses the network path from source endpoint to destination endpoint.

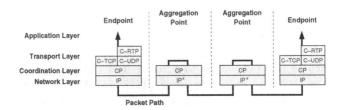

Fig. 3. CP network architecture.

- **As packets originate from source endpoints.**
  The CP header may be used to communicate requests to the local AP. For instance, an endpoint may request to join or leave a cluster, have a membership or bandwidth usage report issued, or post a message to all endpoints within the local cluster. If no request is made, then cluster, flow, and protocol information are simply included in the CP header for identification.
- **As packets arrive at the local AP.**
  CP header and packet information is processed. Part of the CP header will then be overwritten, allowing the AP to communicate congestion probe information with the remote AP.

- **As packets arrive at the remote AP.**
  The CP header is processed and used to detect network conditions. Again, part of the CP header is overwritten to communicate network condition information with the remote endpoint.
- **As packets arrive at the destination endpoint.**
  Network condition information is obtained from the CP header and passed on to the transport-level protocol and the application.

4.2   Detecting Network Conditions

A primary function of CP is to measure congestion and delay along the cluster-to-cluster data path. To accomplish this objective, each packet passing from one AP to another will have two numbers inserted into its CP header. The first number will be a sequence number that increases monotonically for every packet sent. The second number will be an echo of the last sequence number received from the other AP.

By recording the time when a new sequence number is sent and the time when its echo is received, the AP can approximate the round trip time and infer network delay. Similarly, missing sequence numbers can be used to detect packet loss and infer congestion.

Because sequence numbers in the CP header do not have any transport-level function, CP can use whatever packet is being transmitted next to carry this information as long as the packet is part of a flow associated with the C-to-C application. Since the packets of multiple flows are available for this purpose, this mechanism can be used for fine-grained detection of network conditions along the cluster-to-cluster data path.

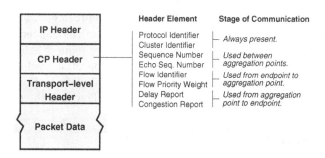

Fig. 4. CP packet structure.

4.3   Transport-Level Interface

An important aspect of CP is the design of its interface with transport-level protocols. CP provides transport-level protocols with information about network conditions, including congestion and delay measurements. These measurements are delivered whenever packets pass from CP to the transport-level protocol through this interface.

Variants of existing transport-level protocols will be developed on top of this interface. For example, a coordinated version of TCP (C-TCP) will consider acknowledgements only as an indicator of successful transfer. Congestion detection will be relegated entirely to CP.

Because an application will need to provide CP-related information to the transport-level protocol, some aspects of the transport-level interface will be exposed to the networking API (i.e., the socket layer). For instance, an application will need to supply a cluster identifier that associates the flow with a given C-to-C application. In the reverse direction, some transport-level protocols will make delay, jitter, loss, or other CP-derived information available to the application layer.

4.4   Cluster Membership Services

An AP maintains a cluster membership table for each C-to-C application. This table is created when a CP packet for a C-to-C application with no current table is received and is maintained as soft state. Endpoints are dynamically added and deleted from this table. Storing the table as soft state avoids explicit configuration and makes the mechanism lightweight and robust

A cluster membership table performs two important functions. First, it maintains a list of known cluster endpoints. This allows the AP to broadcast network condition information to all C-to-C application participants. Endpoints may also request a membership report from the AP to receive a current listing of other endpoints. This list may be used in application-specific ways, for example to communicate point-to-point with cluster participants or to track cluster size.

The second function is that of bandwidth monitoring. An AP will monitor bandwidth usage for each cluster endpoint and use the cluster membership table to store resulting statistics. An endpoint may request a bandwidth report to obtain information on bandwidth usage among other endpoints, as well as aggregate statistics on the cluster as a whole. This information can be used in application-specific ways to configure and manage flow coordination dynamically.

5   Design Rationale

5.1   Benefits of CP

We believe the benefits of our approach to be substantial and include:

- **Locally deployable.**
  CP requires changes to protocol stacks within application clusters only. No changes are required of forwarding nodes along the Internet path between clusters. Furthermore, cluster endpoints can coexist with non-CP communication and computing devices.

- **Available to all transport protocols.**
  A consistent view of network conditions is accessible by all flow endpoints, regardless of the transport-level protocol used by a given flow.
- **Flexible.**
  Our approach does not dictate how an application handles flow coordination. Nor does it enforce coordination schemes through external traffic shaping or packet scheduling at switching points. Instead, flow endpoints are informed of network conditions and adjust in application-defined ways.
- **Dynamic membership and configuration.**
  The number of endpoints within a cluster may change dynamically, along with the traffic characteristics of any given flow endpoint.
- **Sensitive to router performance issues.**
  While the CP architecture does require per-flow and per-cluster state to be maintained at the aggregation points, the work involved is limited to simple accounting operations and does not involve packet scheduling, queue management, or other complex processing. Furthermore, the performance of routers along the Internet path between clusters remains entirely unaffected.

It is important to note that CP is only one possible implementation of a mechanism to satisfy the networking requirements of C-to-C applications outlined in Section 3. The need for a transport-level coordination mechanism is motivated by the needs of C-to-C applications like tele-immersion distributed sensor arrays, and CSCW, which represent an important class of future Internet applications. The specific design of CP is our attempt to satisfy those needs.

5.2   Design Justification

We anticipate several questions about why we designed CP in the manner that we have and justify its design below.

5.3   *Why Do This below the Transport-Level?*

The primary reason for implementing CP below the transport-level is to preserve end-to-end semantics of the transport-level. Another possible approach would be to deploy CP at the application level by having all streams of a cluster sent to a multiplexing agent which then incorporated the data into a single stream sent to a demultiplexing agent on the remote cluster. This approach, however, has several drawbacks. By breaking the communication path into three stages, end-to-end semantics of the individual transport-level protocols have been severed. This approach also mandates that application-level control is centralized and integrated into the multiplexing agent.

A secondary reason for implementing CP below the transport-level is because that is where the CP mechanisms logically belong. The transport-level is associated with the end-to-end semantics of individual streams. The network-level protocol (i.e., IP) is associated with the next-hop forwarding path of individual packets. CP deals with streams that are associated together and share a significant number of hops along their forwarding paths, but do not share exact end-to-end paths. This relaxed notion of a stream bundle logically falls between the strict end-to-end notion of the transport-level and the independent packet notion of the network-level.

5.4   Why Do This at Packet Granularity?

By using every packet from every flow of data associated with a C-to-C application we can achieve fine-grained sampling of current network conditions. Fine-grained sampling is important because Internet network conditions are highly dynamic at almost all time scales. Sampling across the flows as an aggregate allows each transport-level protocol to have a more complete picture of current network conditions. Also, since each packet payload needs to be delivered to its intended endpoint destination, each CP packet provides a convenient and existing vehicle for probing network conditions and communicating resulting information to application endpoints. Endpoints are given the opportunity to react to changing conditions in a fine-grained manner.

5.5   Why Not Have the Endpoints Exchange Information?

Another possible architecture for a transport-level protocol coordination mechanism would be to exchange delay, loss, and bandwidth information among endpoints. This presupposes, however, that the endpoints are aware of each other. Our CP design, on the other hand, allows for loosely-coupled C-to-C applications in which this may not be the case. Endpoints of a C-to-C application are only required to use the same cluster identifier which can be distributed through a naming service like DNS or some other application-specific mechanism. The aggregation points are a natural place for cluster-wide accounting of loss, delay, and bandwidth since all packets of the cluster will pass through them. The design of CP is cognizant of the additional processing load this places on the aggregation point which is reflected in its relatively simple accounting mechanism.

5.6   Related Work

The ideas behind CP were primarily inspired by the Congestion Manager (CM) architecture developed by Balakrishnan [2]. CM provides a framework for different protocols to share information concerning network conditions. The CM is an excellent example of a coordination mechanism, but operates only when the transport-level flows share the entire end-to-end path.

In [6], Kung and Wang propose a scheme for aggregating traffic between two points within the backbone network and applying the TCP congestion control algorithm to the whole bundle. The mechanism is transparent to applications and does not provide a way for a particular application to make interstream tradeoffs.

Pradhan et al. propose a way of aggregating TCP connections sharing the same traversal path in order to share congestion control information [8]. Their scheme takes a TCP connection and divides it into two separate ("implicit") TCP connections: a "local subconnection" and a "remote subconnection." This scheme, however, breaks the end-to-end semantics of the transport protocol (i.e., TCP).

Active networking, first proposed by [11] allows custom programs to be installed within the network. Since their original conception, a variety of active networking systems have been built [14, 1, 3, 12, 15, 5, 7, 10]. They are often thought of as a way to implement new and customized network services. In fact, CP could be implemented within an active networking framework. Active networking, however, mandates changes to routers along the entire network path. This severely hinders deployment. CP requires changes only at the endpoints and at the aggregation points.

6   Summary

In this position paper, we motivated the need for transport-level protocol coordination for a particular class of distributed applications that we described as cluster-to-cluster applications. In particular, C-to-C applications are characterized by many independent, but semantically related, flows of data between clusters of computation and communication devices. This application architecture requires that end-to-end transport-level semantics be preserved, while at the same time, providing each stream with a consistent view of current networking conditions. To achieve this, each transport-level protocol needs measures of congestion, delay, and loss for the aggregate bundle of data flows.

We described the design of the Coordination Protocol (CP) which provides for the unique networking requirements of C-to-C applications. The main features of CP are:

- Transport-level protocol independent.
- Locally deployable.
- Fine grained sampling of network conditions.
- Flexible.
- Supports dynamic membership and configuration.

CP provides cluster endpoints with a consistent view of network conditions, as well as cluster membership and bandwidth usage information. With this information, a C-to-C application can make coordination decisions according to specific objectives and a privileged understanding of application state. CP will facilitate the development of next generation Internet applications.

References

[1] D.S. Alexander et al. Active bridging. *Proceedings of SIGCOMM'97*, pages 101–111, September 1997.

[2] Hari Balakrishnan, Hariharan S. Rahul, and Srinivasan Seshan. An integrated congestion management architecture for internet hosts. *Proceeding of ACM SIGCOMM*, September 1999.

[3] D. Decasper et al. Router plugins: A software architecture for next generation routers. *Proceedings of SIGCOMM'98*, pages 229–240, September 1998.

[4] J. Grudin. Computer-supported cooperative work: its history and participation. *Computer*, 27(4):19–26, 1994.

[5] M. Hicks et al. Plannet: An active internetwork. *Proceedings of INFOCOM'99*, pages 1124–1133, March 1999.

[6] H.T. Kung and S.Y. Wang. Tcp trunking: Design, implementation and performance. *Proc. of ICNP '99*, November 1999.

[7] E. Nygren et al. Pan: A high-performance active network node supporting multiple code systems. *Proceedings of OPENARCH'99*, 1999.

[8] P. Pradhan, T. Chiueh, and A. Neogi. Aggregate tcp congestion control using multiple network probing. *Proc. of IEEE ICDCS 2000*, 2000.

[9] Ramesh Raskar, Greg Welch, Matt Cutts, Adam Lake, Lev Stesin, and Henry Fuchs. The office of the future: A unified approach to image-based modeling and spatially immersive displays. *Proceedings of ACM SIGRAPH 98*, 1998.

[10] B. Schwarts et al. Smart packets for active networks. *Proceedings of OPENARCH'99*, 1999.

[11] D. L. Tennenhouse and D. Wetherall. Towards an active network architecture. *Multimedia Computing and Networking*, January 1996.

[12] J. van der Merwe et al. The tempest - a practical framework for network programmability. *IEEE Network Magazine*, 12(3), May/June 1998.

[13] M. Weiser. Some computer science problems in ubiquitous computing. *Communications of the ACM*, 36(7):75–84, July 1993.

[14] David Wetherall. Active network vision and reality: lessons from a capsule-based system. *Operating Systems Review*, 34(5):64–79, December 1999.

[15] Y. Yemini and S. da Silva. Towards programmable networks. *International Workshop on Distributed Systems Operations and Management*, October 1996.

[16] T.-P. Yu, D. Wu, K. Mayer-Patel, and L.A. Rowe. dc: A live webcast control system. *To appear in Proc. of SPIE Multimedia Computing and Networking*, 2001.

Data to the People - It's a Matter of Control

Mauricio Cortes and J. Robert Ensor

Bell Laboratories, Lucent Technologies
600 Mountain Avenue, Murray Hill, New Jersey 07974, USA
{mcortes, jre}@lucent.com

Abstract. This paper highlights some early results from our current research. We are building prototype multimedia services, *e.g.*, digital television, video on demand, and teleconferencing, for metropolitan area networks. Our work illustrates that application-aware resource management plays a critical role in providing such services economically. The paper describes a middleware system—called *Narnia*—that supports the development and deployment of these application-aware resource controls. Using Narnia programming abstractions, application developers can create flexible, dynamic resource managers as part of multimedia service implementations. The paper also presents a brief summary of our experiences using Narnia to build applications.

1 Introduction

Our goal is to provide multimedia services to communities of people. More precisely, we intend to make multimedia services, *e.g.*, digital television, video on demand, multimedia teleconferencing, and multi-party games, available through packet networks. Towards this goal, we are building a prototype data center, which is illustrated in Figure 1. It contains a switch/router complex that supports data distribution among its users' endpoint devices, local application servers, and interfaces to external networks. Its application servers store and/or cache data as well as perform specialized manipulations. Its software manages loads on its network and computing resources.

Our experience building the data center has shown us that flexible, dynamic, application-aware controls of network and computing resource managers are necessary for economical deployment of multiple services to a large number of people. Without such controls, switches and routers can become overloaded as servers try to deliver large files or real-time data streams to users. Similarly, controls are needed to protect application servers from too many user requests. Simply adding switches and application servers to meet uncontrolled service loads would typically be too expensive. On the other hand, control software can effectively manage service loads. For example, a controller can balance the request load among a group of application servers. In addition, this controller could filter and/or aggregate requests, further reducing the load to any application server.

D. Shepherd et al. (Eds.): IDMS 2001, LNCS 2158, pp. 23-28, 2001.
© Springer-Verlag Berlin Heidelberg 2001

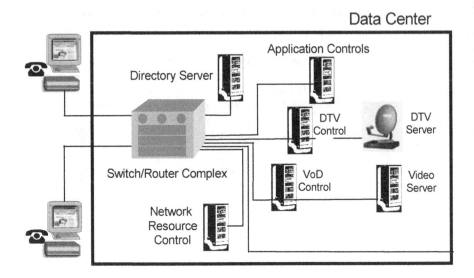

Figure 1: Data Center Components

We have built middleware, which we call *Narnia*, to support development of application-aware controls for network and computing resources. According to the Narnia reference architecture, each resource control is built as a specialized application. As Figure 2 indicates, a typical application is built as a collection of controllers and gateways.

Controllers receive requests from users and other controllers. Therefore, they are able to enforce rules (policies) concerning an application's behavior. Controllers call upon gateways to manage specific resources, such as network elements or media servers. Gateways interact with these resources according to the resources' command interfaces. A collection of controllers and gateways can run on one or more physical machines, according to specified deployment configurations. Different collections can be created to form different applications; thus, these components can be reused.

2   System Components

Narnia provides an extensible set of abstractions to support a variety of multimedia applications. Its base abstractions are sessions, events, event handlers, and shared resources. Controllers and gateways are built upon these abstractions.

Sessions. Each controller and gateway executes one or more sessions. Sessions are a mechanism for rendezvous and communication among users and servers. They maintain state, which provide contexts for these communications, and they have memory, which can be shared among communicating parties. A session also contains a set of event handlers and shared resources (see below).

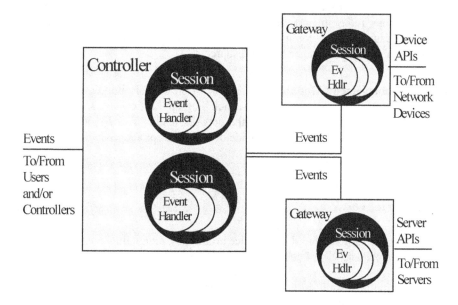

Figure 2: Basic Components of a Control Application

Events. Events are messages sent to and received from sessions; they are Narnia's communication primitives. Each event is a request sent to a session within a control application or a response sent to an earlier requestor's site. Narnia connection managers and event readers/writers handle underlying communication details and provide each session with its own priority ordered event queue. The application developer, therefore, deals with events, not their transmission.

Event Handlers. Event handlers process events; they give semantics to the events and implement service behaviors and policies. Each session defines a set of events and the handlers for those events; thus, a session is the basic context for a service (application). A service can be modified—perhaps during its execution—by creating a new session with updated event handlers.

Shared Resources. Sessions can contain shared resources. Each shared resource represents a specific hardware or software entity. A resource is implemented as a named set of event handlers within a session. *Edge resources* control non-Narnia entities. Their event handlers manage each such entity through the entity's own control interface, *e.g.*, signal ports or API. Narnia gateways use edge resources to monitor and control non-Narnia based system components, such as network routers and video servers. Narnia controller sessions can also contain shared resources. These non-edge resources may refer, in turn, to edge and non-edge resources. Multiple non-edge resources can access a common (edge or non-edge) resource; however, an edge resource does not access other Narnia resources.

Service Management Modules. In addition to these basic building blocks, Narnia provides service management modules, including application and session directories and performance monitors for events and network loads. These monitors, which are built as controllers and gateways, provide data needed for adaptive, dynamic behavior of application-aware resource controls.

3 Experience

We have used Narnia to build two service prototypes: a digital television service and a video on demand service. Each of these services is based on a collection of controllers and gateways.

The digital television service provides users with standard and premium (restricted access) channels. Programs are delivered as MPEG-2 streams at a nominal rate of 6Mbps. The digital television server distributes only those programs that have been requested by viewers, and it sends each channel's data to a multicast group representing the viewers of that channel. The digital television controller is responsible for defining and maintaining these multicast groups. It uses a network resource manager (a gateway) to control the relevant network elements (*e.g.*, switches).

The video on demand service allows users to select movies for downloading. The service operates via a "controlled blast," in which a movie is downloaded to a user's local store at a rate that can be faster than the movie's real-time streaming rate. Users and the video on demand control negotiate to find a suitable download rate (up to 80Mbps). In our service movie downloads begin at controller-determined intervals. This service definition allows the video on demand controller, like the digital television controller, to manage multicast groups for data distribution.

We are now using Narnia to build a multimedia chat room service, which gives users a means of exchanging text messages, talking, and viewing shared video during real-time interactions. The chat room controller coordinates the actions of other controllers to manage each chat room session. A text message controller manages posting, storing, and distribution of text messages. An audio controller manages an audio bridge (through an audio bridge gateway). The bridge is a shared resource that is responsible for mixing audio for chat room participants. The video controller interacts with a video gateway to control distribution of videos from a standard server.

Our work with these various multimedia services has shown that Narnia provides a suitable foundation for building application-aware controls.   The programming abstractions of Narnia offer a small, but powerful base for communication among users and service program elements. Furthermore, Narnia's support for event handlers—event handler classes, factories, and loaders—create a convenient platform for application development and execution. In fact, our directory server, performance monitor, and event logger controllers are the same except for the events and event handlers each one needs. Furthermore, Narnia core components exhibit good performance. Using a Sun Enterprise 450 with two 450MHz CPUs, we have run a controller that receives small (a hundred bytes or so) requests, writes them to a disk log, and sends similar-sized responses back to its clients. The controller can handle approximately 8000 events per second. This level of communication performance gives developers great flexibility in distributing their program modules over different machines.

4   Related Work

Several middleware platforms for the support of multimedia services have been described. Some of these platforms include communication primitives similar to those provided by Narnia, and we have selected representatives of these platforms for comparison to our present work.

CINEMA[4] defines sessions as the basis for access to remote services. A session represents the collection of resources needed to provide a service. To provide a service, a CINEMA session locates and reserves the service's required resources. Then it establishes the needed flow of data among the resources. Narnia sessions, in contrast, do not have inherent flow-building capabilities (these are programmed as part of controller and gateway event handlers) and are not limited to a single user interaction (they can persist without active users).

Several event-based middleware platforms, such as JEDI[2], Siena[2], and CORBA events[3], decouple event producers and consumers. The latter must register with an event dispatcher, specifying the types of events they are interested in processing. The former send events to the dispatcher, which in turn forwards them to all the consumers registered for that event type. Narnia does not contain such an event dispatcher. Rather, programmers can build such infrastructure using Narnia primitives. One would simply develop a controller with the dispatcher's functionality. Other controllers and gateways can register their interest in sets of events with the new dispatch controller. However, Narnia does not provide a specification language to describe how an event handler should forward events.

JAIN[6] is a collection of Java APIs to help developers build applications for multi-network (i.e. IP, ATM, and PSTN), multi-protocol and multi-party environments. JAIN is based on the JTAPI[5] call model. In contrast, our control applications are based on sessions that have no knowledge of the underlying networks and types of endpoint devices. It is possible to develop a Narnia gateway to uses JAIN-based applications as resources.

5 Summary

This paper has presented a brief description of the Narnia middleware system, which supports both the development and the deployment of application-aware controls. Narnia's basic abstractions—sessions, events, event handlers, and shared resources—provide the foundation for development of these control applications. Sessions form the basic context mechanism for applications, and events provide the basis for communication among system components.   Event handlers act on events to provide service behaviors and policies. Shared resources represent underlying devices accessed by multiple users.

The paper has also described our experiences using this middleware to build applications. By building these applications, we have learned that Narnia abstractions create a helpful base for programming controllers and gateways.   Performance measurements show that Narnia communication primitives are sufficiently efficient to support distributed applications. Our planned future work includes further application development and performance tests.

References

1. Carzaniga, A., Rosenblum, D., Wolf, A., Challenges for Distributed Event Services: Scalability vs. Expressiveness, Engineering Distributed Objects '99, Los Angeles CA, USA, May 1999.

2. Cugola, G., Di Nitto, E., Fuggetta, A., Exploiting an event-based infrastructure to develop complex distributed systems, Proceedings of the 1998 International Conference on Software Engineering, pp. 261-270, 1998.

3. Object Management Group. CORBAservices: Common object service specification. Technical report, Object Management Group, July 1998.

4. Rothermel, K., Barth, I., and Helbig, T. CINEMA: An Architecture for Configurable Multimedia Applications. in Spaniel, O., Danthine, A., and Effelsberg, W. (eds.). Architecture and Protocols for High-Speed Networks, 253-271 Kluwer Academic Publisher, 1994.

5. Sun Microsystems, Java Telephony Specification (JTAPI), ver. 1.3, June 1999.

6. Tait, D., de Keijzer, J., Goedman, R., JAIN: A New Approach to Services in Communication Networks, IEEE Communications Magazine, pages 94-99, Jan. 2000.

An Access Control Architecture for Metropolitan Area Wireless Networks

Stefan Schmid, Joe Finney, Maomao Wu, Adrian Friday, Andrew Scott, and
Doug Shepherd

DMRG, Computing Department, Lancaster University,
Lancaster LA1 4YR, U.K.

{sschmid,joe,maomao,adrian,acs,doug}@comp.lancs.ac.uk

Abstract. This paper introduces a novel access control architecture for publicly accessible, wireless networks. The architecture was designed to address the requirements obtained from a case study of ubiquitous Internet service provisioning within the city of Lancaster. The proposed access control mechanism is based on the concepts of secure user authentication, packet marking, and packet filtering at the access routers. The paper demonstrates to what extent this token-based, soft-state access control mechanism improves security and robustness, and offers improved performance over that provided by existing approaches within roaming networks. Early indications show the access control mechanism can better be implemented through the use of active routers, in order to facilitate dynamic rollout and configuration of the system. In addition, extensions to Mobile IPv6 are proposed, which provide support for roaming users at a fundamental level.

1 Introduction

A wireless network infrastructure, based on 802.11 wireless LAN technology, was installed throughout Lancaster city centre as part of the Guide project [1,2] with the aim of supporting tourists via an online tourist guide application. The second phase of the project, Guide II [3], is intended to interact with the recently formed Mobile IPv6 Testbed collaboration between Cisco Systems, Microsoft Research, Orange and Lancaster University [4]. The new challenge is to "open up" the network and provide general-purpose, ubiquitous services and applications to Lancaster citizens, including public Internet access. In order to control access to the publicly available wireless network, secure user authentication and fine grained access control is essential.

The core of the wireless network is based on 11Mbps IEEE 802.11 wireless LAN technology. The network infrastructure consists of numerous base stations distributed around Lancaster covering most of the city centre. Each base station is directly connected to a PC-based router, forming an *access router*. These access routers are linked back to the university campus backbone via DSL and SDH.

For the original tourist guide application (Guide I), the network was simply managed as an Intranet, without globally routable network addressing. However, as Guide

D. Shepherd et al. (Eds.): IDMS 2001, LNCS 2158, pp. 29-37, 2001.
© Springer-Verlag Berlin Heidelberg 2001

II aims to provide public Internet services to citizens, several crucial changes to the network implementation are required. (1) Globally routable network addressing must be introduced. (2) A secure access control mechanism that prevents unauthorised or even malicious users from using the network must be incorporated. (3) Further base stations need to be installed to improve coverage. And finally (4) the network protocol needs to incorporate support for host mobility to enable roaming between cells. While the original Guide architecture managed mobility within the Guide application, Guide II requires a transparent mobility mechanism to support general-purpose applications.

2 Requirements

This section summarises the key requirements for our access control architecture:

Secure Access Control – As the network is publicly available throughout the city centre, a secure mechanism is required to ensure authorised access only.

Transparent Access Control – The access control mechanisms must operate fully transparent to any correspondent node on the public Internet.

Minimum User Inconvenience – End users of the access network should, apart from the initial authentication at login time, not notice any changes when using the network (i.e., standard applications must be fully supported).

Support for Mobile Handoffs – Many of the applications that will be used within the testbed will be multimedia oriented, and may therefore have stringent quality of service constraints. In particular, these applications are likely to be sensitive to the packet loss and delay effects caused by mobile terminals performing handoffs between cells. Consequently, any access control mechanism introduced must not adversely affect the performance of such handoffs.

Protection of Access Network – Protection against internal and external security threats such as denial-of-service attacks must be considered.

3 Architecture

The access control approach proposed here is based on the concept of packet marking and packet filtering. Access routers are placed at the periphery of the network to enforce packet filtering policies on the data traffic traversing the nodes. As a result, data packets sent by authorised users are forwarded, while packets of unauthorised clients are simply discarded.

Authorisation for access to the network is granted by the authentication server. Upon successful authentication of a user, the server issues a short-lived *access token* to the user's end system and informs the relevant access router(s) about the approval. The access token is a transitory credential that grants data packets from a particular user node access to the network. It is a soft-state mechanism, which requires the end systems to periodically refresh their authorisations.

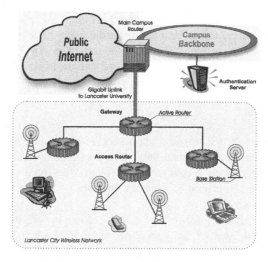

Fig. 1. The access control infrastructure proposed for our wireless network deployed around the City of Lancaster.

The key components of our access control architecture are described here. Figure 1 illustrates how this will be implemented for our wireless network at Lancaster:

- The *Authentication Server* is responsible for authenticating and authorising users of the access network. It provides a remote management interface for the set-up and configuration of user accounts.
- The *Gateway* connects the access network with the public Internet or a private Intranet (i.e., Campus network). As an extension of the firewall concept it is concerned with external security threats of arbitrary nodes on the Internet.
- The *Access Routers* (ARs) control access to the publicly accessible, wireless network. They block traffic originating from unauthorised end nodes based on network-level packet filtering. Co-locating the ARs directly with the base stations enables network-level protection to be applied on a per cell basis.
- The *End Systems* (i.e., handheld devices, laptops, etc.) request periodic authentication on behalf of the users and perform packet marking for authorised users. While the latter is realised through minor modification of the network stack, the former can be accomplished either through extensions to the network stack or by means of a user-level system service.

3.1 User Authentication

User authentication is carried out between the user's end system and the authentication server. As user authentication is needed on a periodic basis to refresh the access tokens, a lightweight mechanism is preferable. We therefore propose the use of a very simple request/response protocol (that consists of only one small message in each direction).

The authentication request sent from a mobile node to the authentication server includes the user's *username* and *password* as well as the node's *MAC address* and *IP address*. While the username and password are required to authenticate a client, the MAC and IP addresses are used to authorise the client node on the access routers. To prevent malicious users from spoofing the secret password of another user, the authentication protocol encrypts the user's credentials, using a public key mechanism.

3.2 Access Tokens

Access tokens are issued to users upon successful authentication and authorisation. The tokens are the *credential* that grants data packets originating from authorised user nodes to pass through the access router. A token is essentially a random value that is large enough to make it hard to guess or discover by a brute force search within the lifetime of the token[1].

Upon successful authorisation, the authentication server generates an access token and sends it to the user for the packet marking. However, before those packets can pass the access router, the router's access control list must also be updated. Consequently, the authentication server will also send an access list update to the respective access router (and its neighbouring routers) upon generation of a new access token. The access list update includes the triple *(access token, IP address, MAC address)*.

For security and robustness reasons, we chose to restrict the validity period of the access tokens to a configurable time interval (referred to as *expiration time*). The soft-state authentication protocol takes care of the periodic refresh of the user authorisation. The *refresh time* of the soft-state protocol must therefore be sufficiently smaller than the expiration time.

The main advantage of short-lived access tokens is that they are hard to spoof; especially in a roaming network, where a node's physical location changes frequently.

3.3 Packet Filtering

As the access control mechanism is based on network level packet filtering within the access routers, each access router maintains an access control list (ACL). This list accommodates the *(access token, MAC address, IP address)* filter information required to identify 'authorised packets' (packets that originate from authorised users). Access routers maintain separate ACLs for each network for which it is responsible.

When an access router receives an 'upstream' packet from a wireless device, it checks the relevant ACL to decide how to process the packet. If no ACL entry is present for the received packet, then the packet is simply discarded. There is however, one exception to this rule - packets destined for selected well-known servers on the network are allowed to pass. This enables unauthenticated mobile nodes access to limited network services (for example, the authentication server).

Upstream packets with MAC addresses matching an access list entry are further inspected. The router checks whether or not the IP address and access token included in the packet is valid. If so, the packet is granted access to the network.

---

[1] Since we envision a tokens lifetime in the order of a few minutes, we suggest a value of 32 bits for now.

Downstream packets (destined for wireless devices) are also subject to packet filtering. Thus, packets routed to the wireless networks force an ACL lookup. If no entry for the destination address exists, then the packet is dropped. Again, there is an exception for packets sourced from trusted hosts, such as the authentication server.

3.4 Roaming Support

We believe that in order to manage a large scale public access network, a set of boundaries must be in place, between areas of different administration. For example, it may be necessary to prevent users from gaining access to a certain part of the network for security reasons, or it may be necessary to use different link layer wireless technologies in different scenarios. As a result, by far the easiest way to separate these administrative areas is by placing each of them into a different layer 3 network. This allows for much more fine-grained and scalable management of the network.

As a result of this however, the mobile terminals require now a layer 3 mobile routing protocol, such as Mobile IPv4/v6, to roam between administrative domains. Therefore, upon a network handoff, mobile devices obtain a new care-of-address (CoA) for their new physical network location[2]. Consequently, network access may well be controlled by a different access router, which will have no knowledge of the user's previous authorisation. The access control scheme described so far however, could take up to several minutes before the user regains network access (i.e., until the next authentication refresh is carried out), which would clearly be unacceptable.

In order to overcome this weakness, we propose two special measures for roaming networks:

1. The mobile node must immediately perform an authentication refresh upon a network handoff.
2. When an access control triple is sent to an access router by the authentication server (in order to authorise a user), a copy of that triple is also sent to all *neighbouring* access routers[3]. Consequently, a node's new access router will already have an entry in its ACL when the node moves into its coverage area. If the respective access router then receives a packet from the mobile node, which has a valid ACL entry that matches the MAC address and access token, but not the IP address, it will still grant access for a short 'reprieve time'. However, if the router does not receive a fresh access list update for the node's new IP address before the reprieve time expires, traffic will be blocked. This technique preserves safety by granting access to packets based on a node's previous authorisation.

These extensions have the advantage that they do not interfere with or slow down network-level handoffs. The initial user authentication required when entering a new area is simply delayed (i.e. carried out in the background) to avoid extra latency.

---

[2] This is usually achieved either through DHCP (v4/v6) or the auto-configuration mechanisms of IPv6.

[3] Neighbouring routers are initially configured manually on the authentication server. However, an automated discovery protocol is subject to further research.

The reprieve time must be chosen carefully. On the one hand, the interval should be minimal as it gives provisional access to users based on their previous authorisation while, on the other hand, it must be long enough to complete an authorisation cycle.[4]

3.5 Enhanced Security

The access control solution described so far provides effective access control, but is subject to attack – the scheme is vulnerable to MAC address spoofing. Since the access token is transmitted in clear text, a malicious user in the same cell could snoop the network to obtain another user's "secret" credential. The combination of this credential and 'spoofing' the user terminal's MAC address would grant an attacker access to the network. Although the soft-state nature of the access control alleviates the problem because access tokens are only a short-lived authorisation, an impostor could develop an automated mechanism to snoop periodically for valid credentials.

As a consequence, to fully secure the access control mechanism even against MAC address spoofing, the access token must be encrypted whenever it is sent across the public wireless network. This gives us two areas of vulnerability. Firstly, the request/response protocol between a wireless device and the authentication server, and secondly, when the wireless terminal sends the tagged packets with the access token.

The interaction between a mobile device and the authentication server uses a combination of public and secret key mechanisms to avoid the need for a public key distribution infrastructure. The authentication server has a well known public key. Upon initiating an authentication request, the mobile device chooses a random *session key*. This key is then encrypted (along with the rest of the authentication request) using the server's public key, and sent to the authentication server. The response from the authentication server (which contains the mobile device's access token) is then encrypted using this shared session key (based on a symmetric encryption algorithm). This secures the conveyance of the access token.

In order to secure the second condition (where the mobile node sends a packet), the access token is also encrypted using the session key. In order to verify the authorisation of a packet, the relevant access router therefore also needs to know this session key. This is conveyed to the access router from the authentication server as part of the ACL update message.

In order to prevent replay-attacks (whereby the encrypted access token could simply be copied by an attacker), the access token is encrypted together with the packet's checksum. The checksum is derived from a CRC of the dynamic fields in the packet, such as the length field in the IP header, the sequence number of the TCP header, etc.

In network environments where the communication channels between the authentication server and the access router cannot be trusted, the access control list up date, which also includes the access token, must be encrypted as well. Standard end-to-end encryption techniques such as IPsec are recommended.

In cases where users demand a high level of security (for example, full privacy), the architecture supports an additional layer of protection based on data encryption on the

---

[4] We recommend a reprieve time of approximately 2-5 seconds depending on the network performance and authentication server.

last hop. Thus, end users can choose to encrypt the whole data packet using the shared session key by tunnelling the data to the access router. The access router decrypts the data packets before forwarding them.

Finally, it is worth noting that standard IPsec authentication and encryption are entirely complementary to our access control architecture. They can be used in addition to achieve secure end-to-end communication.

4 Implementation

This section outlines the implementation of the key components of our access control architecture. Due to the lack of space, we provide only a brief description here.

Client Software. We incorporate the network protocol extensions required for the access control mechanism within the Microsoft and Linux Mobile IPv6 stacks. We have chosen these particular protocol stacks, since we implemented both within previous projects [5].

Secure user authentication is accomplished by means of encryption. A client node uses the public key of the authentication server (which can be loosely configured at the client to avoid the need for a key distribution service) to encrypt the secret data of the authentication request. The RSA [6] public-key encryption algorithm is used to securely propagate the secret key to the authentication server. For the encryption of the authentication response, we use symmetric encryption based on the shared session key. This is accomplished via the triple-DES [7] encryption algorithm.

The enhanced MIPv6 stack also carries out the packet marking. It adds the most recent access token into every outgoing packet. To prevent MAC address spoofing and replay attacks, the access token is encrypted using the shared session key along with a packet checksum. The 32-bit checksum is taken from dynamic protocol fields of the IPv6 header. In order to simplify the filtering in the access routing, we place the 64-bit access credentials *(access token, checksum)* in front of the actual IPv6 header.

Authentication Server. A user-level application manages the user accounts and performs the actual authentication of the users on the client nodes. The user authentication protocol is based on a lightweight request/response protocol. The client node sends a request message (using UDP) to the authentication server including the encrypted user password, its IPv6 address and MAC address. Upon successful authentication, the server then replies with an access list update (which includes a new access token).

Access Router. The access router is based on the LARA++ active router architecture [8] supporting dynamic programmatic extension of router functionality. The access control service is implemented as a collection of active components. The control component is responsible to handle ACL updates from the server and to configure the packet filter component accordingly. The filter component in turn deals with the actual access control. It registers to receive all packets in order to enforce the access rules.

Gateway. The gateway connecting the wireless network covering the city centre with the campus backbone is also based on LARA++. Several active components are responsible for securing the access network from malicious external nodes. The router, for example, tries to detect denial-of-service attacks by external nodes based on packet analysis.

5 Related Work

Due to the restriction in this short paper, we merely mention directly related approaches here.

- Stanford's web-based access control solution, called SPINACH [9], is a simple approach without the need for specialised hardware or client software, but at the cost of inferior security (i.e., vulnerable to MAC address spoofing).
- Microsoft's CHOICE [10] is based on a proprietary Protocol for Authentication and Negotiation of Services (PANS). The architecture involves, separate PANS Authoriser and PANS Verifier gateways in addition to a global authentication server. The authoriser gateway enables restricted access to the authenticator only. Upon successful authorisation of a client node, the verifier gateway grants full access to the network. It filters packets based on the PANS tags. A custom client module is used to attach the tag to the data packets.
- Carnegie Mellon's Netbar system [11] is based on a remote configurable VLAN switch that is used to enable/disable individual ports depending on the authorisation of the connected machine.
- UC Berkeley has proposed a design [12] based on an enhanced DHCP client, an intelligent hub that supports enabling/disabling of individual ports, and a DHCP server that has been extended to remotely configure the hub based on the client's authorisation.

6 Conclusion

This paper has introduced a novel access control architecture for a publicly available, wireless network. Our architecture distinguishes itself from other approaches through the following features:

- Soft-state based authorisation in conjunction with the periodic authentication protocol offers a high level of security, as secret credentials (i.e. access tokens, secret keys) are re-issued in a configurable period.
- Support for roaming users in a mobile environment is inherent to the architecture. A short reprieve time allows previously authorised client nodes to smoothly roam between networks without adding extra latency.
- Configurable levels of security allow network administrators and/or end users to decide whether no encryption, encryption of the access credentials only (prevents MAC address spoofing), or full encryption of the data (provides privacy) should be used on the wireless link.

The design of our access control implementation is unusual in that we integrate the client-side functionality (i.e. authentication protocol, packet tagging) into our Mobile IPv6 stack (in order to better improve the performance of cell handoff) and build the access router functionality on top of an active router (for reasons of flexibility and extensibility).

References

1. Davies, J. et. Al: Caches in the Air: Disseminating Information in the Guide System. In Proceedings of IEEE Workshop on Mobile Computing Systems and Applications (WMCSA '99), New Orleans. (1999)
2. Cheverst, K. et. Al: Developing a Context-aware Electronic Tourist Guide: Some Issues and Experiences. In Proceedings of CHI '00, Netherlands, pp 17-24. (2000)
3. Guide II: Services for Citizens. Research Project. Lancaster University, EPSRC Grant GR/M82394. (2000)
4. Mobile IPv6 Research Collaboration with Cisco, Microsoft and Orange. Lancaster University, available via the Internet at "http://www.mobileipv6.net/testbed". (2001)
5. The LandMARC Project. Research Collaboration with Microsoft Research, Cambridge, available via the Internet at "http://www.LandMARC.net". (1999)
6. Kaliski, B., Staddon, J.: PKCS #1: RSA Cryptography Specifications. RFC 2437. (1998)
7. Schneier, B.: Applied Cryptography. Second Edition, John Wiley & Sons, New York, NY. (1995). ISBN 0-471-12845-7.
8. Schmid, S., Finney, J., Scott, A., Shepherd, D.: Component-based Active Network Architecture. In Proceedings of 6th IEEE Symposium on Computers and Communications (ISCC '01), Hammamet, Tunisia. (2001)
9. Poger, E., Baker, M.: Secure Public Internet Access Handler (SPINACH). In Proceedings of the USENIX Symposium on Internet Technologies and Systems. (1997)
10. Miu, A., Bahl, P.: Dynamic Host Configuration for Managing Mobility between Public and Private Networks. In Proceedings of the 3rd Usenix Internet Technical Symposium, San Francisco, California. (2001)
11. Napjus, E. A.: NetBar – Carnegie Mellon's Solution to Authenticated Access for Mobile Machines. White Paper, available at "http://www.net.cmu.edu/docs/arch/netbar.html".
12. Wasley, D. L.: Authenticating Aperiodic Connections to the Campus Network. Available at "http://www.ucop.edu/ irc/wp/wpReports/wpr005/wpr005_Wasley.html". (1996)

Design and Implementation of a QoS-Aware Replication Mechanism for a Distributed Multimedia System

Giwon On[1], Jens B. Schmitt[1] and Ralf Steinmetz[1,2]

[1]Industrial Process and System Communications
Dept. of Electrical Eng. & Information Technology
Darmstadt University of Technology
Merckstr. 25, D-64283 Darmstadt, Germany

[2]GMD IPSI
German National Research Center for Information Technology
Dolivostr. 15, D-64293 Darmstadt, Germany
{Giwon.On, Jens.Schmitt, Ralf.Steinmetz}@KOM.tu-darmstadt.de

Abstract. This paper presents the design and implementation architecture of a replication mechanism for a distributed multimedia system *medianode* which is currently developed as an infrastructure to share multimedia-enhanced teaching materials among lecture groups. The proposed replication mechanism supports the quality of service (QoS) characteristics of multimedia data and the availability of system resources. Each type of data handled and replicated are classified according to their QoS characteristics and replication requirements. The main contribution of this paper is the identification of new replication requirements in distributed multimedia systems and a multicast-based update propagation mechanism by which not only the update events are signalled, but also the updated data are exchanged between replication managers. By prototyping the proposed replication mechanism in medianode, we prove the feasibility of our concept for combining the QoS concept with replication mechanisms.

1 Introduction

One major problem about using multimedia material in lecturing is the trade-off between actuality of the content and quality of the presentations. A frequent need for content refreshment exists, but high quality presentation can not be authored by the individual teacher alone at the required rate. Thus, it is desirable that teachers presenting the same or at least similar topics but work at different locations can easily share their multimedia-enhanced lecture materials. The medianode project[1] is intended to provide such means for sharing to lecturers at the universities of the German state Hessen.

The design of the medianode system addresses issues of availability, quality of service, access control and distribution of data. To support teachers, it must allow for transparent access to shared content, and it must be able to operate in disconnected mode since lecturers do not have access to the network at all times during their presentations. The medianode system architecture is intended for de-centralized operation of a widely distributed system. Within this distributed system, each participating host is called a medianode and conceptually equal to all other participating nodes, i.e. a medianode is not considered a client or a server. Client or

D. Shepherd et al. (Eds.): IDMS 2001, LNCS 2158, pp. 38–49, 2001.

server tasks are taken on by medianodes in the system depending on the their resources and software modules.

Replication is the maintenance of on-line copies of data and other resources[2, 5]. Replication of presentation materials and meta-data is an important key to providing high availability, fault tolerance and quality of service (QoS) in distributed multimedia systems[21], and in particular in medianode. For example, when a user requires access (read/write) to a presentation which comprises audio/video data and some resources which are not available in the local medianode at this point of time, a local replication manager copies the required data from their original location and puts it into either one of the medianodes located nearby or the local medianode without requiring any user interaction (user transparent). This function enhances the total performance of medianode by reducing the response delay that is often caused due to insufficient system resources, such as memory, CPU time, and network bandwidth, at a given service time. Furthermore, because of the available replica in the local medianode, the assurance that users can continue their presentation in a situation of network disconnection, is significantly higher than without replica.

The structure of the paper is as follows. In Section 2, we give an overview of related work. The merits and limitations of existing replication mechanisms are discussed and a comparison of our approach with previous work is given. Section 3 presents our replication system model. We define the scope of our replication mechanism in medianode and present the characteristics of presentational media types, for which we identify a need for new replica units and granularity. We also describe the proposed replication maintenance concept, e.g. how and when replicas are created and how the updates are signalled and transported. In Section 4, we present our prototype implementation architecture. It describes operation flows in medianode with and without replication system. We conclude the paper with a summary of our work and an outlook towards possible future extensions of our replication mechanism in Section 5.

2 Related Works

Several approaches to replication have already been proposed. The approaches differ for distributed file systems from those for Internet-based distributed web servers and those for transaction-based distributed database systems. Well-known replication systems in distributed file systems are AFS[6], Coda[7], Rumor[13], Roam[14] and Ficus[16] which keep the file service semantics of Unix. Therefore, they support to develop applications based on them. They are based either on a client-server model or a peer-to-peer model. Often they use optimistic replication which can hide the effects of network latencies. Their replication granularity is mostly the file system volume, with a large size and low number of replicas. There is some work on optimization for these examples concerning of update protocol and replica unit. To keep the delay small and therefore maintain real-time interaction, it was desirable to use an unreliable transport protocol such as UDP. In the earlier phases, many approaches used unicast-based data exchange, by which the replication managers communicated with each other one-to-one. This caused large delays and prevented real-time interaction. To overcome this problem, multicast-based communication has used recently [9, 11, 12,

17]. For Coda, the RPC2 protocol is used for multicast-based update exchange, which provides with the *Side Effect Descriptor* transmission of large files.

For limiting the amount of storage used by a particular replica, Rumor and Roam developed the selective replication scheme[18]. A particular user, who only needs a few of the files in a volume, can control which files to store in his local replica with selective replication. A disadvantage of selective replication is the 'full backstoring' mechanism: if a particular replica stores a particular file in a volume, all directories in the path of that file in the replicated volume must also be stored.

JetFile[9] is a prototyped distributed file system which uses multicast communication and optimistic strategies for synchronization and distribution. The main merit of JetFile is its multicast-based callback mechanism by which the components of JetFile, such as file manager and versioning manager interact to exchange update information. Using the multicast-based callback, JetFile distributes the centralized update information which is normally kept by the server over a number of multicast routers. However, the multicast callbacks in JetFile are not guaranteed to actually reach all replication peers, and the centralized versioning server, which is responsible for serialization of all updates, can lead to a overloaded system state. Furthermore, none of the existing replication systems supports quality of service (QoS) characteristics of (file) data which they handle and replicate.

3 Replication System Model

3.1 Design Goals and Scope of Our Replication System

By analysing the service requirements distributed multimedia systems for the example of medianode, we identified a number of issues that the design of our replication system needs to address:

- **High availability:** The replication system in medianode should enable data/service access in both connected and disconnected operation modes. Users can keep multiple copies of their files on different medianodes that are distributed geographically across several universities in the state of Hessen.

- **Consistency:** Concurrent updates and system failures can lead to replicas not being consistent any more, i.e. *stale* state. The replication system should offer mechanisms for both resolving conflicts and keeping consistency between multiple replicas and their updates.

- **Location and access transparency:** Users do not need to know where presentation resources are physically located and how these resources are accessed.

- **Cost efficient update transport:** Due to the limitation of system and network resources, the replication system should use multicast-based transport mechanism for exchanging updates to reduce resource utilization.

- **QoS support:** The specific characteristics of presentational data, especially of multimedia data should be supported by the proposed replication mechanism.

In medianode, we mainly focus on the replication service for accessing data in terms of '*inter-medianode*', i.e. between medianodes, by providing replica maintenance in each medianode. Consequently, a replication manager can be implemented as one or a set of medianode's bow instances in each medianode. The replication managers communicate among each other to exchange update information through the whole medianodes.

3.2 Different Types of Presentation Data

Data organization comprises the storage of content data as well as meta information about this content data in a structured way. The typical data types which can be identified in medianode are described in [3]. Table 1 shows an overview of these data types with their characteristics.

Table 1: Data categories and their characteristics in medianode

target data	availability req.	consistency req.	persistency	update frequency	data size	QoS playback
presentation description	high	middle (high)	yes	low	small/ middle	not required
organizational data	high	high	yes	low	small	not required
file/data description	high	middle	yes	middle	small	not required
multimedia resources	high	middle	yes	middle	large	required
system resources	middle (low)	middle	no	high	small	not required
user session/ token	high	high	no	high	small	not required

3.3 Classification of Target Replicas

As argued in subsection 3-1, the main goal of replication is to provide availability of medianode's services and to decrease the response time for accesses to data located on other medianodes. To meet this goal, data which is characterized by a high availability requirement (See Table 1) should be replicated among the running medianodes. We classify different types of target replicas according to their granularity (data size), requirement of QoS support, update frequency and whether their data type is 'persistent' or not ('volatile'). Indeed, there are three classes of replicas in medianode:

- *Truereplicas* which are persistent and of large size. Content files of any media type, which also may be parts of presentation files are Truereplicas. Truereplicas are the only replica type from the three types, to which the end users have access for direct manipulation (updating). On the other side, these are also the only replica type which requires the support of really high availability and QoS provision.

- *Metareplicas* (replicated metadata objects) that are persistent and of small size. An example would be a list medianodes (sites) which currently contain an up-to-date copy of a certain file. This list itself is replicated to increase its availability and improve performance. A metareplica is a replica of this list.

- *Softreplicas* which are non-persistent and of small size. This kind of replicas can be used for reducing the number of messages exchanged between the local and remote medianodes, and thereby reducing the total service response time. I.e., if a local medianode knows about the available local system resources, then the local replication manager can copy the desired data into the local storage bow, and the service that is requested from users which requires exactly the data can be processed in a shorter response time. Information about the available system resource, user session and the validity of user tokens are replicas of this type.

All replicas which are created and maintained by our replication system are an identical copy of original media. Replicas with errors (non-identical copy) are not allowed to be created. Furthermore, we also do not support any replication service for function calls, and elementary data types.

3.4 The Replication Mechanism

3.4.1 Replication Model

Basically, our replication system does not assume a client-server replication model, because there are no fixed clients and servers in the medianode architecture; every medianode may be client or server depending on its current operations. Peer-to-peer model with the following features is used for our replication system:

(a) Every replica manager keeps track of a local file table including replica information.

(b) Information whether and how many replicas are created is contained in the every file table. I.e. each local replica manager keeps track of which remote replica managers (medianode) are caching which replicas.

(c) Any access to the local replica for reading is allowed, and guaranteed that the local cached replica is valid until notified otherwise.

(d) If any update happens, the corresponding replica manager sends a multicast-based update signal to the replica managers which have the replica of the updated replica and therefore members of the multicast group.

(e) To prevent excessive usage of multicast addresses, the multicast IP addresses through which the replica managers communicate can be organized in small replica sub-groups. Examples for such sub-groups are file directories or a set of presentations about a same lecture topic.

3.4.2 Update Distribution and Transport Mechanism

The update distribution mechanisms in medianode differs between the three replica types and their concerning managers. This is due to the fact that the three replica types have different levels of requirements on and characteristics of high availability, update frequency and consistency QoS (see Table 1). Experience from GLOVE[4] and [5] also shows that differentiating update distribution strategies makes sense for web and other distributed documents. The medianode's replication system offers an unique interface to the individual update signalling and transport protocols which are selectively and dynamically loaded and unloaded from the replica transport manager that is implemented as an instance of medianode's access bow. Possible update transport and signalling protocols are:

- RPC protocol [2,10]as a simple update distribution protocol. This mechanism is mainly used at the first step of our simple and fast implementation.
- A *multicast based RPC* communication mechanism. In this case, the updates are propagated via multicast other replica managers which are members of the multicast group. *RPC2* [7,11] is a good candidate for the first implementation. *RPC2* also offers the transmission of large files, such as the updated AV content files or *diff*-files, by using the *Side Effect Descriptor*. But, the *RPC2* with *Side Effect Descriptor* does not guarantee any reliable transport of updates.
- LC-RTP based reliable multicast protocol: LC-RTP (Loss Collection-Realtime Transport Protocol)[12] is originally developed as an extension of RTP protocol to support the reliable video streaming within the medianode project. Therefore, we adopt LC-RTP and check the usability of the protocol, depending on the degree of reliability required for the individual groups of replicas.

3.4.3 Approaches for Solving Conflicting Updates and for Resolving Conflicts

The possible conflicts that could appear during the shared use of presentational data and files are either (a) update conflict when two or more replicas of an existing file are concurrently updated, (b) naming conflict when two (or more) different files are given concurrently the same name, and (c) update/delete conflict that occur when one replica of a file is updated while another is deleted. In most existing replication systems, the conflict resolving problem for update conflicts was treated as a minor problem. It was argued that most files do not get any conflicting updates, with the reason that only one person tends to update them[9]. Depending on the used replication model and policy, there are different approaches of which our replication system uses the following strategies [7,8,13,14,15]:

- Swapping - to exchange the local peer's update with other peer's updates;
- Dominating - to ignore the updates of other peers and to keep the local update as a final update;
- Merging - to integrate two or more updates and build one new update table;

4 Implementation

We have implemented a prototype of the proposed replication system model on a Linux platform (SuSe 7.0, Redhat 6.2). Implemented are the media (file) and its replica manager (ReplVerifierBow), update transport manager (ReplTransportBow), replica service APIs which are Unix-like file operation functions such as open, create, read, write, close (ReplFileSysBow), and a session information storage bow (VolatileStorBow) which maintains user's session and token information.

4.1 Bow Description

Table 2 gives a short descriptions of bows which implement medianode's basic functions and the services of our replication system.

Table 2: A summary of medianode's bows used for our replication system

Bow	Description
MNBow	• addressable via an unique bow identifier and version number • uses request and response queues and dispatcher threads • defines request processing routine
MNAccessBow	• child class of MNBow and implements access bow API • offers RPC server modules and enables RPC connection from web server • HTML-based presentation files are provided via this bow
ReplTransportBow	• child class of MNBow and a variant of access bow • implements the transport managers for replication service • offers transport protocol modules such as RPC, RPC2, and LC-RTP (LC-FTP)
(GUI)TelnetBow	• child class of MNBow and a variant of access bow • offers TCP server modules • acts as telnet server and provides information which medianode maintains such a list of bows loaded by the core, memory usages of a certain medianode's process running etc. • GUIBow implements a TelnetBBow with a graphical user interface
MNVerifierBow	• child class of MNBow and implements verifier bow API • offers modules needed for user authentication
ReplVerifierBow	• child class of MNBow and a variant of verifier bow • implements the media (file) and replica managers for replication service • maintains the three replica tables
MNStorageBow	• child class of MNBow and implements storage bow API
FileBow	• child class of MNStorageBow • implements functions for local file operation • no interface routine support for replication service
XMLBow	• child class of MNStorageBow • offers modules for dynamic generation of presentation files • no interface routine support for replication service
ReplFileSysBow	• child class of MNStorageBow • implements functions for local file operation • implements interface routines for replication service
VolatileBow	• child class of MNStorageBow • implements functions for maintaining volatile data such as memory usage information • implements interface routines for replication service

4.2 Presentation Service without Replication Support

The interaction model for medianode's bows is based on a 'request-response' communication mechanism. A bow which needs to access data or services creates a request packet and sends it to the core. According to the request type, the core either processes the request packet directly, or forwards it to a respective bow. The processing results are sent to the origin bow in a response packet. The request and response packets contain all necessary information for the communication between bows as well as for processing the requests.

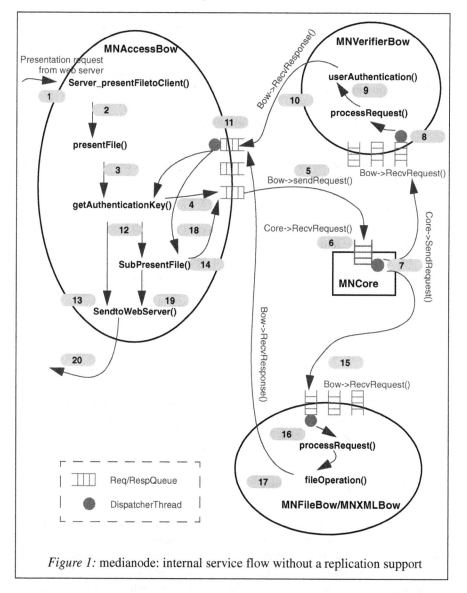

Figure 1: medianode: internal service flow without a replication support

Based on this request-response mechanism, we experimented some presentation scenarios with and without a replication service. Figure 1 shows one example of presentation services without a replication system. Upon receiving a presentation request from user via web server, the MNAccessBow creates first a request packet to check user's authentication (steps 1~4) and sends it via the core (steps 5~7) to MNVerifierBow which puts authentication test value into a response packet and sends it to the origin bow, MNAccessBow (steps 8~11). In the case of a successful authentication, MNAccessBow creates a request packet to get the required presentation data and sends it via the core to a corresponding storage bow (steps 12~15). Either MNFileBow or MNXMLBow, it depends on the requested (media) data type, checks whether the data exists locally, and then creates a response packet which contains either a file handle or an error message, sends it to the MNAccessBow (steps 16~18). MNAccessBow sends then to the web server a response which is either an authentication failure message or a presentation file.

4.3 Presentation Service with Replication Support

4.3.1 Initialization of MediaList and Replica Tables
In this subsection, we describe the medianode's operation flow with the replication service. Basically, the replication service in medianode begins by creating media list and replica tables of the three replica types in each medianode. As shown in Figure 2, ReplFileSysBow sends a request packet via the core to ReplVerifierBow for creating a media list for media data which locate in the local medianode's file system (steps 1~2). Upon receiving the request packet, ReplVerifierBow creates media list which will be used to check the local availability of any required media data (step 3). ReplVerifierBow then builds the local replica tables for the two replica types, *Truereplicas* and *Metareplicas,* if the replica information exists already. A medianode configuration file can specify the default location where replica information is stored. Every type of replica table contains a list of replicas with the information about organization, replica volume identifier, unique file name, file state, version number, number of replicas, a list of replica, a multicast IP address, and some additional file attributes, such as access right, creation/modification time, size, owner, and file type. The third replica table for the *Softreplicas* to which the local system resource, user session and token information belong may be needed to be created in terms of memory allocation, and the contents of this table can be partly filled when users request some certain services. Once the replica tables are created, they are stored in the local file system and accessible persistently.

4.3.2 Maintaining Replica Tables

In medianode, these three replica tables are maintained locally by the local replication manager. So, there is no need to exchange any update-related messages for the files of which there is no replica created. This approach increases the system resource utiliza-tion, especially network resources, by decreasing the message numbers exchanged between the replication managers among the distributed medianodes. But, when any medianode wants to get a replica from the local replica tables, the desired replica elements are copied to the target medianode, and the replication manager at the target medianode keeps these replica elements separate in another replica table which is used only for the management of remote replicas, i.e. for the management of replicas for which their original files are stored in a remote medianode.

4.3.3 Acquiring a Replica to Remote Replication Managers

Upon receiving the service requests (data access request) from users, the local medianode attempts to access the required data in a local storage bow (ReplFileSysBow) (step 4~5).

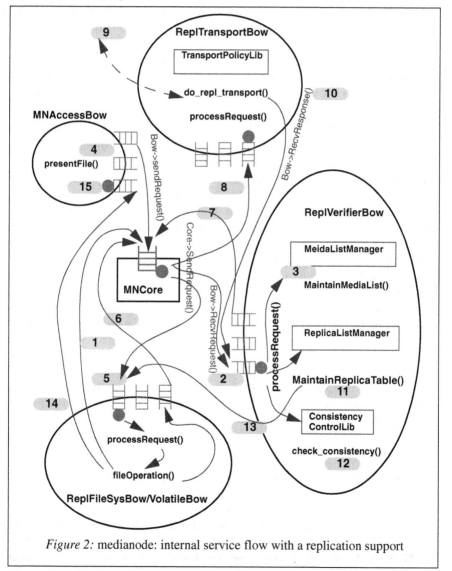

Figure 2: medianode: internal service flow with a replication support

In the case, when the data is not available locally, the local ReplFileSysBow sends a request packet to ReplVerifierBow to get a replica for the data. The ReplVerifierBow then start a process to acquire a replica by creating a corresponding request packet which is passed to ReplTransportBow (steps 6~8). The ReplTransportBow multicasts a data search request to all the peer replication managers and waits for replication managers to respond (step 9). The list of medianodes to which the multicast message is sent can be read from the medianode's configuration file. Whether the ReplTransportBow waits for all responses or receives the first one is dependent on the optimization policy which is given as configuration flag. After receiving the target replica, the ReplTransportBow sends a response packet to the ReplVerifierBow which then updates the corresponding replica tables, i.e. ReplVerifierBow adds the new replica element to the Truereplicas table and its metadata to the Metareplicas table, respectively (steps 10~13). Finally, the local ReplFileSysBow which originally issued replica creation request creates a response packet including the replica handle and then sends it to the MNAccessBow (steps 14~15).

5 Summary and Future Works

In this paper, we presented the replication mechanism of our distributed media system *medianode*, and described the design and implementation architecture of the prototyped replication system. The main contributions of this paper are (1) to identify the new replication requirements for distributed multimedia systems, and (2) to build a replication mechanism for distributed multimedia systems, which supports the individual QoS characteristics of multimedia data and uses system resource usage information. To achieve these targets, we first studied the characteristics of presentational media types which are handled in medianode, identified replica units and granularity. These have not been considered and not supported in existing replication mechanisms. We then built a QoS-aware replication mechanism, in which the decision whether and when a replica should be created from original file is made by checking the QoS characteristics of the requested media and the current usages of available system resources, for distributed multimedia systems based on the new requirements and the result of feature surveys.

The next working steps would be to design other replication services which provide service implementations such as predictive replication to increase access availability and to reduce latency. Similar approaches are Hoarding[7, 19], prefetched caching and resource reservation in advance[20].

References

1. The medianode project. (web site http://www.httc.de/medianode).
2. G. Coulouris, J. Dollimore and T. Kindberg. *Distributed Systems*, 3rd Ed., Chapter 1,8,14 and 15, Addison-Wesley, 2001.
3. G. On, M. Zink, M. Liepert, C. Griwodz, J. Schmitt, R. Steinmetz. Replication for a Distributed Multimedia System. In *Proc. of ICPADS2001*, pp.37-42, 2001.
4. G. Pierre, I. Kuz, M. van Steen and A.S. Tanenbaum. Differentiated Strategies for Replicating Web documents, In *Proc. of 5th International Workshop on Web Cach-*

ing and Content Delivery, Lisbon, May 2000.

5. P. Triantafillou and D.J. Taylor. Multiclass Replicated Data Management: Exploiting Replication to Improve Effciency. In *IEEE Trans. on Parallel and Distributed Systems*, pages 121-138, Vol.5, No.2, Feb.1994.

6. R. Campbell. *Managing Andrew File System (AFS)*, Prentice Hall PTR, 1998.

7. M. Satyanarayanan, J.J. Kistler, P. Kumar, M.E. Okasaki, E.H. Siegel, and D.C. Steer. Coda: A Highly Available File System for a Distributed Workstation Environment. In *IEEE Transaction on Computers*, 39(4), April 1990.

8. J. Yin, L. Alvisi and C. Lin. Volume Leases for Consistency in Large-Scale Systems. In *IEEE Trans. on Knowledge and Data Engineering*, 11(4), 1999.

9. B. Groenvall, A. Westerlund and S. Pink. The Design of a Multicast-based Distributed File System. In *Proceedings of Third Symposium on Operating Systems Design and Implementation, (OSDI'99), New Orleans, Louisiana,* pages 251-264. February, 1999.

10. K.P. Birman and B.B. Glade. Reliability Through Consistency. In *IEEE Software*, pages 29-41, May 1995.

11. M. Satyanarayanan and E.H. Siegel. Parallel Communication in a Large Distributed Environment. In *IEEE Trans. on Computers*, pages 328-348, Vol.39, No.3, March 1990.

12. M. Zink, A. Jones, C. Girwodz and R. Steinmetz. LC-RTP (Loss Collection RTP): Reliability for Video Caching in the Internet. In *Proc. of ICPADS 2001: Workshop,* pages 281-286. IEEE, July 2000.

13. R. Guy, P. Reiher, D. Ratner, M. Gunter, W. Ma, and G. Popek. Rumor: Mobile Data Access Through Optimistic Peer-to-Peer Replication. In *Workshop on Mobile Data Access,* November 1998.

14. D. Ratner, P. Reiher, and G. Popek. Roam: A Scalable Replication System for Mobile Computing. In *Workshop on Mobile Databases and Distributed Systems (MDDS),* September 1999.

15. P. Triantafillou and C. Neilson. Achieving Strong Consistency in a Distributed File System. In *IEEE Transaction on Software Engineering*, pages 35-55, Vol.23, No.1, January 1997.

16. T.W. Page,Jr., R.G. Guy, G.J. Popek, and J.S. Heidemann. Architecture of the Ficus scalable replicated file system. *Technical Report CSD-910005, UCLA,* USA, March 1991.

17. M. Mauve and V. Hilt. An Application Developer's Perspective on Reliable Multicast for Distributed Interactive Media. In *Computer Communication Review*, pages 28-38, 30(3), July 2000.

18. D.H. Ratner. Selective Replication: Fine grain control of replicated files. *Master's thesis, UCLA,* USA, 1995.

19. G.H Kuenning. Seer: Predictive File Hoarding for Disconnected Mobile Operation. *PhD. dissertation, UCLA-CSD-970015. UCLA,* USA, 1997.

20. C. Griwodz. Wide-Area True Video-on-Demand by a Decentralized Cache-based Distribution Infrastructure. *PhD. dissertation*, TU Darmstadt, April 2000.

21. J. Chung-I and M.A. Sirbu. *Distributed Network Storage with Quality-of-Service Guarantees.* web site http://www.ini.cmu.edu/~sirbu/pubs/99251/chuang.h

Distribution of Video-on-Demand in Residential Networks*

Juan Segarra and Vicent Cholvi

Departament de Llenguatges i Sistemes Informàtics
Universitat Jaume I
CP 12071 Castelló (Spain)
{jflor,vcholvi}@uji.es

Abstract. In this paper, we study how to distribute cache sizes into a tree structured server for transmitting video streams through video-on-demand (VoD) way. We use off-line smoothing for videos and our request rates are distributed according to a 24 hour audience curve. For this purpose we have designed a slotted-time bandwidth reservation algorithm, which has been used to simulate our experiments. Our system tests the quality of service (QoS) in terms of starting delay, and once a transmission has started, the system guarantees that it will be transmitted without any delay or quality loss. We tested it for a wide range of users (from 800 to 240 000) and also for a different number of available videos. We demonstrate that a tree structured system with uniform cache sizes performs better than the equivalent system with a proxy-like configuration. We also study delay distribution and bandwidth usage in our system on a representative case.

1   Introduction

New net connections at homes are increasingly becoming faster and having more bandwidth. This allows multimedia applications for these connections, from on-line radio stations which are widely available nowadays, to heavier applications such as video playing.

Previous Studies Much work has already been done on the delivery of video–on–demand (VoD). Maybe the most simple technique consists of using a centralized single–server intended to deliver all video requests to users. However, it is known that this approach does not scale well as the number of users and videos grows. In order to solve this problem, Vassilakis et al. [13] use a hierarchical network of servers so that most popular videos are located as close to the users as possible. They found that such an approach is preferable to using a centralized server.

Dan and Sitaram presented a framework for dynamic caching [5]. Basically, this does not require the whole video to be stored on the same server, but rather

---

* This study is partially supported by the CICYT under grant TEL99-0582 and Bancaixa under grant P1-1B2000-12.

D. Shepherd et al. (Eds.): IDMS 2001, LNCS 2158, pp. 50–61, 2001.

only parts of the video. They try to retain in a server the parts brought in by a request for reuse by a closely followed request and then those parts are subsequently discarded. However, this approach does not guarantee real video–on–demand delivery, but rather a good performance of the overall system.

New video compression formats such as MPEG2 [8] also allow for the storage and transmission of high quality video streams requiring relatively low capacity. One major problem with compression formats in streams is that their bit rate variability is increased. Transmitting real-time VBR flows is no trivial matter, because a different amount of bandwidth will be needed during the transmission. Naive approaches to this problem use a pessimistic evaluation, as they reserve enough bandwidth for the stream to be transmitted as if it were always in its worst case. Obviously, this is quite inefficient.

One of the methods to improve these transmissions is the *smoothing* [7, 12] of streams before their transmission. This is done by transmitting frames into the client playback buffer in advance of each burst so that peak and rate variability requirements are minimized. Rexford and Towsley show how to compute an optimal transmission schedule for a sequence of nodes by characterizing how the transmission rate varies as a function of the playback delay and the buffer allocation at the server and client nodes [9]. By also using smoothing, several techniques have been proposed which develop a *transmission plan* [12] consisting of time periods so that, in each period, the transmission may be performed by using a constant–bit–rate (CBR) network service. In [14], the authors present a technique that makes use of this approach. They also develop a video delivery technique via intelligent utilization of the link bandwidth and storage space available at the proxy servers (i.e., servers which are attached to the gateway router that connects the final users).

Our Study In our study, we follow an approach similar to [14]. First, we consider that, for each video, we have a transmission plan. Additionally, we split the video into parts, each one corresponding with each time period of the transmission plan. We also allow each part to be placed at the different video servers located along the network. Unlike [14], we do not restrict these servers to being attached to the gateway router that connects the final users (i.e., they do not have to be proxies).

In this paper we focus, given the above mentioned scenario, on the analysis of both how to place video parts at the different video servers and how to distribute resources (storage space) throughout the whole system. We also analyze the system behavior by varying both the number of videos and users. Finally, we examine the behavior of the system through the day.

The rest of our paper is organized as follows. In Section 2 we describe the scenario we use. In Section 3 we present our video–on–demand delivery system and in Section 4 we show our results. Finally, our conclusions are presented in Section 5.

2   Scenario

For our study, we use a hierarchical network architecture for the distribution network. This architecture is used nowadays in residential networks, so it meets our needs.

Our tree structure is a binary tree with four depth levels. At the top of the tree, there is a central server, storing all videos, ranging from 100 to 10 000. Furthermore, at each node of the tree there is a cache server, which acts as a client to the upper caches servers. These caches must be understood as static caches; their content is specified off–line, and it does not change in time. Server caches at leafs serve the same number of users, ranging from 50 to 15 000 (so, the total number of users ranges from 800 to 240 000). Links between nodes have a bandwidth of 1.5 Gbps downstream. A moderate bandwidth is also needed upstream in order to send user requests to the central server. Note that final users share a bandwidth of 1.5 Gbps because they share the link to their nearest node. Fig. 1 shows our tree structure.

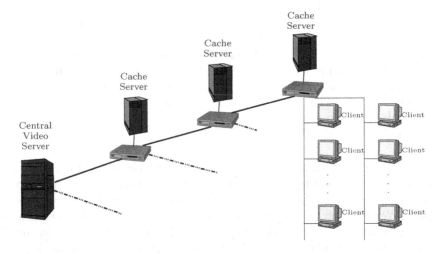

Fig. 1. Tree structure of our system.

In our approach to the video transmission problem we study the performance in a 24 hour period. Previous studies on video demand rates [1, 6] have determined the behavior of these rates in this period; so our simulations work with a rate distribution according to these studies. We also consider that a user makes a request only if he is not waiting nor receiving a video (i.e., nobody can receive more than one transmission at a time). In Fig. 2 we can see the request rate distribution obtained in a simulation with one request per day for each user.

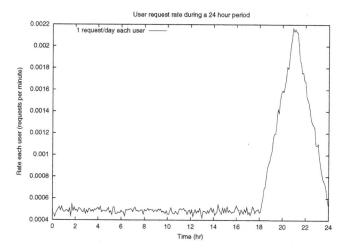

Fig. 2. Request rate distribution in a 24 hour period

3   Placement of Video Streams and the Reservation Algorithm

In this section we analyze how to distribute videos throughout the whole system. Since bandwidth usually becomes a bottleneck in stream transmissions, the placement policy is a major issue of the system we are proposing for delivery of video on demand.

In order to avoid the rate variability problem we described in the introduction, we use smoothed versions of video streams [12]. Thus, each video is characterized by a collection of tuples $\langle time, rate \rangle$, whose first parameter denotes a time period and whose second one is the CBR rate associated with such a time period.

Our distribution policy is applied off–line and it acts on the different video–parts corresponding to the tuples of each video. Basically, it first assigns, at start up, a weight value to each video. That weight value is based on the video *popularity*, which represents the probability of being requested according to Zipf's law [3]. This distribution has been found to statistically fit video program popularities estimated through observations from video store statistics [4]. Once such an assignment is done, it distributes the video–parts in the tree, sorting them out by weight value: the higher the weight value, the nearer to users they are placed. When storing these video–parts in places other than the main server, they are replicated in all other caches at the same level. Thus, the video–parts with the highest weight value are placed in all caches next to users.

For the above proposed video stream placement policy, it is necessary to use a *reservation algorithm*. Such an algorithm manages video requests, guaranteeing that, once a video is accepted (maybe after some start–up time delay), it will be delivered without interruption to the final user/s.

Our reservation algorithm is constructed around a *bandwidth reservation table* which represents the bandwidth that will be used by each link at each *time–slot*, the units of time to provide a bandwidth reservation (in our case it is of 1 minute). Initially, all values in this table are 0, due to there being no bandwidth reservation. This table changes over time, since rows of time–slots are added and removed as videos are requested and served.

When a video request is received, we first map out the route which each video–part will follow. Then, we test (for each video–part) to see whether it is already planned for transmission at the same time by the same links. If so, that request is added to the multicast transmission of this video–part without any additional bandwidth requirements. Otherwise, we check whether there is enough bandwidth in each link of the route during the slots of the transmission. In that case, bandwidth is reserved by adding the new video–part rate to the bandwidth used in the table. In order to use a single video stream to serve several near arriving requests, we intentionally delay the playback for an amount of time of 2 minutes (such an amount of time is called *batch–time*). Fig. 3 shows the code of this algorithm.

Step #1: A user requests a video.
Step #2: If that video has already been requested and it has not started yet, the start time of the new request will be the same as the previous one. Otherwise, the new request will start after a batch–time.
Step #3: The system calculates the transmission path of each video–part, and the exact time when they have to be transmitted.
Step #4: **For each** video–part **do**
    For each link in the transmission path **do**
        If there is a reserve for this video–part in this link at the same time, add our request as a multicast. Otherwise, reserve the bandwidth needed for this video–part in this link during the required time–slots.
Step #5: Accept video for transmission or go to Step #3 in the next time slot (in which case, all reserves and multicasts for this request performed in Step #4 are canceled).

Fig. 3. Algorithm for the acceptance of video requests.

It must be pointed out that, in general, it may be necessary to synchronize the different video–parts that make up a video during the playback. That is because they may be placed at different servers throughout the system. Whereas this can be done in a number of ways by using protocols such as RTP [10] and RTSP [11], in this paper we will not go into details about how to carry them out.

4   Results

In this section we present the results generated by our simulations. The performance of the system is obtained using the starting delay (or serving time). That is, the time between a video request and the beginning of its transmission. Due to space limitations, we show only the mean value of this magnitude (which follows a similar pattern to both the maximum and 90% starting delays).

4.1   Storage Distribution in the Cache Servers

In these simulations we test the system performance against the number of users with four different cache sizes. All these simulations have a request rate of 1 video/day each user. We have analyzed two possible configurations: uniform cache sizes in all the system, and a proxy–like configuration.

Fig. 4 shows how those configurations behave against a centralized system (i.e, a system without caches where all videos are stored in the main server).

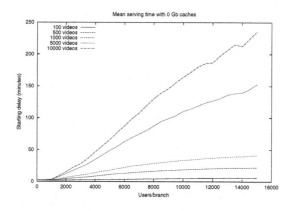

Fig. 4. System performance without storage capacity in caches

Performance with Uniform Cache Sizes Our first approach to the problem of distributing cache sizes consists of using the same size in all caches.

Figures 4, 5, 6 and 7 show the system performance with 0, 100, 250 and 500 Gb cache size respectively. They show that, when the number of users is low, the system works without any congestion. That is what explains why its performance is independent of the number of videos. However, when we increase

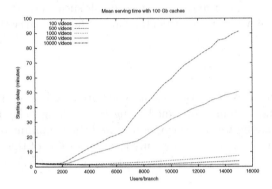

Fig. 5. System performance with 100 Gb cache size

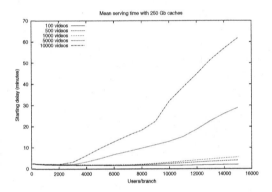

Fig. 6. System performance with 250 Gb cache size

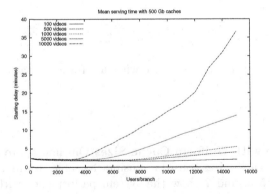

Fig. 7. System performance with 500 Gb cache size

the number of users, the system becomes unable to serve their requests without any congestion. In any case, it can be readily seen that the bigger the cache size, the better the serving times offered by the system. With a more accurate view, we can see that the change in times between Fig. 4 and Fig. 5 is the bigger one. This indicates that having a minimum cache size in each node greatly improves our serving times. Thus, adding cache size always increases the system performance, but this increment is lower when the system already has a large cache size.

Performance with Proxy–like Configuration In this section, we compare the approach followed in the previous sections with one using proxy servers (i.e., cache servers attached to the gateway router that connects the finals users). In order to be fair, we will compare *equivalent* systems (i.e., systems with the same global capacity). For instance, given a system with uniform caches sizes of 100 Gb in 14 cache servers, the proxy–like equivalent system would have 175 Gb in its 8 proxy servers. Thus, Fig. 8 would be equivalent to Fig. 5, Fig. 9 to Fig. 6 and Fig. 10 to Fig. 7.

As can be seen, in all cases the performance in proxy–like systems is slightly lower than in systems with uniform caches. Starting delays with uniform caches are about 40% lower than with proxy–like caches. The main reason for this is that when we do not have intermediate caches and we request a video which is not in the first cache level, it has to be transmitted from the main server. This results in a faster congestion of upper links. Moreover, because of the tree structure, adding storage size to leaf caches is always more expensive than adding the same size to intermediate caches, so this added size is not enough to compensate the lack of intermediate caches.

4.2   System Behavior Through the Day

As previously pointed out (see Fig. 2), the request rate varies through the day. Consequently, it seems quite reasonable to expect a different system behavior during a 24 hour period.

In this section, we analyze the system behavior through the day. For this task, we take a system with 100 Gb of storage capacity in each cache, 1000 different videos and 10 000 users in each final branch (that is 160 000 total users). In order to start this simulation with a non-empty system, we have simulated a period of 48 hours and we have used the results from the last 24 hours.

Fig. 11 shows the starting delay distribution of this system. It follows the same pattern as Fig. 2, which is what we expected[1]. The first part of the figure corresponds to the end of the maximum audience peak of the previous day. Another interesting point is that, when the request rate is low, starting delay is always below the batch time (2 minutes). This fact demonstrates that some requests are added to previous plans and the system is not congested during this period.

---

[1] Note that local peaks are due to the multicast effect in transmission plans in a high request rate.

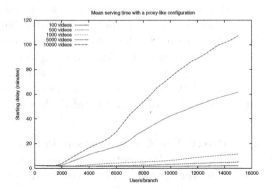

Fig. 8. Starting delay in a proxy–like system equivalent to 100 Gb cache sizes

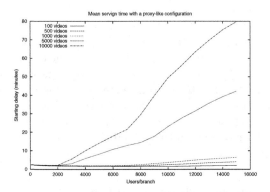

Fig. 9. Starting delay in a proxy–like system equivalent to 250 Gb cache sizes

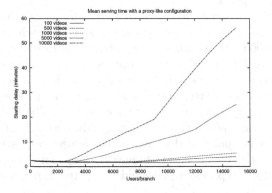

Fig. 10. Starting delay in a proxy–like system equivalent to 500 Gb cache sizes

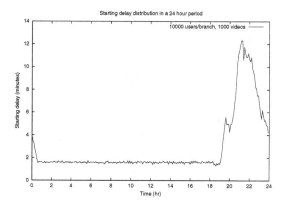

Fig. 11. Serving time distribution in a 24 hour period

Fig. 12 shows the percentage of used bandwidth in the links of each level. Whereas *level* 4 represents the links between the main server and the next two caches (2 links of 1.5 Gb each one), *level* 1 represents the links which share each user branch (16 links of 1.5 Gb each one).

It can be seen that links are used below 100% during the low request rate period. For that reason the minimum delays in Fig. 11 are all around the batch time. It also shows that links at *level* 4 constitute the bottleneck of the system, because it is the first level which reaches a usage of 100%. This indicates that although intermediate caches serve many requests, 100 Gb each cache is not enough to avoid this bottleneck. This is quite logical, because if each video size is about 1.5 Gb, in 3 cache levels (300 Gb) we could only store 200 of the 1 000 videos there. Thus, to watch the other 800 videos, transmissions must be made from the main server. Note also that bandwidth usage in lower levels may grow even when the upper ones have reached a usage of 100%. This indicates that lower caches are serving the videos which they have stored locally.

5   Conclusions

In this paper we have studied the benefits of using caches in a tree structured system for video–on–demand. We test two ways of distributing the cache size, and we compare our results with the centralized system as a reference.

Our simulations demonstrate that a system with 100 Gb in each cache has a performance of about 5 times better than without it, and about 10 times when we use 500 Gb in each cache. We also demonstrate that a uniform distribution offers results about 40% better than a proxy–like configuration. However, there are many other ways of distributing this size, and the performance variation with different configurations can be important.

Some other issues need further research. As demonstrated above, links at the main server are the bottleneck. Thus, studies for adjusting the system charac-

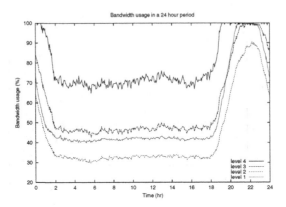

Fig. 12. Bandwidth usage at each level of the tree

teristics to avoid this situation are needed. Furthermore, it will be necessary to add the possibility of changing the video locations on-line, thereby adding more videos or modifying their popularity value without shutting down the system. Finally, in this paper we have used the popularity value for linearly distributing the videos in the caches, but other methods should be tested as well.

References

[1] Bell Atlantic. Fact sheet:results of bell atlantic video services. video–on–demand market trial. trial results, 1996.

[2] L. Berc, W. Fenner, R. Frederick, and S. McCanne. Rpt payload format for jpeg-compressed video. Request for Comments 2035, Network Working Group, October 1996.

[3] Lee Breslau, Pei Cao, Li Fan, Graham Phillips, and Scott Shenker. Web caching and Zipf-like distributions: Evidence and implications. In *Proceedings of the IN-FOCOM '99 conference*, March 1999.

[4] A. Dan, D. Sitaram, and D. Shahabuddin. Dynamic batching policies for an on–demand video server. *Multimedia Systems*, 4:112–121, 1996.

[5] Asit Dan and Dinkar Sitaram. A generalized interval caching policy for mixed interactive and long video environments. *Multimedia Computing and Networking*, January 1996.

[6] PG de Haar et al. DIAMOND project: Video–on–demand system and trials. Eur Trans Teleccommun (8)4: 337–244, 1997.

[7] W. Feng, F. Jahanian, and S. Sechrest. An optimal bandwidth allocation strategy for the delivery of compressed prerecorded video. *Multimedia Systems*, 5(5):297–309, 1997.

[8] D. Gall. Mpeg: a video compression standard for multimedia applications. *Communications of the ACM*, 34(4):46–58, April 1991.

[9] Jeniffer Rexford and Don Towsley. Smoothing variable–bit–rate video in an internetwork. *IEEE/ACM Transactions on Networking*, pages 202–215, April 1999.

[10] H. Schulzrinne, S. Casner, R. Frederick, and S. McCane. RTP: A transport proto-col for real–time applications. Request for Comments RFC 1889, Network Work-ing Group, 1994.

[11] H. Schulzrinne, A. Rao, and R. Lanphier. Real–time streaming protocol (RTSP). Internet Draft, IETF, 1997.

[12] Arun Solleti and Kenneth J. Christensen. Efficient transmission of stored video for improved management of network bandwidth. *International journal of network management*, 10:277–288, 2000.

[13] Constantinos Vassilakis, Michael Paterakis, and Peter Triantafillou. Video place-ment and configuration of distributed video servers on cable TV networks. *Mul-timedia Systems*, 8:92–104, 2000.

[14] Yuewei Wang, Zhi-Li Zhang, David H.C. Du, and Dongli Su. A network–conscious approach to end–to–end video delivery over wide area networks using proxy servers. *IEEE/ACM Transactions on Networking*, 8(4):429–442, August 2000.

A QoS Negotiation Scheme for Efficient Failure Recovery in Multi-resolution Video Servers

Minseok Song, Heonshik Shin, and Naehyuck Chang

School of Computer Science and Engineering,
Seoul National University, Seoul 151-742, Korea
mssong@cselab.snu.ac.kr,{shinhs,naehyuck}@snu.ac.kr

Abstract. In this paper, we present a Quality of Service (QoS) negotiation scheme for efficient failure recovery in multi-resolution video servers with disk arrays. This scheme exploits multi-resolution property of video streams by negotiating service resolutions in order to provide graceful QoS degradation when a disk fails. Using the proposed scheme, not only can we increase the number of admitted clients greatly when all disks are operational but also utilize server resources efficiently. Furthermore, it can provide each client with acceptable QoS even in the presence of disk failure while maximizing server-perceived rewards. The effectiveness of the proposed algorithm is evaluated through simulation-based experiments.

1 Introduction

One of the crucial requirements for a Video-on-Demand (VOD) service is the ability to support heterogeneous clients with different Quality of Service (QoS) parameters, such as display size, resolution level, and frame rate. As described in [3], [5], the most viable way to satisfy various QoS requirements of clients is to use multi-resolution video stream whose video sequences are encoded such that subsets of a full-resolution video bit stream can be decoded to extract lower resolution streams.

Video data is inherently voluminous and requires high bandwidth throughput. Therefore, most VOD servers employ Redundant Array of Inexpensive Disks (RAID). A fundamental problem, though, is that large disk arrays are highly vulnerable to disk failures [8]. Since delivery and playback of video streams should be performed in a real-time fashion, the VOD server must guarantee the playback rate of accepted video streams even in the presence of disk failures.

To guarantee continuous delivery of video streams in the degraded mode (i.e., when a disk has failed), current approaches for the fault-tolerant VOD servers tend to reserve contingent bandwidth or buffers [1], [7], [8], [11]. Thus, they admit too few streams thereby under-utilizing the server resources in the normal mode (i.e., when all disks are operational). Furthermore, they do not consider the buffer and the disk bandwidth constraints simultaneously albeit important for admission control.

In this paper, we propose a QoS negotiation scheme for efficient failure recovery in multi-resolution video servers. The proposed scheme exploits multi-resolution property of video streams and uses resources such as disk bandwidth and buffer efficiently. It

D. Shepherd et al. (Eds.): IDMS 2001, LNCS 2158, pp. 62–73, 2001.

defines a spectrum of resolution levels and permits acceptable performance when a disk fails by using a smaller amount of resources; thus, it can improve resource utilization in the normal mode. It also considers the priority of clients and thus provides graceful degradation in the degraded mode.

The rest of this paper is organized as follows: In Section 2, we present system models to aid further description of our fault tolerance schemes. Next, we propose an admission control algorithm in Section 3 and resource adjustment algorithms in Section 4, respectively. We validate the proposed schemes through the simulation in Section 5 and conclude in Section 6.

2 Multi-resolution Video System Model

2.1 Multi-resolution Video Stream Model

An efficient method for extracting multi-resolution video streams is to use *sub-band coding schemes* [9]. The sub-band coding schemes provide high scalability as well as compression ratios which are comparable to MPEG-2 compression. Further discussion on the video server will be based on this scheme.

Multi-resolution video streams can be modeled as follows [9]. We refer to the video segment as the amount of data retrieved during one round. Let us assume that a given video V has g segments such that
$$V = \{S_0 \bigcup \ldots \bigcup S_i \bigcup \ldots \bigcup S_{g-1}\}.$$
Let us assume that each segment S_i has up to Q display resolutions of data such that
$$S_i = \{S_i^0 \bigcup \ldots \bigcup S_i^j \bigcup \ldots \bigcup S_i^{Q-1}\},$$
where S_i^j represents the jth *enhancement* ($0 < j \leq Q-1$) for the segment S_i. We refer to S_i^0 as the *base resolution* of the segment S_i. To display a video stream with resolution k, it requires a reading of data from the base resolution as well as that of all the data from the first enhancement to the kth enhancement. For example, to view the resolution k of S_i, we need to retrieve $\{S_i^0 \bigcup S_i^1 \bigcup \ldots \bigcup S_i^k\}$. Let each S_i^j be composed of b_j bits, and then total bits for the resolution k is $\sum_{j=0}^{k} b_j$. We define a *Unit Request Size* for resolution k, NB_k, to be

$$NB_k = \frac{\sum_{j=0}^{k} b_j}{\min_{m \in [0, Q-1]} b_m}.$$

2.2 Data Placement for Multi-resolution Video Stream

Two data placement schemes for multi-resolution video streams have been proposed in the literature. Chang *et al.* [3] propose a periodic interleaving placement scheme, and Paek *et al.* [12] define a balanced placement scheme for the multi-resolution video streams. We assume that the disk array consists of D homogeneous disks. The periodic interleaving scheme accesses only one disk during a round for a segment, whereas a segment is divided into D equal amounts of data and placed across D disks in the balanced placement. We employ the periodic interleaving scheme for our data placement policy because it achieves high disk throughput and low system delay time [5].

For data availability, a parity encoding technique of RAID 5 is also used. Since a stripe unit size is equal to the data size for the full-resolution video stream requested during a round, *any partial resolution stream as well as the full resolution stream can be retrieved contiguously from the surviving disks in the degraded mode.* Figure 1 shows our data placement which stores three display resolutions of video streams. The parity blocks are computed on a segment basis, e.g., $P1 = S_0 \oplus S_1 \oplus S_2 \oplus S_3$.

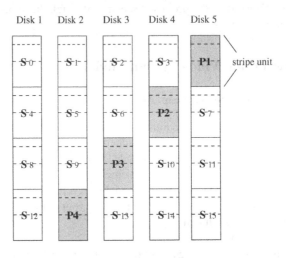

Fig. 1. RAID for periodic interleaving data placement

Let us consider the variation in the load on each disk in the periodic interleaving scheme. Since each access unit is completely stored on a single disk, each client retrieves data from a single disk during a round. Examining the load on disks for any two consecutive rounds, we find that due to the round-robin placement of access units, the clients retrieving data on the same disk will all move to the neighboring disk during the next round. To express such a load shifting property efficiently, we refer to the clients accessing the same disk during a round as a *client group.* Therefore, we can partition clients into D client groups (say CG_1, CG_2,...,CG_D, respectively).

2.3 QoS Model

Feasibility of the multi-resolution presentation gives an opportunity for graceful degradation when there are not enough resources for supporting video streams. QoS degradation, however, should be enforced judiciously because some applications cannot accept video streams below some resolution levels [2]. Furthermore, VOD servers should consider priority requirements of the clients [6].

To efficiently express the priority of the client, we apply the notion of *reward* [6] to our QoS model. That is, every client is assigned with several rewards indicating its value to the system (e.g., monetary value) when the video stream is serviced with the assigned QoS level successfully. To explicitly describe QoS requirements of clients, we assume that every client is aware of the following information:

- A maximum resolution level is assigned to every client, and the video server retrieves a video stream with the maximum resolution level in the normal mode.
- A minimum resolution level is assigned to every client, and the video server can degrade the resolution to the minimum resolution level in the degraded mode; however, resolutions below the minimum resolution level are not allowed.
- A reward value is assigned to every resolution ranging from the minimum resolution level to the maximum resolution level.

Let C_i^m denote the mth client in the client group CG_i ($i = 1, ..., D$). Let max_i^m and min_i^m be the maximum resolution level and the minimum resolution level for the client C_i^m, respectively, where $0 \leq min_i^m \leq max_i^m \leq Q - 1$. Each client C_i^m has resolution levels $min_i^m, ..., max_i^m$ with rewards $RW_i^m(min_i^m), ..., RW_i^m(max_i^m)$, respectively, where $0 \leq RW_i^m(min_i^m) \leq ... \leq RW_i^m(max_i^m)$. We limit the difference between the maximum resolution level and the minimum resolution level, and refer to it as $diff$. That is, $\forall C_i^m$, if $max_i^m \geq diff$, then $min_i^m = max_i^m - diff$. Otherwise, $min_i^m = 0$.

3 Admission Control Algorithm

The proposed scheme guarantees the video services above the minimum resolution levels in the degraded mode and the maximum resolution level in the normal mode for all the clients while maximizing the sum of rewards in the degraded mode. To satisfy these objectives, we first describe an admission control algorithm in this section, and reward maximization algorithms in the next section.

3.1 Admission Control Condition

We consider two constraints, disk bandwidth and buffer, for admission control.

Disk Bandwidth Constraint Round-based scheduling is used for data retrieval: The time is divided into equal-sized time intervals and each admitted client is served once every time interval, named *round*. If we ignore the degraded mode, the service time, which represents total read and seek times requested by the clients in one round, must not exceed the round duration R. However, a *contingent disk bandwidth* for reconstruction should be reserved to prepare for the degraded mode. Since additional disk load is the same as the load of the failed disk, approximately twice the disk load are required for surviving disks in the degraded mode [8]. Therefore, *the service time for the clients in each client group must not exceed $\frac{1}{2}R$.*

Let N_i be the number of clients *to be serviced* from the client group CG_i. Let us define ST_i^{min} and ST_i^{max} to be the service time for the client group CG_i when all the clients in the group retrieve the video streams of the minimum resolution and the maximum resolution level, respectively. Let us assume that the server disk is characterized as shown in Table 1. We use typical seek time model described in [4], in which *every*

Table 1. Notations and parameter values for a disk

Transfer rate	r_t	80Mbps
Typical disk seek and rotation time	T_s	14 ms

client requires a seeking overhead (seek time + rotational delay) T_s for one read. The
following inequality that represents ST_i^{min} should hold for every client group to guarantee that all the clients retrieve their streams with the minimum resolution level even
in the degraded mode:

$$ST_i^{min} = \sum_{m=1}^{N_i} (T_s + \frac{\sum_{j=0}^{min_i^m} b_j}{r_t}) \leq \frac{1}{2}R \tag{1}$$

To service the maximum resolution levels in the normal mode, the following relationship should hold for every client group:

$$ST_i^{max} = \sum_{m=1}^{N_i} (T_s + \frac{\sum_{j=0}^{max_i^m} b_j}{r_t}) \leq R \tag{2}$$

Buffer Constraint To schedule the video streams in any order during a service round,
we use dual-buffer mechanism [5]. Let B be the total buffer size, and CG_{mh} be the most
heavily loaded client group. In the degraded mode, the buffer requirement becomes the
maximum when the clients in the CG_{mh} retrieve data from the failed disk. Therefore,
the following inequality for the buffer constraint should hold to service streams with
the minimum resolution levels even in the degraded mode:

$$2(\sum_{\{i|1\leq i\leq D, i\neq mh\}} \sum_{m=1}^{N_i} \sum_{j=0}^{min_i^m} b_j) + (D-1)(\sum_{m=1}^{N_{mh}} \sum_{j=0}^{min_i^m} b_j) \leq B \tag{3}$$

In the normal mode, there should be sufficient buffer to service the maximum resolution levels. Therefore, the following inequality should hold:

$$2(\sum_{i=1}^{D} \sum_{m=1}^{N_i} \sum_{j=0}^{max_i^m} b_j) \leq B \tag{4}$$

3.2   Admission Control Decision

When a client requests a video stream, the server assigns the client to the client group
accessing a disk on which the first segment requested by the client is stored. If the admission of the client violates the admission control conditions described in Inequalities
(1),(2), (3) and (4), the server delays admitting the client considering the client's acceptable initial delay. That is, if a suitable group can be found within the client's acceptable
initial delay time, the new client is admitted and becomes a member of that client group;
otherwise, it is rejected. After the admission, the client remains a member of the client
group until it closes a video stream.

4   Resolution Adjustment Algorithms

The selected resolutions for the admitted clients may be changed in the following three situations.

- When a disk fails.
- When admitting a new client in the degraded mode.
- When a client closes a video stream.

4.1   When a Disk Fails

We define FR_i^m to be the selected resolution for the client C_i^m in the degraded mode, and ST_i^{FR} to be the service time for the client group CG_i when all the clients in the group retrieve the video streams with FR_i^m. Then, the four inequalities below indicate the conditions imposed on FR_i^m.

$$ST_i^{max} \leq \frac{1}{2}R \qquad (5)$$

$$ST_i^{FR} = \sum_{m=1}^{N_i}\left(T_s + \frac{\sum_{j=0}^{FR_i^m} b_j}{r_t}\right) \leq \frac{1}{2}R \qquad (6)$$

$$2\left(\sum_{\{i|1\leq i\leq D, i\neq mh\}}\sum_{m=1}^{N_i}\sum_{j=0}^{max_i^m} b_j\right) + (D-1)\left(\sum_{m=1}^{N_{mh}}\sum_{j=0}^{max_i^m} b_j\right) \leq B \qquad (7)$$

$$2\left(\sum_{\{i|1\leq i\leq D, i\neq mh\}}\sum_{m=1}^{N_i}\sum_{j=0}^{FR_i^m} b_j\right) + (D-1)\left(\sum_{m=1}^{N_{mh}}\sum_{j=0}^{FR_i^m} b_j\right) \leq B \qquad (8)$$

The degradation of resolutions is incurred by the shortage of either buffer or disk bandwidth. When a disk fails, for every client group, the server checks whether Inequality (5) is satisfied or not. Let Sd be the set of client groups which do not satisfy Inequality (5). The server degrades the resolution for the clients in each client group $CG_i \in Sd$ *on a per client group basis*. The server also checks a buffer condition described in Inequality (7). If Inequality (7) is not satisfied, the server degrades the resolution by examining *all the clients admitted by the server*. There can be the following cases for the resolution degradation.

1. Case 1: $Sd \neq \phi$, and Inequality (7) is satisfied.
2. Case 2: $Sd = \phi$ and Inequality (7) is not satisfied.
3. Case 3: $Sd \neq \phi$, and Inequality (7) is not satisfied.

We now define Resolution Degradation Problems ($\mathcal{RDP}$) as follows.

Definition 1 Resolution Degradation Problems ($\mathcal{RDP}$)
*1. In Case 1, the resolution degradation problem is to find FR_i^m for every client C_i^m
in each client group $CG_i \in Sd$, that maximizes $\sum_{m=1}^{N_i} RW_i^m(FR_i^m)$ while satisfying
Inequality (6).*
*2. In Case 2, the resolution degradation problem is to find FR_i^m for every client C_i^m
that maximizes $\sum_{i=1}^{D} \sum_{m=1}^{N_i} RW_i^m(FR_i^m)$ while satisfying Inequality (8).*

In Case 3, the server first determines FR_i^m for every client C_i^m in each client group
$CG_i \in Sd$, that maximizes $\sum_{m=1}^{N_i} RW_i^m(FR_i^m)$ while satisfying Inequality (6). Then,
if Inequality (8) is not satisfied yet, the server further degrades the resolutions by examining all the clients admitted by the server.

In the degraded mode, every client C_i^m should receive a stream with one resolution
between min_i^m and max_i^m while maximizing the sum of rewards. Hence, $\mathcal{RDP}$ is
reduced to a *multiple choice knapsack problem* which is known to be NP-complete [10].
For this reason, we now present heuristic algorithms for $\mathcal{RDP}$. To describe heuristic
algorithms, let us define *Impact Factors* $IF_i^m(k)$ ($k = min_i^m, ..., max_i^m - 1$) for the
client C_i^m to be

$$IF_i^m(k) = \frac{RW_i^m(max_i^m) - RW_i^m(k)}{NB_{max_i^m} - NB_k}.$$

A denominator of the $IF_i^m(k)$ represents the difference of unit request sizes, while a
numerator represents the difference of rewards when the resolution is degraded from
the maximum resolution level to the k. Therefore, *a client with a smaller impact factor
should be degraded first because it can return more disk bandwidth to the server while
minimizing the reward loss.* Let AI_i be a set of impact factors for all the clients in the
client group CG_i ($i = 1, ..., D$). Sets of impact factors DI_i for the client group CG_i
($i = 1, ..., D$) are maintained for later resolution enhancement and are initialized to ϕ.
The heuristic algorithm for resolution degradation when a disk fails, called RDF, is as
follows:

Algorithm *RDF: Resolution Degradation algorithm when a disk Fails*
1.   Set of impact factors : TI_{all}, TI_i ($i = 1, ..., D$);
2.   **for** all the clients C_i^m in each client group CG_i, ($i = 1, ..., D$)
3. $FR_i^m \leftarrow max_i^m$;
4.   **for** each client group CG_i ($i = 1, ..., D$)
5. $TI_i \leftarrow sort(AI_i)$; (* with the increasing order of impact factors *)
6.   **if** $Sd \neq \phi$, and Inequality (7) is satisfied.   (* Case 1 *)
7.   **for** each client group $CG_k \in Sd$
8.   **repeat**
9.   Find the least impact factor, $IF_k^L(v) \in TI_k$;
10.   **if** ($v < FR_k^L$)
11. $FR_k^L \leftarrow v$;
12. $TI_k \leftarrow TI_k - \{IF_k^L(v)\}$;
13. $DI_k \leftarrow DI_k \bigcup \{IF_k^L(v)\}$;
14.   **until** (Inequality (6) is satisfied)
15.   **if** $Sd = \phi$, and Inequality (7) is not satisfied.   (* Case 2 *)

16. $TI_{all} = TI_1 \bigcup ... \bigcup TI_D;$

17. $TI_{all} \leftarrow sort(TI_{all});$ (* with the increasing order of impact factors *)

18.   **repeat**

19.   Find the least impact factor, $IF_k^L(v) \in TI_{all};$

20.   **if** ($v < FR_k^L$)

21. $FR_k^L \leftarrow v;$

22. $TI_{all} \leftarrow TI_{all} - \{IF_k^L(v)\};$

23. $DI_k \leftarrow DI_k \bigcup \{IF_k^L(v)\};$

24.   **until** (Inequality (8) is satisfied)

When a disk fails, FR_i^m is initialized to max_i^m for every client C_i^m. In addition, impact factors in the AI_i are sorted in the ascending order and added to the TI_i ($i = 1, ..., D$). After initialization (lines 2-5), RDF determines whether Case 1 or Case 2 occurs (line 6 and 15). If Case 1 occurs, for each client group $CG_k \in Sd$, the RDF chooses the *least* value of impact factor $IF_k^L(v) \in TI_k$ and removes it from the TI_k. Then, if $FR_k^L > v$, it degrades the resolution to v. The steps for Case 1 above are repeated until Inequality (6) satisfied (lines 7-14). If Case 2 occurs, the degradation is performed by examining all the clients admitted by the server (lines 16-24).

4.2 When Admitting a New Client in the Degraded Mode

Just after admitting a new client in the degraded mode, the resolutions for the admitted clients may be degraded to accommodate the new client. We assume that the new client is serviced from the client group CG_w. If $CG_w \in Sd$, the server finds FR_w^m for the clients in the CG_w by using the RDF. If Case 2 occurs, then the server enforces the method described from the line 16 to the line 24 in the RDF.

4.3 When a Client Closes a Video Stream in the Degraded Mode

When a client closes a video stream in the degraded mode, returned disk bandwidth or buffer is reclaimed to increase the resolutions for the clients. Assuming that an outgoing client C_u^p belongs to the client group CG_u, the heuristic algorithm for resolution enhancement, called REA, is as follows:

Algorithm *REA: Resolution Enhancement Algorithm*

1.   Set of impact factors : $DI_{all};$

2.   Removes impact factors for the client C_u^p from DI_u and $AI_u;$

3.   Removes the client C_u^p from the client group CG_u and recalculates $ST_u^{FR};$

4.   **if** $CG_u \in Sd$, and Inequality (7) is satisfied. (* Degradation for the clients in the client group CG_u is due to Case 1 *)

5.   **while** ($ST_u^{FR} \leq \frac{1}{2}R$)

6.   Find the greatest impact factor, $IF_u^G(v) \in DI_u;$

7.   **if** ($v > FR_u^G$)

8. $FR_u^G \leftarrow v;$

9. $DI_u \leftarrow DI_u - \{IF_u^G(v)\};$

10. **if** $CG_u \notin Sd$, and Inequality (7) is not satisfied. (* Degradation is due to Case 2 *)

11. $DI_{all} = DI_1 \bigcup ... \bigcup DI_D$;
12. $DI_{all} \leftarrow sort(DI_{all})$; (* with the decreasing order of impact factors *)
13.   **while** (Inequality (8) is satisfied)
14.   Find the greatest impact factor, $IF_k^G(v) \in DI_{all}$;
15.   **if** ($v > FR_k^G$)
16. $FR_k^G \leftarrow v$;
17. $DI_{all} \leftarrow DI_{all} - \{IF_k^G(v)\}$;
18. $DI_k \leftarrow DI_k - \{IF_k^G(v)\}$;

REA first determines the reasons for the resolution degradation (line 4 and 10). If degradation for the clients in the client group CG_u is due to Case 1, the REA chooses the *greatest* impact factor, $IF_u^G(v)$ in DI_u and removes it from the DI_u. Then, if $v > FR_u^G$, it increases the resolution to the v. Above steps are repeated while $ST_u^{FR} \leq \frac{1}{2}R$ (lines 5-9). If degradation is due to Case 2, resolution enhancement is enforced by examining all the clients admitted by the server (lines 13-18).

5   Experimental Results

To evaluate the effectiveness of our schemes, we have performed simulation-based experiments. The server consisting of 32 disks stores 1000 video clips, and each of the video length is 50 minutes. Arrival of client requests is assumed to follow the Poisson distribution and the mean arrival rate is assumed to be 20 arrivals/min, where the choice of video clips is random. Each segment has 11 display resolutions whose bit rates are shown in Table 2 [5], and the maximum resolution level for every client is assumed to be random. The objectives for the simulation are as follows:

1. Number of admitted clients according to the degree of resolution degradation
2. Effectiveness of heuristic algorithms

Table 2. Scalable video data rates

Resolution index	0	1	2	3	4	5	6	7	8	9	10
Current bit rate (kb/s)	190	63	63	64	126	127	127	127	126	127	190
Total bit rate (kb/s)	190	253	316	380	506	633	760	887	1013	1140	1330

5.1   Number of Admitted Clients According to the Degree of Resolution Degradation

Figure 2 shows the number of admitted clients for 10 hours according to the buffer size and $diff$ when R is 2 seconds. The number of admitted clients increases with the $diff$ value. The reason for this is that greater $diff$ provides more opportunity for the resolution degradation. The number of admitted clients also increases with the buffer size.

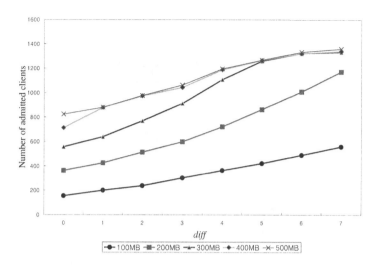

Fig. 2. Effects of buffer size and $diff$

5.2 Effectiveness of Heuristic Algorithms

An optimal solution for $\mathcal{RDP}$ can be found by exhaustively enumerating the feasible solutions and selecting the one with the highest reward sum. However, its computational complexity is $O((diff+1)^{N_i})$ for the client group CG_i. Since the number of admitted clients in a client group is approximately 35, finding the optimal solution when $diff > 1$ is almost impossible. Thus, we only compare our heuristic algorithm with the optimal solution when $diff = 1$. A reward value of 40 is assigned to the maximum resolution level, and the rewards are assumed to decrease by random values between 1 and 5 for one resolution degradation. The metric used here is the sum of rewards for a client group. Figure 3 shows the sum of rewards according to the round length, and the sum of rewards by our methods is very close to the optimal sums.

To evaluate our heuristic algorithm for $diff > 1$, let us consider the following algorithm, called *RDWF*. For simplicity, we ignore Case 2.

Algorithm *RDWF: Resolution Degradation algorithm considering reWard diFference*
1. **for** all the clients C_i^m in each client group CG_i, $(i = 1, ..., D)$
2. $FR_i^m \leftarrow max_i^m$;
3. **for** each client group $CG_k \in Sd$
4.   **repeat**
5.   For the client whose FR_k^m is greater than min_k^m, find a client C_k^p whose $RW_k^p(max_k^p) - RW_k^p(FR_k^p - 1)$ is minimum;
6. $FR_k^p \leftarrow FR_k^p - 1$;
7.   **until** (Inequality (6) is satisfied)

Figure 4 shows the sum of rewards according to the number of admitted clients in a client group when $diff = 4$. RDF shows better performance than $RDWF$ because

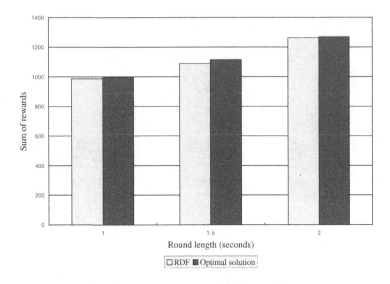

Fig. 3. Comparison between optimal solution and RDF when $diff = 1$

the RDF reflects both rewards and bandwidth for the degradation, whereas the $RDWF$ only considers the difference of rewards.

6   Conclusions

In this paper, we have proposed a QoS negotiation scheme for multi-resolution video servers to provide efficient failure recovery. The proposed scheme defines a QoS model which includes both a range of resolution levels and their respective rewards to the system in order to provide QoS degradation in the degraded mode. It also estimates the additional disk load and the buffer size in the degraded mode at admission time, and thus it can guarantee acceptable performance even in the degraded mode. To maximize the server-perceived rewards, we have presented heuristic algorithms for resolution degradation and enhancement. We have demonstrated the effectiveness of the scheme through simulations. Our simulation results show that it increases the admission ratio as well as server-perceived rewards. We are currently working on the QoS negotiation scheme for VBR video streams in multi-resolution video servers.

References

[1] S. Berson, L. Golubchik, and R. Muntz. Fault tolerant design of multimedia servers. In *Proceedings of the ACM SIGMOD Conference on Management of Data*, pages 364–375, May 1995.
[2] R. Boutaba and A. Hafid. A generic platform for scalable access to multimedia-on-demand systems. *IEEE Journal on Selected Areas in Communications*, 17(9):1599–1613, September 1999.

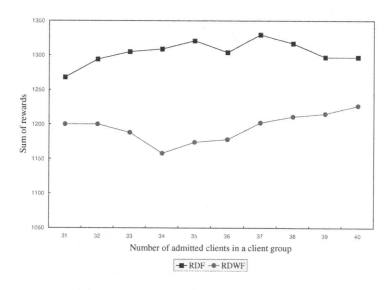

Fig. 4. Comparison between RDF and $RDWF$ for R = 2 seconds

[3] E. Chang and A. Zakhor. Scalable video data placement on parallel disk arrays. In *Proceedings of IS/SPIE International Symposium on Electronic Imaging: Science and Technology*, pages 208–221, December 1994.

[4] E. Chang and A. Zakhor. Cost analyses for vbr video servers. *IEEE multimedia*, 3(4):56–71, 1996.

[5] E. Chang and A. Zakhor. Disk-based storage for scalable video. *IEEE Transactions on Circuits and Systems for Video Technology*, 7(5):758–770, October 1997.

[6] I. Chen and C. Chen. Threshold-based admission control policies for multimedia servers. *The Computer Journal*, 39(9):757–766, 1996.

[7] A. Cohen and W. Burkhard. Segmented information dispersal (sid) for efficient reconstruction in fault-tolerant video servers. In *Proceedings of ACM International Multimedia Conference*, pages 277–286, November 1996.

[8] L. Golubchik, J. Lui, and M. Papadopouli. A survey of approaches to fault tolerant vod storage servers: Techniques, analysis, and comparison. *Parallel Computing*, 24(1):123–155, January 1998.

[9] J. Lui K. Law and L. Golubchik. Efficient support for interactive service in multi-resolution vod systems. *The VLDB Journal*, 24(1):133–153, January 1999.

[10] S. Martello and P. Toth. *Knapsack Problems: Algorithms and Computer Implementations*. John Wiley & Sons, 1990.

[11] B. Ozden, R. Rastogi, P. Shenoy, and A. Silberschatz. Fault-tolerant architectures for continuous media servers. In *Proceeding of the ACM SIGMOD Conference on Management of Data*, pages 79–90, 1996.

[12] S. Paek, P. Bocheck, and S. Chang. Scalable mpeg2 video servers with heterogeneous qos on parallel disk arrays. In *Proceedings of International Workshop on Network and Operating System Support for Digital Audio and Video*, pages 363–374, April 1995.

Tolerance of Highly Degraded Network Conditions for an H.323-Based VoIP Service

Peter Holmes, Lars Aarhus, Eirik Maus

Norwegian Computing Center, P.O. Box 114 Blindern, Oslo, Norway
{peter.holmes, lars.aarhus, eirik.maus}@nr.no

Abstract. The empirical work presented here concerns the effects of very large packet loss and delay conditions upon the performance of an H.323-based VoIP service. Specifically, it examines call establishment performance and audio voice quality under these conditions. The work was performed as part of an investigation concerning the effects of GEO satellite environments upon H.323-based VoIP, but its findings are relevant to all kinds of networks which may suffer or become subject to highly aberrant transmission conditions. The call establishment tests showed that the H.323 protocols could establish calls successfully under severely impaired conditions. The listening tests showed that uncontrolled jitter was the most destructive parameter to listening quality. Packet loss was also influential, though somewhat less dramatically.

1   Introduction

The empirical work presented here concerns the effects of very large packet loss and delay conditions upon the performance of an H.323-based VoIP system. It was performed during Q2-Q4 2000 within the IMMSAT project ("*Internet Protocol based MultiMedia Services over a Satellite Network*") [1] [2], a project carried out by Norsk Regnesentral [14] and Nera SatCom AS [16].

Two primary types of VoIP tests were carried out: *call establishment* and *audio voice quality*. The main objectives of prototype testing were:

- To verify that the H.323 protocols could be used to establish calls with an acceptable voice quality, in an environment that approximates the characteristics of a GEO (Geosynchronous Earth Orbit) satellite-based IP network.
- To find the *parametric limits* for delay, jitter, and packet loss where the H.323 protocols could no longer provide an acceptable VoIP service. That is, where call establishment becomes severely impaired / fails and where audio voice quality degrades such that usability of the service is severely or wholly impaired.

Regarding other related work, Bem, et.al. [3] provide a thorough introduction to the area and issues of broadband satellite multimedia systems, clarifying the basic physical and architectural distinctions amongst satellite systems, as well as some of the technical and legal issues to be addressed. Farserotu and Prasad [5] provide a more brief survey, and include concise descriptions of the basic issues and references to the latest work in areas such as enhancements to TCP/IP, enhanced QoS awareness,

D. Shepherd et al. (Eds.): IDMS 2001, LNCS 2158, pp. 74–85, 2001.

IP security over SATCOM, onboard processing, switching and routing, and service enabling platforms. Metz [7] offers another concise introduction.

The IMMSAT results can perhaps be best contrasted to recent work by Nguyen, et.al. [8]. There, the work studied the effects of link errors and link loading upon link performance (e.g., packet and frame loss, delay, etc.) for an H.323-based VoIP service. The IMMSAT study focused upon identifying the levels of link delay, jitter and packet loss which could be *sustained* and *tolerated*.

2   H.323 Call Establishment

H.323 calls [9] can be established according to a variety of call models. A call model basically defines the system entities to and from which signals are exchanged. Readers can find a comprehensive H.323 tutorial at [10]. This section focuses upon signaling procedures and timers relevant to H.323 call establishment.

2.1   Basic Signaling Procedures for H.323 Call Establishment

The provision of H.323-based communication proceeds in 5 phases:

- phase A: call setup (RAS and H.225 messages [13]); connection of endpoints; H.245 call control channel establishment [11])
- phase B: initial communication and capability exchange (H.245 procedures); master/slave determination
- phase C: establishment of audio visual communication (H.245 procedures); media stream address distribution; correlation of media streams in multipoint conferences and communication mode command procedures
- phases D and E: call services and call termination, respectively [9].

In IMMSAT, call establishment testing concerned itself specifically with the success or failure of phases A-C. That is, call establishment was judged successful when voice could be transmitted between the endpoints.

2.2   Signaling and Timing Details within Call Setup

The discussion in this section specifically focuses upon call setup (phase A) within a Direct Endpoint Call Signaling via Gateway call model. This was the call model used during prototype testing. *It is important to note that in this call model, the Gateway is both a callee endpoint and a calling endpoint.* The RAS and H.225 signal exchanges in phase A for that call model are illustrated in Figure 1.

Timers. System entities start and stop various timers as they send and receive different signals. These include the T303, T310 and T301 timers, as specified for use within call setup by H.225 and Q.931[1].

Each calling endpoint starts a T303 timer at the moment it issues a *Setup* signal. By default [13], each calling endpoint should receive an *Alerting, Call Proceeding, Connect, Release Complete* (or other message) from its respective called endpoint within 4 seconds. Should a calling endpoint receive a *Call Proceeding* signal before T303 timeout, it should start a T310 timer. Its T310 timer runs until it receives an *Alerting, Connect* or *Release Complete* signal. Typical timeout values for the T310 timer are about 10 seconds [15].

If a calling endpoint receives an *Alerting* signal before a T310 timeout, it should start a T310 timer. This timer runs until a *Connect* or *Release Complete* signal is received. Its timeout value should be 180 seconds or greater [13].

Mandatory vs. optional signaling. Not all signals appearing in Figure 1 are mandatory; certain are optional, and certain can be omitted in special cases. For instance, the *Alerting* ("terminal is ringing") signal can be omitted should the callee answer the phone (*Connect*) before it has time to ring. Otherwise, H.225 requires the callee endpoint to send an *Alerting* signal, regardless of call model. H.225 also states that a Gateway should forward an *Alerting* signal (as shown in Figure 1).

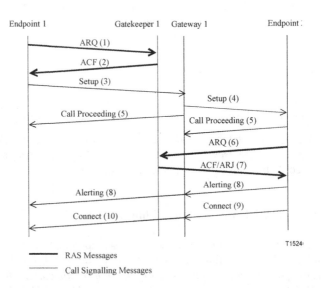

Fig. 1. Direct endpoint call signaling via Gateway: phase A (adapted from [9])

---

[1] It has been pointed out that certain equipment implementations use two timers in place of the three timers mentioned here (T303, T310 and T301) [15]; the discussion in this section accords with H.225 and Q.931.

When call setup signaling transpires via a Gateway, H.323 requires the Gateway to send a *Call Proceeding* signal to the calling endpoint, whenever the Gateway judges that it might require more than four seconds to respond to that endpoint. This is required in order to help prevent a T303 timeout (or its equivalent) within the calling endpoint. Perhaps surprisingly, H.225 does *not* require that the callee endpoint (e.g., endpoint 2) issue a *Call Proceeding* signal. In network environments with extraordinarily long delays, the absence of a *Call Proceeding* signal from a callee endpoint could yield a T303 timeout (or its equivalent) in the Gateway. In many implementations, a T303 timeout causes call setup to fail[2].

In short, use of the *Call Proceeding* signal by the callee endpoint can be highly valuable when facing *very* large delay conditions. Use of this signal helps serve to alleviate, though not decouple, end-to-end call setup timing constraints. In satellite environments, issuance of this message from callee endpoints helps mitigate the effects of multiple satellite hops during H.323 call setup.

3   Prototype Testing

The satellite-based environment parameters in focus within IMMSAT were delay, jitter, packet loss and bit error rate (BER). For a typical GEO satellite-based environment, measured values[3] for these parameters are:

- *Delay*: 550 ms one-way delay (includes processing delay)
- *Jitter*: ±15 ms (standard deviation)
- *BER*: 10^{-6} average bit error rate
- *Packet Loss*: 1% average packet error (assuming 10^{-6} BER and 100 byte packets on average).

3.1 Prototype Configuration

The network configuration and prototype elements within the IMMSAT prototype are given in Figure 2. Details about the specific kind of equipment used is provided in the figure, and explicated in [6]. References to the equipment include [17][18][21] [22].

In the figure, the H.323 client types are indicated with **NM** for the Microsoft NetMeeting 3.01 clients, **IPT** for Siemens LP5100 IP telephones [20], and **ISDN** for Siemens Profiset 30 ISDN telephones[4] [19]. The configuration enabled testing the effects of both *one* and *two hop* calls[5].

---

[2] H.225 and Q.931 allow the *Setup* signal to be retried. Since TCP underlies the H.225 call signaling messages, however, many implementations choose to abort and clear the call, rather than retry *Setup* [15].

[3] Information as to which system these values were measured from is confidential.

[4] These acronyms are followed by a number (1 or 2) which distinguishes different instances of the same kind of system entity.

[5] Two hop calls can occur, for example, when two mobile satellite terminals require (e.g., audio) media transcoding in order to communicate. In such cases, the audio media is transmitted from the first terminal to the satellite gateway via the satellite, transcoded in the

All testing was performed using various combinations of H.323 clients, IP telephones, ISDN telephones, H.323 Gateway, and Gatekeeper (for most tests). A Direct Endpoint Call Signaling via Gateway call model was employed. Voice encoding and decoding was fixed to G.711 in the ISDN/H.320 network, and to G.723.1 (6.3Kb/s), in the IP/H.323 network. During testing, transcoding was always performed in the H.323 Gateway.

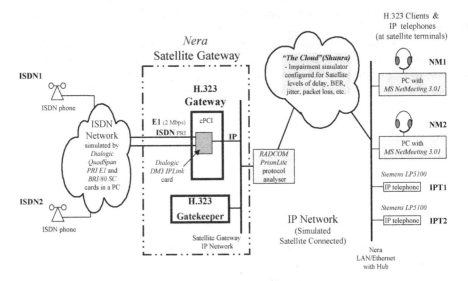

Fig. 2. IMMSAT Prototype, including network and telephony configuration details

3.2   Test Strategy and Approach

A test strategy was chosen in which an effort was made to independently identify critical values for each individual parameter[6]. For call establishment tests, a critical value was a value for a single parameter (e.g., delay, packet loss, etc.) at which call establishment began to fail. Once a critical value was identified for a specific parameter during a test series, two or three calls were made in the parametric space neighboring upon that critical value. Unfortunately, time available for testing yielded only very small sample sizes for each test series.

Early, yet significant experimentation with the impact of varying BER upon call establishment indicted that it was necessary to raise this rate to values greater than 1/50000, in order that call establishment should *occasionally* fail. The same was true

---

gateway, then transmitted on to the second terminal, again via the satellite. In this example, this process transpires for audio media transmission in each direction.
[6] Clearly, certain parameters (e.g., delay and jitter) are interdependent. In this document, the term 'individual parameter' is use to mean a parameter which could be independently adjusted within the satellite simulator.

in regard to the perception of BER's effect upon audio voice quality[7]. Since such a rate is far outside the expected performance range for most networks, including GEO satellite, further independent testing of this variable was terminated.

Complete details about the approach and test process for call establishment and audio voice quality testing can be found in [6]. Some details about audio voice quality testing are included below, however, due to their relevance in this context.

The voice quality tests included two aspects, one-way *listening quality* and two-way *conversational quality*. To rate the subjective listening quality of audio voice, Recommendation P.800's *Quantal-Response Detectability Testing* scale was employed (see [12], Annex C). An abbreviated version of this scale is included in the legend for Figure 4.

In order to employ a consistent audio reference during listening quality tests, playback of a pre-recorded audio source via the Gateway was used. *It must be noted that the time and resources available for listening quality testing were so limited that only a single subject was employed to perform the listening tests and to rate performance. Testing procedures were made as "blind" as possible [6].*

As part of the listening quality tests:

- silence suppression was turned off in all prototype elements (whenever and wherever possible)
- audio frame size was 30 msec
- number of audio frames per packet was clearly noted as a significant variable (either 1 or 2 audio frames per packet)
- listening quality for both one and two hop calls was checked.

4   Analysis of Results

Since the total number of trials in each test series was so very limited, a judgement was made to analyze the results on the basis of apparent, rather than statistical trends.

4.1   Call Establishment

Figure 3 summarizes two major sets of call establishment tests. Each major set included eight *test series*. These two major sets include:

- investigations of the effects of varying delay (test series A-H) and
- investigations of the effects of varying packet loss (test series J-R).

The relevant variables for each test series are: the type of client terminal initiating the call (the *caller*), the type of client terminal answering the call (the *callee*), whether the call involved one or two simulated satellite hops and the settings for the satellite simulator. When reviewing Figure 3, it is important to note that the horizontal axes employed therein are not linear.

---

[7] This is consistent with the findings of Nguyen, et.al. [8].

Effects of delay. In regard to the effects of delay upon call establishment, there were two major observations. The first was that in the face of delay, call establishment performance did not seem to be influenced by the addition of a second (simulated) satellite hop. This can be seen in Figure 3 by comparing: test series C to D, test series C to E, and test series F to H. It is expected that this behavior is related to the characteristics of a Direct Endpoint Call Signaling via Gateway model which fully employs the *Call Proceeding* signal, as explained in section 2.2.

With respect to this first observation, the comparison of F to G is *not* conformant. It is presumed that this result is a consequence of the second observation described below.

The second major observation is that increases in delay apparently seemed to impact calls employing IPT (as either caller or callee) *more adversely* than calls which did not involve IPT. Rather than including here a detailed clarification involving signal exchanges and timing, a higher-level explanation is offered instead.

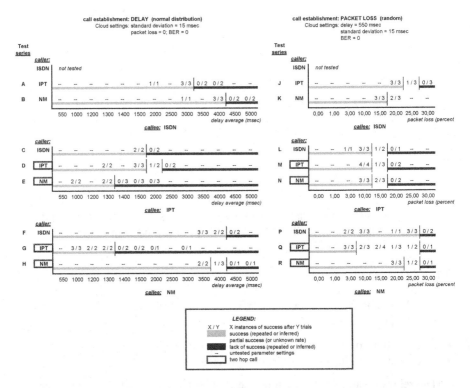

Fig. 3. Results of call establishment testing for delay and packet loss

IPT as a caller endpoint: In test series F, G and H, the *second* leg of the call involves signaling between the Gateway and NetMeeting. Series F and H both demonstrate that the second call leg *can* tolerate up to 4000 ms delay. Series G begins to fail at 1400 ms, however, which implies that the cause of failure lies on the first leg of the call. A reasonable hypothesis in this case is that timeouts occurred within the IPT terminal, the originating caller.

IPT as a callee endpoint: In test series B, E and H, the *first* leg of the call involves signaling between NetMeeting and the Gateway. Series B and H both demonstrate that the first call leg *can* tolerate up to 4000 ms delay. Series E begins to fail at 1400 ms, which implies that the cause of failure lies on the second leg of the call. It is also interesting to notice that the other two series having IPT as callee endpoint (series C and D) also demonstrated failure at 2000 ms. A reasonable hypothesis in this case is that IPT did not issue a *Call Proceeding* signal to the Gateway, a situation which caused the Gateway to timeout and clear the call. As mentioned earlier, H.225 does not require that callee endpoints issue the *Call Proceeding* signal. Still, these test series seem to demonstrate the value of that signal being issued by the callee endpoint.

It must be mentioned here that though reasonable, the two hypotheses above could not be *completely* verified. The circumstances regarding this condition are explained further in [6].

Effects of packet loss. Analysis of the call establishment testing for packet loss did not reveal any apparent trends with respect to the variables under study (e.g., caller vs. callee type, hop count, etc.). The only apparent trend is that the success rate of call establishment seemed to significantly diminish when packet loss reached 15-20%. It should be mentioned here that some of the *successful* call establishment trials employing packet loss rates of 20-25% took one minute or more to establish. Despite the lack of usable audio quality at this level of loss (see below), successful call establishment could still be of value in other kinds of contexts (e.g., a "sign of life" in an emergency).

4.2   Listening Quality

Figure 4 summarizes six major *cases* of listening tests: one matrix for each major case (case matrices A-F). The approach used for testing is completely described in [6]. In the figure, each case matrix is also colored according to a "usability scale" defined for IMMSAT. The colors essentially map P.800's seven point quantal-response detectability scale ([12], Annex C) onto a three point scale; this was done in order to ease perception of the significance of the listening test results. The legend in Figure 4 explains this mapping. Note that in certain case matrices, parts of the matrix are colored despite the fact that no trial was performed. These instances of coloring were *inferred*, based upon the performance of other trials within the same matrix.

The parameters which *distinguish* each major case are: the type of client terminal initiating the call (the caller), the type of client terminal answering the call (the callee), whether the call involved one or two (simulated) satellite hops, whether the listening test was performed using a headset or a handset, and the number of audio frames per packet. For the cases in which IPT was the callee, an additional parameter was the setting for the HiNet jitter buffer; this buffer could be set to either 'Long' or 'Short'. The HiNet jitter buffer is a buffer internal to the Siemens IP telephones. The parameters which distinguish the trials *within* each major case are the settings for the satellite simulator. It is important to note that the axes employed for each major case matrix are not linear.

The analysis here is discussed using *comparisons* amongst major cases A-F (i.e., "Case Comparisons I-V" in Figure 4's legend); these are depicted as directed arcs in the figure. The legend succinctly describes the variation in parameter values for each case comparison. Note further that the case comparisons can be viewed as tree rooted at case B.

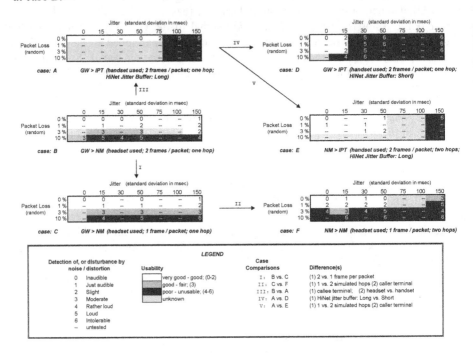

Fig. 4. Results of listening tests for jitter and packet loss

Case B depicts a listening test where the configuration supported "good – very good" audio quality for jitter values as high as 150 msec and packet loss up to 1%. Audio quality began to noticeably degrade to "fair" when packet loss reached 3%. Comparison with case C (comparison I) indicates that use of two vs. one audio frames per packet does not appear to be of any significance.

Differences are noticeable in comparison II, however; case F involves two hops, while case C involves only one. This comparison illustrates that audio quality degrades quite noticeably when a second hop is introduced, an expected result due to the cumulative effects of packet loss, delay and jitter across hops. Worth noting in case F is the near-usability of the trial having 150 msec jitter and 0% packet loss per hop. This result seems to indicate that NetMeeting is internally operating with a relatively "large" jitter buffer. No user-level access to this parameter was available via the NetMeeting application, however, in order to confirm this hypothesis.

Consider now comparison III (case B vs. case A). In case A, the most significant difference from case B is that instead of NetMeeting, the Siemens LP5100 telephone is used as the callee terminal. For the LP5100 telephone, jitter has a severely destructive impact upon audio quality as soon as it reaches 100 msec. This was the case even though the HiNet jitter buffer was set to 'Long'. When that buffer was set to 'Short' (see case D, comparison IV), the effect of jitter was devastating.

In contrast to the LP5100 telephone's poor performance in the face of jitter, the results seem to indicate that its audio quality was somewhat better than NetMeeting, when faced with the same levels of packet loss. Though this is not explicitly shown in comparison III, one may choose to infer this by considering how well the LP5100 performed with respect to packet loss in case E — a two hop call (comparison V).

In summary, the one-way listening tests showed that uncontrolled jitter was the most *destructive* parameter to audio quality. Packet loss was also influential, though somewhat less dramatically.

4.3   Conversational Quality

Even when the intelligibility of audio is unaffected by its transmission medium, the exclusive effect of delay can have severe consequences upon the character of a conversation (see e.g., [4]). Since this area has already been so well investigated, the tests for conversational quality were only quick, general checks performed using the typical values expected for delay, BER, packet loss, etc. In general, the conversational quality between clients at these levels was satisfactory. Of note, the two hop calls tended to included some (very) small amount of added noise / distortion, when compared to the one hop calls.

For the sake of experience, conversational quality was occasionally tested when delays were varied between 1500-4000 msec and other satellite parameters were held at their typical values. As expected, users could ultimately manage to successfully communicate. With such large delays, however, it was necessary for them to adopt an unnatural "single duplex" mode of conversation.

5   Conclusions

Generally, all tests performed using the IMMSAT prototype indicated that H.323-based VoIP services in a GEO satellite-based IP network are practical and usable. The effects of *typical*, GEO satellite environment conditions upon H.323-based VoIP services are expected to be negligible. These results are consistent with those of Nguyen, et.al. [8]. Further remarks about call establishment and audio voice quality follow below.

5.1   Call Establishment

The call establishment tests showed that the H.323 protocols could establish calls successfully under severely impaired conditions — conditions which were at least an order of magnitude worse than in typical GEO satellite-based environments.

The call establishment tests also indicated that the client type on each end of the call can have great significance with respect to the amount of delay which can be tolerated during call establishment. For example, it appeared that one of the clients failed to issue the *Call Proceeding* signal. This signal is not required by the standard but, when facing extreme conditions, its use can yield greater tolerance of delay.

Lastly, it was interesting to see that both one and two hop call configurations performed equally well in the face of delay. It is expected that this behavior is due to the characteristics of a Direct Endpoint Call Signaling via Gateway model which fully employs the *Call Proceeding* signal.

5.2   Audio Voice Quality

The experiments showed that audio quality appreciably degrades when moving from a one hop call to a two hop call. This kind of result is expected due to the cumulative effects across multiple hops. The experiments showed that client type also has an impact upon voice quality; use of headset instead of a handset also makes a difference here.

Still, jitter is the network characteristic that seemed to have the greatest impact on listening quality. Even though the highly adverse conditions tested in this investigation are not likely to be observed in most networks, the ability to handle jitter is crucial for offering an acceptable VoIP service. Using a larger jitter buffer in certain system entities may help alleviate the problem, though at the cost of an increase in overall delay.

The experience of large delays when trying to converse can be frustrating and confusing, even to users who have been informed of and prepared in advance for such conditions. Users practiced with large delays *can* adapt and reconcile themselves with the condition and ultimately use the service, but conversations must transpire in a "single duplex" mode in order that communication be achieved.

Acknowledgements

The authors wish to thank the project team at Nera SatCom: Ronald Beachell, Harald Hoff and Paul Mackell. A special thanks as well to Ronald Beachell, for his diagram of the IMMSAT prototype configuration (Figure 2).

References

1. Beachell, R.L., Bøhler, T., Holmes, P., Ludvigsen, E., Maus, E., Aarhus, L., "1551-IMMSAT; IP Multimedia over Satellite Study Report", Copyright 2000, Nera SatCom AS / Norsk Romsenter. Also available as: "IP Multimedia over Satellite: Study Report", NR Report 967, December 2000, ISBN 82-539-0473-8. See: http://www.nr.no/publications/nrrapport967.pdf
2. Beachell, R.L., Holmes, P., Thomassen, J., Aarhus, L., "1523-IMMSAT-TR; IP Multimedia over Satellite: Test Report for the IMMSAT Prototype", Copyright 2000, Nera SatCom AS /

Norsk Romsenter. Also available as: " IP Multimedia over Satellite: Test Report", NR Technical Note IMEDIA/10/00 (Classified), December 2000.

3. Bem, D., Wieckowski, W., Zielinski, R., *Broadband Satellite Systems*, IEEE Communications Surveys & Tutorials, vol.3, no.1, 2000, pp. 2-15; see: http://www.comsoc.org/pubs/surveys/1q00issue/pdf/zielinski.pdf

4. Douskalis, B., IP Telephony - *The Integration of Robust VoIP Services*, Prentice-Hall, 2000.

5. Farserotu, J., Prasad, R., *A Survey of Future Broadband Multimedia Satellite Systems, Issues and Trends*, IEEE Communications, vol. 38, no. 6, June 2000, pp. 128-133.

6. Holmes, P., Aarhus, L., Maus, E., "An Investigation into the Effects of GEO Satellite Environments upon H.323-based Voice over IP", NR Report 973, May 2001, ISBN 82-539-0479-7. Available as: http://www.nr.no/publications/report973.pdf

7. Metz, C., *IP-over-Satellite: Internet Connectivity Blasts Off*, IEEE Internet Computing, July-August 2000, pp.84-89.

8. Nguyen, T., Yegenoglu, F., Sciuto, A., Subbarayan, R., *Voice over IP Service and Performance in Satellite Networks*, IEEE Communications, Vol. 39, No. 3, March 2001, pp. 164-171.

9. *Packet-based multimedia communications systems*, ITU-T Recommendation H.323 v3 (with change marks), ITU-T October 1999.

10. From DataBeam: "A Primer on the H.323 Series Standard", see: http://www.h323analyser.co.uk/h323_primer-v2.pdf

11. *Control protocol for multimedia communication*, ITU-T Recommendation H.245 v5 (with change marks), ITU-T 1999.

12. *Methods for Subjective Determination of Transmission*, ITU-T Recommendation P.800, ITU-T August 1986: http://www.itu.int/itudoc/itu-t/rec/p/p800.html

13. Call signaling protocols and media stream packetization for packet based multimedia communication systems, ITU-T Recommendation H.225.0 draft v4 (with change marks), ITU-T 1999.

14. Norsk Regnesentral (Norwegian Computing Center) WWW site; see: http://www.nr.no/ekstern/engelsk/

15. Personal communication from Espen Kjerrand, Ericsson AS Norway, May 2001.

16. Nera SatCom AS WWW site; see: http://www.nera.no/

17. Dialogic IPLink cPCI Solutions; see: http://www.dialogic.com/products/d_sheets/4798web.htm

18. Dialogic QuadSpan™ Voice Series; see: http://www.dialogic.com/products/d_sheets/3967web.htm

19. Siemens Profiset 30isdn: see http://www.siemens.no/telefoni/isdn/profi30.htm

20. Siemens optiPoint 300 advance IP telephone (formerly LP5100 IP); see: http://www.ic.siemens.com/CDA/Site/pss/1,1294,208375-1-999,00.html

21. The Cloud, from Shunra Software Ltd.; see: http://www.shunra.com/products/thecloud.htm

22. RADCOM Prism and PrismLite protocol analyzers; see: http://www.radcom-inc.com/radcom/test/prism.htm

Conception, Implementation, and Evaluation of a QoS-Based Architecture for an IP Environment Supporting Differentiated Services

Fabien Garcia[1], Christophe Chassot[1], Andre Lozes[1], Michel Diaz[1], Pascal Anelli[2], Emmanuel Lochin[2]

[1]LAAS/CNRS, 7 avenue du Colonel Roche, 31077 Toulouse cedex 04. France
{fgarcia, chassot, alozes, diaz}@laas.fr

[2]LIP6, 8 rue du Capitaine Scott, 75015 Paris. France
{pascal.anelli, emmanuel.lochin}@lip6.fr

Abstract. Research reported in this paper deals with the design of a communication architecture with guaranteed end-to-end quality of service (QoS) in an IPv6 environment providing differentiated services within a single Diff-Serv domain. The paper successively presents the design principles of the proposed architecture, the networking platform on which the architecture has been developed and the experimental measurements validating the IP level mechanisms providing the defined services. Results presented here have been obtained as part of the experiments in the national French project @IRS (Integrated Architecture of Networks and Services).

1 Introduction

Technical revolutions in computer science and telecommunications have led to the development of several new types of distributed applications: multimedia and co-operative applications, interactive simulation, etc. These new applications present challenging characteristics and constraints to network designers, such as higher bandwidths, the need for bounded delays, etc. As a result, the Internet community formed two research and development efforts (IETF[1] Int-Serv [1] and Diff-Serv [2] working groups) whose goal is to develop a new generation of protocols within a revised architecture for the TCP/IP protocol suite. One of the key points of that architecture is that the new "differentiated" or "integrated" services respond to the needs of new applications. Performed within the national French project @IRS[2], work presented within this article straddles this context. More precisely, it deals with the

---

[1] IETF: Internet Engineering Task Force
[2] The @IRS project (Integrated Networks and Services Architecture) is a national project of the France's RNRT (*Réseau National de la Recherche en Télécommunications*), whose objective is the development and experimentation of innovative Internet mechanisms and protocols within an heterogeneous telecommunications infrastructure (ATM, satellite, wireless, LAN, etc.). Initiated in December 1998, project @IRS has ended in April 2001.

D. Shepherd et al. (Eds.): IDMS 2001, LNCS 2158, pp. 86-98, 2001.

conception, the implementation and the evaluation of a communication architecture providing a guaranteed end-to-end QoS in an IPv6 differentiated services environment constituting a single Diff-Serv domain. Several other works have been initiated to target the QoS problem within the Internet. Among them, let's cite the TF-TANT activity [3] and the GEANT, TEQUILA, CADENUS, AQUILA and GCAP IST projects [4,5,6,7,8].

The article is structured as follows. Section 2 presents the architecture principles. Section 3 describes the experimental platform over which the architecture has been developed. Section 4 details the experimental scenarios for the validation of the IP QoS mechanisms providing the defined services; results of the corresponding measurements are also provided and analysed. Conclusions and future work are presented in Section 5.

2   General Architecture

The following two major sections (2.1 and 2.2) successively present the architecture defined at the end-to-end level and then at the network level.

2.1   End-to-End Level

The basic underlying principle that supports the proposal of the @IRS end-to-end architecture is one of many dedicated to the transport of multimedia flows [9,10,11,12]. The idea is that the traffic exchanged within a distributed application can be decomposed into several data flows each one requiring its own specific QoS (i.e. delay, reliability, order, ...). That is, each application can request a specific QoS for each flow via a consistent API (Application Programming Interface) offering parameters and primitives for a diverse set of necessary services. By way of a session (see Figure 1), the application layer software is then allowed to establish one or many end-to-end communication channels, each being: (1) unicast or multicast, (2) dedicated to the transfer of a single flow of application data, and (3) able to offer a specific QoS.

Besides the API, three other modules are defined:
- the first one provides multiple transport layer possibilities, such as TCP, UDP, or the partial-order, partial-reliable POC (Partial Order Connection [13,14]);
- the second one implements the mechanisms linked to the utilisation of QoS services at the IP layer (e.g., RSVP, RSVP light, manual configuration);
- the third one associates a given transport channel with a given IP QoS service.

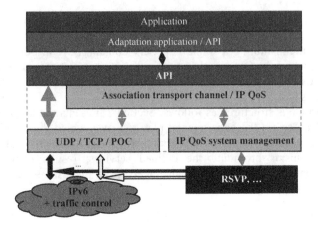

Figure 1. Architecture of the End-to-End Communication System

Two types of modifications have been defined for the applications: the translation of transport layer function calls (e.g. socket) to the new API, and the insertion of an adaptation layer managing the establishment of end-to-end QoS-based communication channels, along with translating the applications' needs into generic parameters understood by the API.

Since the experimental results presented in the paper are "IP QoS" rather than "Transport QoS" oriented, we do not present the API in detail. However, we precise that the QoS specified for each end-to-end channel is expressed by the following parameters:

- a partial order, expressed as both an intra and inter flow order since a user may want a logical synchronisation service either within each flow (e.g., logical synchronisation of two media transported within the same end-to-end channel) or between flows (e.g., logical synchronisation of voice and video);
- a partial reliability defined, for example, by a maximum number of consecutive lost packets, and/or by a maximum running percentage of lost packets;
- a maximum end-to-end transmission delay.

Although the question is pertinent, the goal of this paper is not to describe and enforce ordering relationships within channels that may lose packets to tackle synchronisation needs associated with multimedia applications, or to reduce the transit delay of application level data units. Identically, the paper does not study the usefulness of RTP based propositions.

Finally, in addition to QoS parameters, an application must specify four service parameters:

- the first one characterises the traffic generated by the application sender; for this, the token bucket model is used;
- the second one designates which transport protocol to use (e.g. UDP, TCP or POC). One of the proposed future research activities is to determine if it is possible and/or efficient to have the system automatically select the transport protocol. For now, this choice must be specified by the application;

- the third one designates the IP layer's QoS management desired by the application (e.g. Best Effort service, Int-Serv Guaranteed or Controlled Load services, Diff-Serv Premium or Assured services, etc.). Here again, automatic selection is a proposed research activity outside the scope of the work presented here;
- the final parameter identifies the address, either unicast/multicast, of a set of destination application softwares.

Although the architecture is designed so as to allow several kinds of Transport protocols or IP level management systems, the architecture implemented within the project only includes UDP and TCP at the Transport level and a Diff-Serv proposition (described in section 2.2) at the IP level.

2.2   Network Level

QoS functions performed at the network level can be divided in two parts: those related to the *data path* and those related to the *control path* [15]. On the data path, QoS functions are applied by routers at the packet level in order to provide different levels of service. On the control path, QoS functions concern routers configuration and act to enforce the QoS provided. If studies performed during the @IRS project tackle the two areas (data and control paths), only the data part has been implemented and evaluated over the experimental platform. In this section, we first describe the defined services at the IP level. Then we detail the different functions required for the services implementation, with a clear separation between the control path and the data path.

Services. Three services have been defined at the IP level:

- GS (Guaranteed Service) - analogous to the *Premium Service* [16] - is used for data flows having strong constraints in both delay and reliability. Applications targeted by GS are those which do not tolerate QoS variation;
- AS (Assured Service) is appropriate for responsive flows having no strong constraints in terms of delay, but requiring a minimum average bandwidth. More precisely, a flow served in AS has to be provided with an assured bandwidth for the part of its traffic (IN packets) respecting the characterisation profile specified for the flow. Part of the traffic exceeding the characterisation (OUT - or opportunistic - packets) is conveyed in AS as far as no congestion occurs in the network on the path used by the flow;
- BE: Best Effort service offers no QoS guarantees.

Three markings have been defined to differentiate packets: EF (Expedited Forwarding), AF (Assured Forwarding) and DE (Discard Eligibility) [17,18], corresponding to the three services provided at the IP level.

Control Path QoS Functions. In order to implement the mentioned services in the testbed network (described in section 3), the two mechanisms involved in the control path are *admission control* and *route change protection*. Note that the multicast issue is not studied in this paper.

Admission Control. The admission control takes care of the acceptance of new flows in service classes. Its decisions are taken according to the TCA[1] contracted between the user domain and the service provider domain. Our proposition is different for AS and GS:

- for AS, a per flow admission control is applied at the edge of the network (core routers are not implied); this control is based on the amount of AS traffic already authorised to enter the network by the considered edge router. This gives the guarantee that at any time, the amount of *in profile* AS packets (IN packets) in the network will be at most the sum of the AS authorised at each edge router;
- for GS, as a delay guarantee is needed, the admission control involves all the routers on the data path (edge and core routers). As for AS, it is applied per flow, each flow being identified by the couple (*flow_id* field, *source address*).

Route Change Protection. This issue is raised for GS only as a route change can have a heavy impact on the service and even results in the service not being available anymore. As it has been decided in the @IRS project that QoS and routing issues would be considered separately, our solution is to use static routing only.

Data Path QoS Functions. QoS functions involved in the data path are *policing*, *scheduling* and *congestion control*. We first describe these three functions, then we detail their implementation within routers *input* and *output* interfaces.

Data Path Functions Description.
Policing. Policing deals with the actions to be taken when out of profile traffic arrives in a given service class:

- for AS, the action is to mark the out of profile packets with a higher drop precedence than for the IN traffic. OUT packets are called *opportunistic* packets because they are processed like the other IN AS packets, as far as no congestion occurs in the network. If congestion occurs, the congestion control described here after is applied. Targeted applications are those whose traffic is elastic, that is with a variable profile (a minimum still being assured);
- for GS, as a guarantee exists, we must be sure that enough resources are available; therefore the amount of GS traffic in the network must be strictly controlled. To enforce this, the chosen policing method is to shape the traffic at the edge router and to drop out of profile GS packets.

---

[1] TCA - Traffic Control Agreement: part of the SLA (*Service Level Agreement* [19]) that describes the amount of traffic a user can send to the service provider network.

Scheduling. Once again, the scheduling is different for AS and GS packets:

- GS scheduling is implemented by a *Priority Queuing* (PQ) mechanism. This choice is due to the fact that a PQ based scheduler adds the smallest delay to the packet forwarding due to packetisation effect;
- the remaining bandwidth is shared by a *Weighted Fair Queuing* (WFQ) between AS and BE traffic. This ensures that there will not be service denial for BE.

Congestion Control. The congestion control issue is essential for QoS services, as a congestion can prevent the network from offering the contracted QoS to a flow:

- GS traffic does not need congestion control as it benefits from a priority queuing ensuring that all its packets are served up to the maximal capacity of a given router. Associated with a strong policing (drop of out of profile packets) at the network boundary, this guarantees that no congestion will occur in GS queues;
- for AS, as opportunistic traffic is authorised to be sent in the network, the amount of AS packets in any router can't be known a priori. Therefore, a drop precedence system has been implemented; it allows the drop of opportunistic packets as soon as a congestion is about to occur in an AS queue. A *Partial Buffer Sharing* (PBS) has been chosen on the AS queues rather than a *Random Early Discard* (RED) method. This choice comes from recent studies which show that simple systems such as PBS avoid the queue length oscillation problems raised by RED [20,21].

Let us now look at the implementation of these functions over the @IRS platform through the *input interface* of the first router (called edge router as opposed to core routers) and the *output interface* of all routers.

Data Path Functions Implementation
Input Interface of Edge Router. This interface is the first encountered by a packet when it enters the network. Its logical structure is shown in Figure 2.

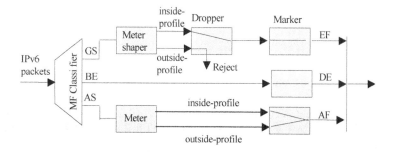

Figure 2. Input Interface Structure

This interface is in charge of:

- packets classification, which is based on information from the IPv6 header (source address and *flow_id*); this is done through a *MultiField Classifier*;
- measuring AS and GS flows to determine whether they are in or out of profile;
- shaping GS packets and dropping them if necessary;
- marking AS and GS packets with the appropriate *Diff-Serv CodePoint* (DSCP)

- marking AS packets with the precedence due to their being in or out profile;
- marking BE packets to prevent them from entering the network with the DSCP of another service class.

Output Interface of All Routers. In the Diff-Serv model, all routers must implement a set of forwarding behaviours called Per Hop Behaviour (PHB). In the @IRS architecture, these behaviours are implemented through scheduling and AS congestion control as described in section (0). They are integrated in the output interface of each router (Figure 3).

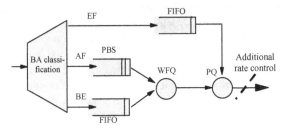

Figure 3. Output Interface Structure

Two additional points must be noted: the *Behaviour Aggregate classifier* which classifies packets according to their DSCP, and the rate control at the output of core routers. As it will appear more clearly in the next section, this rate control is necessary to avoid congestion at the ATM level. Indeed, congestion at the ATM level is due to the fact that ATM *Virtual Paths* (VP) through which the packets are sent have a smaller bandwidth capacity than the ATM cards of the routers. Combined with the limited buffer size in the ATM switches, this could create ATM cell losses when the throughput of the router is not controlled.

3   Experimental Platform

The testing network environment used for applications of the project is shown in Figure 4.

Local equipment is connected by edge routers (R_b) to an *Internet Service Provider* (ISP) represented by the national ATM RENATER 2 platform. Four core routers (R_c) are introduced within the ISP; physically, they are located in the local platforms, but logically they are part of the ISP. By means of its edge router, each site is provided with an access point to the ISP (R_b). This access point is characterised by a statically established traffic contract called *Service Level Agreement* (SLA) [19]. For each service, the SLA consists of:

- classification and packet (re)marking rules;
- a sending traffic profile called *Traffic Conditioning Agreement* (TCA) [19] (for @IRS, the model chosen was the Token Bucket);
- actions the network has to perform when the application violates its traffic profile.

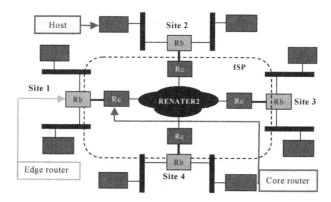

Figure 4. Experimental Platform

It is the edge router's responsibility to implement the SLA as it introduces application flows within the ISP. All the ATM VPs offer a 1Mbit/s Constant Bit Rate (CBR) service.

4   Experimental Scenarios and Measurements

The purpose of the experimental scenarios described in this section is to validate the IP mechanisms developed to provide a *slightly degraded* QoS for AS flows and an *excellent* QoS for GS flows when the network load is increasing.

4.1   Studied Cases

Two cases have been considered:
- **case 1**: the edge router is not in state of congestion and the AS (respectively GS) flow respects its traffic profile. This case is the reference one;
- **case 2**: the edge router is now in state of congestion and the AS (resp. GS) flow still respects its traffic profile; the congestion is due to BE traffic. Here, we want to study the behaviour of the AS (resp. GS) flow when the network is overloaded.

4.2   Tools

The software tool used for the experiments is a traffic generator (named Debit6) developed by LIP6 and LAAS. Debit6 is able to:
- send/receive UDP/IPv6 flows under Free BDS or Window NT operating system;
- send traffic respecting a token bucket type-like profile;
- measure throughput and loss rate for a given experiment session;
- measure transit delay for each packet.

4.3   QoS Validation

Experiment Configuration. Measurements have been realised between LAAS (Toulouse) and LIP6 (Paris) over the IPv6 inter-network environment illustrated on Figure 5.

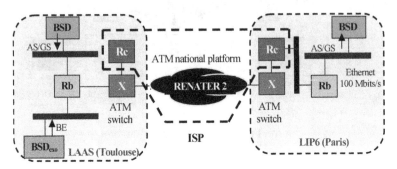

Figure 5. Inter-network Environment

Bandwidth of the link connecting LAAS (resp. LIP6) to the ISP (via an ATM VP) is such that the maximal throughput provided at the UDP level is 107 Kbytes/s. In the following of the paper, we use the term *link bandwidth* to refer to this throughput.

Hypothesis and Measured Parameters. Edge and core routers have been configured with the following hypothesis:
- the maximal amount of GS traffic that can be generated by the edge router (in average) has been fixed to 20 Kbytes/s, i.e. about 20% of the link bandwidth;
- the maximal amount of AS traffic that can be generated by the edge router (in average) has been fixed to 40 Kbytes/s, i.e. about 40% of the link bandwidth;
- the rate control applied by the core router is 107 Kbytes/s (i.e. the link bandwidth);
- weights associated to the AS and BE packet scheduling within the WFQ mechanism are respectively 0.8 and 0.2.

Measured parameters are the loss rate, the transit delay and the throughput; more precisely:
- the loss rate corresponds to the ratio between the number of not received packets and the number of sent packets for the complete experiment session;
- minimal, maximal and average values of the transit delay are calculated for the complete experiment session (about 300 seconds);
- the throughput is measured both at the sending and receiving side and corresponds to the number of user data bytes sent or received for the complete experiment session divided by the communication duration (about 300 seconds).

Note that hosts are synchronised by means of NTP (Network Time Protocol), inducing a +/- 5 milliseconds (ms) uncertainty on the transit delay measurements.

Measurements Specification. Two kinds of measurements have been defined (see Table 1). In both cases, AS and GS flows have to respect their traffic profile and all flows (GS, AS and BE) are generated by bursts of 1 UDP packet whose size is 1024 bytes. The inter-packet delay is the variable parameter used to change the throughput of the generated flows.

1st kind of measure		BE (% of the link bandwidth)				
		0	25	50	75	100
GS (% of the maximal	50	case 1				case 2
amount of GS traffic)	100	case 1				case 2
AS (% of the maximal	50	case 1				case 2
amount of AS traffic)	100	case 1			case 2	
2nd kind of measurements		BE (% of the link bandwidth)				
		100				
AS and GS	50	case 2				

Table 1. QoS Measurements Specification (case 1 = no congestion ; case 2 = congestion)

The first kind of measurements is aimed at validating the protection of an AS (resp. a GS) flow in presence of a BE flow whose load is increased from 0% to 100% of the link bandwidth. AS and GS flows are not generated together. For these measurements:

- the BE flow is sent from the BSD_{exo} PC (LAAS); values of its mean rate are successively 0%, 25%, 50%, 75% and 100% of the link bandwidth;
- AS and GS flows are transmitted using Debit6 from LAAS BSD PC to LIP6 BSD PC; two cases are considered:
  - a single AS (resp. GS) flow is generated with a mean rate corresponding to 50% of the maximal amount allowed by the edge router to AS (resp. GS) traffic, i.e. 20 Kbytes/s (resp. 10 Kbytes/s);
  - a single AS (resp. GS) flow is generated with a mean rate corresponding to 100% of the maximal amount, i.e. 40 Kbytes/s (resp. 20 Kbytes/s).

The second kind of measurements is aimed at validating the protection of an AS flow and a GS flow generated together, in presence of a BE flow whose load corresponds to the totality of the link bandwidth (100%). For these measurements:

- the BE flow is sent from the BSD_{exo} PC (LAAS); its mean rate is 107 Kbytes/s ;
- AS and GS flows are transmitted using Debit6 from LAAS BSD PC to LIP6 BSD PC, each one with a mean rate corresponding to 50% of the maximal amount provided by the edge router (i.e. 20 Kbytes/s for AS and 10 Kbytes/s for GS).

Results and Analysis. For the first kind of measurements, due to space limitation, only the results for 100% of AS (respectively GS) are exposed in this section.

Protection of the AS Flows (vs. BE). Results of the measurements are exposed in Table 2. These results conform to the excepted ones. When the network is not in state of congestion (first three columns), one can conclude that:

- the average transit delay is almost constant (less than 1 ms gap);
- the loss rate is almost null;
- the receiving throughput is almost the same as the sending one;
- the maximum delay is not guaranteed.

Note that the second and third points are compliant to the expectations as we only consider in-profile traffic; measurements with out of profile traffic would show a receiving throughput inferior to the sending throughput (and a loss rate higher than 0)

When the network is in state of congestion, one can see that the transit delay value is slightly increased, which again is correct for the expected service.

AS – 100%		BE (% of the link bandwidth)				
		0%	25%	50%	75%	100%
Transit	- min	0.019	0.019	0.019	0.019	0.019
delay	- max	0.045	0.032	0.030	0.033	0.036
(s)	-	0.020	0.021	0.021	0.024	0.024
Through	-	40765	40963	40964	40963	40964
put	-	40761	40963	40963	40963	40963
Loss rate (%)		0.0	0.0	0.0	0.0	0.0

Table 2. AS - 100% vs. BE

Protection of the GS Flows (vs. BE). Results of the measurements are exposed in Table 3. These results are similar to those exposed for the AS flows, the main difference being that the maximum delay for GS packets seems slightly lower than the maximum for AS packets. This is normal as we only compare AS vs. BE and GS vs. BE; indeed, in both cases, the flow that benefits from QoS goes through the network nearly as quickly as it can.

GS – 100%		BE (% of the link bandwidth)				
		0%	25%	50%	75%	100%
Transit	- min	0.018	0.019	0.019	0.019	0.019
delay	- max	0.024	0.029	0.031	0.032	0.033
(s)	-	0.019	0.020	0.022	0.023	0.025
Through	-	18289	18289	18290	18289	18289
put	-	18289	18289	18289	18289	18289
Loss rate (%)		0.0	0.0	0.0	0.0	0.0

Table 3. GS - 100% vs. BE

Protection of the AS and GS flows (vs. BE). Results of the measurements are exposed in Figure 6, which presents the % of packets received with a delay less than or equal to the value denoted on the x-axis. The difference between AS and GS is now apparent for the maximum delay which is much higher for AS. Moreover, one can observe that the transit delay of the AS packets is more widely spread than the GS one. Note that the BE curve is not shown because it is out of the scale of the graphic.

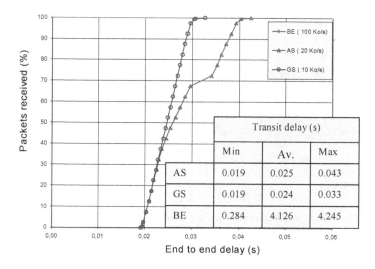

Figure 6. AS - 50% vs. GS - 50% vs. BE - 100%

5   Conclusions and Future Work

Work presented in this paper has been realised within the @IRS French project. It consists in the conception, the implementation and the validation of a communication architecture supporting differentiated IP level services as well as a per flow end-to-end QoS. The proposed architecture has been exposed in section 2; the network over which it is deployed has been described in section 3; finally, an experimental evaluation of the QoS provided by the defined IP services (GS, AS and BE) has been exposed in section 4.

Several conclusions may be stated:

- the first one is that a differentiated services architecture may be easily deployed over a VPN (*Virtual Private Network*)-like environment such as the one described;

- the second conclusion is that if experimental results correspond to the expected ones (as far as the GS, AS and BE services are concerned), the effect of the IP level parameters (router's queue length, WFQ weights, PBS threshold, ...) appears to be a crucial point in the implementation of the services. For instance, size of the AS queues has an influence on the offered service, short queues inducing a delay priority, longer queues inducing a reliability priority. In the same way, the PBS threshold defines the way the network reacts to the out of profile traffic, thus providing a service more or less adapted to applications needing a base assurance and willing to use additional available resources.

Three major perspectives of this work are currently under development:

- the first one is to extend the experimentations exposed in this paper so as to evaluate the IP QoS when several routers are overloaded with best effort traffic;

- the second one is to evaluate the QoS at the application level when several flows requiring a same class of service are generated;
- finally, it is our purpose to formalise the semantic of guarantee associated with the QoS parameters and to develop a mechanism allowing the application to be dispensed from the explicit choice of the Transport and IP services to be used.

Finally, a long term perspective of this work is the extension to a multi-domain environment, by using for example bandwidth brokering.

References

1. IETF: IntServ WG: http://www.ietf.org/html.charters/intserv-charter.html
2. IETF: DiffServ WG: http://www.ietf.org/html.charters/diffserv-charter.html
3. TF-TANT: http://www.dante.net/tf-tant
4. Campanella, M., Ferrari, T., et al: Specification and implementation plan for a Premium IP service. http://www.dante.org.uk/tf-ngn/GEA-01-032.pdf (2001).
5. TEQUILLA: http://www.ist-tequila.org
6. CADENUS: http://www.cadenus.org
7. AQUILA: http://www-st.inf.tu-dresden.de/aquila
8. GCAP: http://www.laas.fr/GCAP/
9. Campbell, A., Coulson, G., Hutchinson, D.: A quality of service architecture. ACM Computer Communication Review (1994).
10. Nahrstedt, K., Smith, J.: Design, Implementation and experiences of the OMEGA end-point architecture. IEEE JSAC, vol.14 (1996).
11. Gopalakrishna, G., Parulkar, G.: A framework for QoS guarantees for multimedia applications within end system. GI Jahrestagung. Zurich (1995).
12. Chassot, C, Diaz, M, Lozes, A.: From the partial order concept to partial order multimedia connection. Journal for High Speed Networks, vol. 5, n°2 (1996).
13. Amer, P., Chassot, C., Connolly, C., Conrad, P., Diaz, M.: Partial Order Transport Service for MM and other Appli. IEEE/ACM Trans. on Net[ing], vol.2, n°5 (1994).
14. Connolly, T., Amer, P., et al.: An Extention to TCP: Partial Ord. Serv. RFC 1693.
15. Zhao W, Olshefski D, Schulzrinne H.: Internet Quality of Service: an Overview. Technical Report CUCS-003-00. http://www.cs.columbia.edu/~hgs/netbib/ (2000).
16. Nichols, K., Jacobson, V., Zhang, L.: A Two-bit Differentiated Services Architecture for the Internet. November 1997.
17. Heinanhen, J., Baker, F., Weiss, W., and al.: An Assured Fwd[ing] PHB. RFC 2597.
18. Jacobson, V., Nichols, K., Poduri, K.: An Expedited Forwarding PHB. RFC 2598.
19. Blake, S., Black, D., Carlson, M.: An Arch. for Differentiated Services. RFC 2475.
20. Bonald, T., May, M., Bolot, J.: Analytic Evaluation of RED Performance. Proceedings INFOCOM'2000, Tel Aviv (2000).
21. Ziegler, T., Fdida, S., Brandauer, C.: Stability Criteria of RED with TCP Traffic. Internal report. http://www.newmedia.at/~tziegler/red_stab.pdf. (2000).

A Service Differentiation Scheme for the End-System[*]

Domenico Cotroneo[1], Massimo Ficco[2], and Giorgio Ventre[1]

[1] Dipartimento di Informatica e Sistemistica, Università degli Studi di Napoli "Federico II"
Via Claudio 121,
80125 Napoli, Italy
{cotroneo, giorgio}@unina.it

[2] ITEM - Laboratorio Nazionale di Informatica e Telematica Multimediali
Via Diocleziano 328
80124 Naples, ITALY
massimo.ficco@napoli.consorzio-cini.it

Abstract. A number of research studies show that the operating system has a substantial influence on communication delay in distributed environments. Thus, in order to provide applications with end-to-end QoS guarantees, network resource management alone is not sufficient. To date, several approaches have been proposed, addressing QoS issues from the end-system point of view. However, while network QoS provisioning has achieved a good level of standardization, no standard proposals exist for the end-systems. We claim that a single architectural model, taking into account both end-system and network resource management is needed. In this paper we propose a QoS architecture, which extends the concept of service differentiation inside the end-system. A system prototype has been developed and tested on a Diffserv network scenario. The prototype incorporates a priority-based communication mechanism inside the end-point operating system and a local marker so to implement an appropriate mapping between local classes of services and network QoS levels. Experimental results have also been provided in order to evaluate the impact of the proposed architecture on Diffserv routers.

1 Introduction

The problem of providing real-time communications between hosts over the Internet has become more understood. In fact, a number of research studies show that operating system has substantial influence on communication delay in distributed environments. These studies have demonstrated that in order to provide application with QoS guarantees, the network resource management alone is not sufficient. End-system resources, such as processing capacity, have also to be taken into account and they have to be managed in concert with the networking ones.

With respect to the network, experiences over the Internet have showed the lack of a fundamental technical element: real-time applications do not work well across the

[*] This work has been performed with the support of the Italian Ministry of Research and University (MURST) under a grant Progetti Cluster "Cluster 16 Multimedialità: LABNET2" and under a grant PRIN "MUSIQUE".

D. Shepherd et al. (Eds.): IDMS 2001, LNCS 2158, pp. 99-109, 2001.

network because of variable queueing delays and congestion losses. The Internet, as originally conceived, offers only a very simple quality of service: point-to-point best-effort data delivery. Thus, before real-time applications can be broadly used, the Internet infrastructure must be modified in order to support more stringent QoS guarantees. Based on these assumptions, the Internet Engineering Task Force (IETF) has defined two different models for network QoS provisioning: Integrated Services [1] and Differentiated Services [2]. These frameworks provide different, yet complementary, solutions to the issue of network support for quality of service.

A number of researchers dealt with the issue of providing Quality of Service guarantees inside network end-points. David K.Y. Yau and Simon S. proposed an end-system architecture designed to support network QoS [3]. They implemented a framework, called Migrating Sockets, composed of an user level protocol that minimize hidden scheduling on the sender side, and an active demultiplexing mechanism with constant overhead on the receiver side. With Migrating Sockets, performance-critical protocol services such as send and receive are accessed as a user level library linked with applications.

An architectural model providing Quality of Service guarantees to delay sensitive networked multimedia applications, including end-systems, has been proposed by K. Nahrstedt and J. Smith [4]. K. Nahrstedt and J. Smith also proposed a new model for resource management at the end-points, called the QoS Broker [5]. The broker orchestrates resources at the end-points, coordinating resource management across layer boundaries. As an intermediary, it hides implementation details from applications and per-layer resource managers. The QoS broker manages communication among the entities to create the desired system configuration. Configuration is achieved via QoS negotiation resulting in one or more connections through the communication system.

While we recognize that the cited works represent fundamental milestones for the pursuit of quality of service mechanisms inside the end-systems, we claim that the time is ripe for taking an integrated view on QoS-enabled communication.

A single architectural model is thus needed, integrating network centric and end-system centric approaches and taking into account the most relevant standards proposed by the research community.

In this work we propose a QoS architecture, which extends the concept of service differentiation inside the end-system. A system prototype, running on Sun Solaris 2.6, has been developed and tested in a Diffserv network scenario. The prototype incorporates a priority-based communication mechanism inside the end-point operating system, called the Priority Broker [6], and a local marker so to implement an appropriate mapping between local classes of services and network QoS levels.

The rest of the paper is organized as follows. In section 2 we briefly introduce the architecture and the services provided by Priority Broker. In section 3 we illustrate the design and the implementation of an enhanced version of the Priority Broker, including local marker and a more efficient buffer management schema. In section 4 we present the DiffServ network testbed we adopted. In section 5 we provide a critical discussion of the experimental results, obtained from the execution of the Priority Broker (PB) on each end-system connected to the Diffserv network. Ultimately, conclusions and future works are described in section 6.

2 The Priority Broker (PB)

The PB, which an earlier prototype is provided in [6], is an architectural model that supports communication flows with a guaranteed priority level. It is conceived as daemon process running on the end-system, which provides an API (Broker Library Interface) enabling applications to request the following three classes of communication services:

1. Best-effort: no Qos guarantees;
2. low priority: for adaptive applications;
3. high priority: for real-time applications.

It is implemented as a new software module residing between applications and the kernel and provides an additional level of abstraction, capable of interacting with the operating system in order to provide the applications with a well-defined set of differentiated services, while monitoring the quality of the communication by means of flow control techniques.

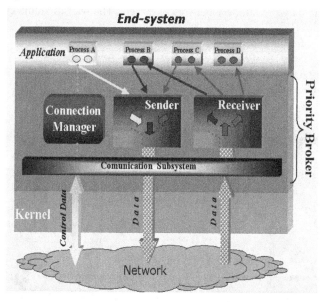

Fig. 1. Conceptual schema of the Priority Broker architecture.

The Priority Broker is composed of four components: the sender-broker, the receiver-broker, the communication subsystem, and the connection manager.

The sender-broker is responsible for the transmission of packets with the priority required by end-users, while the receiver-broker manages incoming packets. The communication subsystem provides the I/O primitives that enable discrimination, in the kernel I/O subsystem, among outgoing packets. Finally, the connection manager is in charge of handling all service requests on behalf of the local and remote processes.

The PB, in turn, relies on the services made available by both the transport provider and the I/O mechanisms of the operating system upon which it resides. Further implementation details can be found in [6].

3   An Enhanced Version of the Priority

As we mentioned, we envision a distributed environment where resources are explicitly required by the applications and appropriately managed by the local OS, which is also in charge of mapping local requests onto the set of services made available by the network.

More precisely, we enforce a correspondence between end-system priorities and network classes of service, thus obtaining an actual end-to-end Per Hop Behavior, where the first and last hops take into account transmission between end hosts and network routers. To the purpose, in this section we propose an extension of architecture described in [6]. The enhancement we propose deals with the sender-broker. We introduced a new module, in charge of mapping local requests onto the set of services made available by the Diffserv network (Marker). The overall architecture is depicted in Figure 2.

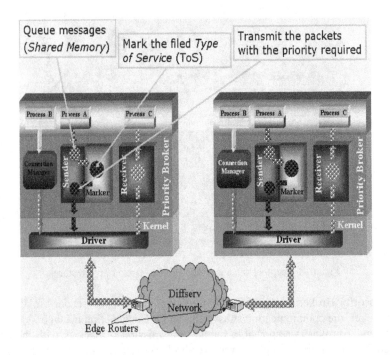

Fig. 2. End-to-end communication schema

As the figure shows, communication in this scenario takes place with the following steps:

1. A sender application selects its desired level of service among the set of available QoS classes and it asks the local connection manager to appropriately setup the required resources.
2. The connection manager is in charge of performing local admission control strategy.
3. Once the application calls the BLI send primitive, data is queued in the part of shared memory assigned to the application.
4. The sender-broker transmits the packets with the required priority.

The sender-broker is structured as a multithreaded process. Each thread is in charge of managing and transmitting data with a required priority level. The Marker is part of sender-broker, it sets the particular DS codepoint corresponding to the required class of service. To cope with this issue, an appropriate mapping has been defined between local classes of service and network QoS levels. The solution we propose is shown in the following figure.

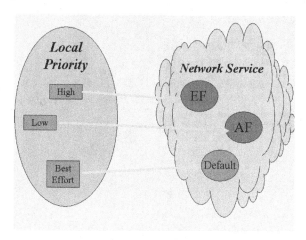

Fig. 3. Marker's mapping schema

To transmit packets with the priority assigned by the user by means of BLI, the Sender-broker uses the following mechanisms, as shown in figure 4:

1. I/O primitives made available by the Operating System to assure flow control on the sender side when accessing the network;
2. Shared memory to avoid multiple copies between applications and kernel to send messages;
3. Synchronization mechanisms to implement the communication protocol between user applications and PB.

As far as I/O primitives are concerned, our PB runs on Solaris 2.6. This kind of system provides a powerful I/O mechanism, the STREAMS framework [10]. STREAMS uses message queuing priority. All messages have an associated priority field: default messages have a priority of zero, while priority messages have a priority band greater than zero. Non-priority, ordinary messages are placed at the end of the queue following all other messages that can be waiting. Priority band messages are placed below all messages that have a priority greater than or equal to their own, but above any with a smaller priority.

To discriminate among three different classes of service, we found, by trial and error, that the best choice was to use a priority of 0 for Best Effort, 1 for Low Priority and 255 for High Priority.

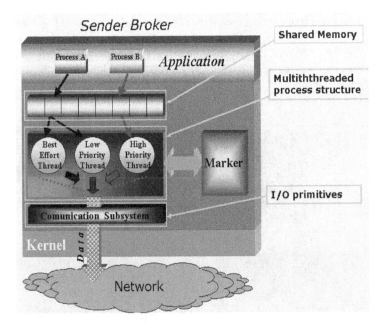

Fig. 4. Sender-Broker architecture.

4   Experimental Testbed

We deployed the system over the heterogeneous platform illustrated in figure 5. The figure illustrates a Diffserv network, composed of three routers (Aphrodite, Gaia, Zeus) based on the Class Based Queuing (CBQ) algorithm [7]. The routers are low-end PCs running FreeBSD. In order to be able to take measurements, a monitor application is installed on each routers.

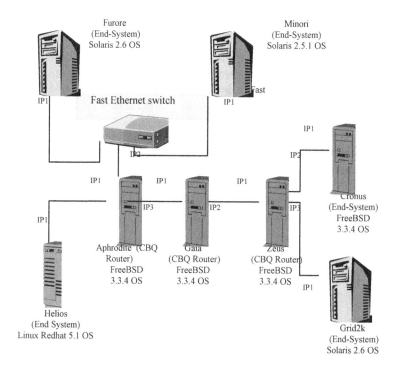

Fig. 5. Testbed DiffServ architecture

During the experiments the following Sun's workstations are involved as end-system: Furore, Minori e Grid2k. Furore and Minori, based respectively on Solaris 2.6 and Solaris 2.5.1, are connected to Aphrodite by a Fast Ethernet switch, while Grid2k is directly wired to Zeus. On each end-system is installed the Priority Broker, which consists of a daemon process and the BLI user-level library. Furore and Minori act as senders, while Grid2k as receiver. Several sender applications can be launched on these end-systems.

On sender sides (Furore and Minori) the PB takes care of marking the outgoing IP packets, by setting the TOS field as mentioned in section 3.

CBQ routers are configured as follow: the 98% of the bandwidth is assigned to the Best Effort (BE) traffic. To the Assured Forwarding (AF) traffic is assigned the 96% of the BE, and the 95% of this, is assigned to the Expedited Forwarding (EF) traffic. Finally, the bandwidth allocation hierarchy is:

1. 2% of the total bandwidth to the BE traffic;
2. 1% of the total bandwidth to the AF traffic ;
3. 95% of the total bandwidth to the EF traffic.

We chose such configuration in order to better discriminate flows inside the monitors.

5   Experimental Results

In this section we present some of the experiments we performed in order to investigate the behaviour of overall architecture. Experiments are performed on the testbed illustrated in section 4. The maximum bandwidth that can be managed by routers is 2 Megabits per second. All the data presented in the following are measured by the monitor application running on the routers.

The first test was run to compare the behaviour of the routing activity in the case of the PB is active or not. Three sender applications run concurrently on workstation Furore. Such senders, A, B and C use different classes of service, respectively BE, AF and EF. Sender applications are launched in the following sequence: the sender A is the first, the sender B is the second, and the sender C is the third. Each application transmits about 20000 messages of 1200 bytes.

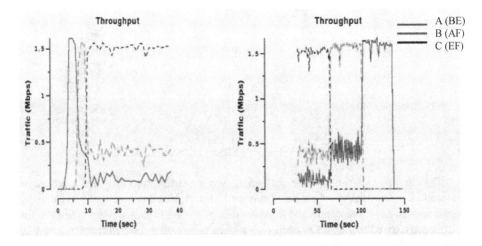

Fig. 6. Test results without the Priority Broker

First, we performed measurements without executing the PB on the end-systems. Figure 6 shows that differentiated services are scheduled by the routers according to the CBQ router configuration.

The two graphics depicted in figure 7, report the same experimental results in the case of the PB was running on the end-systems.

From the left-side of figure 7, it should be noted that the sender A (BE traffic) is able to transmit until B (AF traffic) starts. As soon as sender B starts, the PB pre-empts resources allocated to A, letting only sender B to transmit. In a similar way sender B is pre-empted as soon as C (EF traffic) starts. From the right picture of figure 7, it should be noted that sender A resumes its transmission only when B and C end. Conversely, the two graphics show the impact of the PB on the router activity. Class of Services, belonging to the same end-system, with lower priorities are scheduled directly at the end-system. This is due to PBs running on the end-system. We believe that such behaviour emphasize the differentiation performed inside the Diffserv routers.

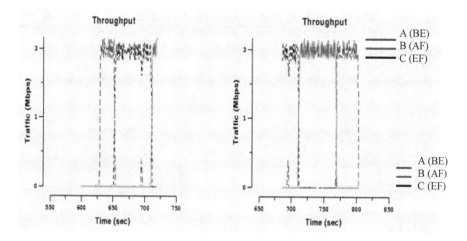

Fig. 7. Test result with the Priority Broker

The second test was run to evaluate the combined effect of PB and Diffserv routers in a real world scenario. In this case four sender applications run concurrently on two different workstations: two of these run on workstation Furore and the others on workstation Minori. Two senders, running on Minori, use respectively BE and AF priority, while priorities used by senders running on Furore are BE and EF.

Senders start transmitting their flows according to the following sequence:

1. BE flow on Furore;
2. BE flow on Minori;
3. AF flow on Minori;
4. EF flow on Furore.

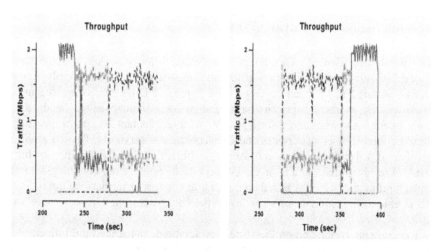

Fig. 8. Test Results in a real world scenario with PB

As soon as Furore and Minori start respectively AF and EF senders, no more BE traffic is scheduled by the routers. This is due to the pre-emption performed by the PB at the end-systems by PBs. The BE traffic is resumed when AF and EF end (second graphics depicted in figure 8).

Figure 9 shows the same experimental results when PBs were not running.

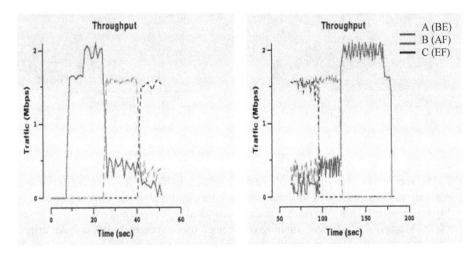

Fig. 9. Test results in a real world scenario without PB

We believe that such behaviour emphasize the differentiation performed inside the Diffserv routers. We are currently investigating benefits of the PB form end-to-end point of view.

6   Conclusion and Future Work

This work has presented a QoS architecture, called Priority Broker, which extends the concept of service differentiation inside the end-system. A system prototype, running on Sun Solaris 2.6, has been developed and tested in a Diffserv network scenario. The prototype incorporates a priority-based communication mechanism inside the end-point operating system and a local marker so to implement an appropriate mapping between local classes of services and Diffserv class of services. The PB architecture consists of a daemon process and user level library, called Broker Library Interface (BLI). We integrated our PB in the Diffserv architecture, thus obtaining a single architectural model, which is based on the central concept of service differentiation. The PB is able to discriminate services inside the end-system, the Diffserv router outside of it.

Experiments conducted on the system prototype demonstrated the influence of the end-system in the router activity. PB running on the end-system "help" the router scheduler to better discriminate its class of services

Future work will aim to:
1. Refine measurements in order to evaluate the end-to-end behaviour of applications using our architecture;
2. Investigate the porting of this architecture to different operating systems. We are current the implementing a new version of the PB running on Linux Real Time. In order to discriminate services inside the end-system, in this case the communication subsystem will exploit the real time features instead of the I/O mechanisms.

References

1. R. Braden, D.Clark, and S. Shenker. "Integrated Services in the Internet Architecture: an Overview". RFC 1633, July 1994.
2. S. Blake, D. Black, M. Carlson, E. Davies, Z. Wang, and W. Weiss. "An Architecture for Differentiated Services". RFC 2475, Dec. 1998.
3. David K.Y.Yau and Simon S. Lam "Migrating Sockets-End System Support for Networking with Quality of Service Guarantees", IEEE/ACM Trans. On Networking. VOL. 6, December 1998.
4. K. Nahrstedt and J. Smith "A Service Kernel for Multimedia Endstations", Technical Report, MS-CIS, University of Pennsylvania.
5. K. Nahrstedt and J. Smith, "The QoS Broker", IEEE Multimedia Spring 1995,Vol.2, No.1, pp. 53-67.
6. D. Cotroneo, M. Ficco, S.P.Romano and G.Ventre, "Bringing Service Differentiation to the End System", IEEE conference ICON 2000, Oct. 2000.
7. S.Floyd and V. Jacobson, "Link-sharing and resource management models for packet networks", IEEE/ACM transaction on Networking, 3(4), August 1995.
8. G. Banga P. Druschel, „Resource containers: New facility for resource management in server system", 3rd USENIX Symposium on Operating Systems Design and Implementation, New Orleans, Feb, 1999.
9. G. Banga, "Operating System Support for Server Application", PhD Thesis, Rice University, May 1999.
10. Uresh Vahalia, UNIX Internals, The new frontiers, Prentice Hall International, 1996.

Enabling the Internet to Provide Multimedia Services

Markus Hofmann

Bell Labs, Holmdel, New Jersey, USA
hofmann@bell-labs.com

Abstract. The Internet as of today is still mostly governed by the end-to-end principle, which demands that the network itself is to be kept as simple as possible and that all intelligence resides at the end-systems. This principle proved to be very successful and beneficial for the evolution of the Internet. Despite its success, we have recently seen more application-specific functionality moving into the network, in particular to the edges of the network. Deployment of network caches and content-aware switches are probably the most widely known examples for this kind of functionality. It helps accelerating the delivery of static web pages by moving content closer to the user.

However, margins for such basic delivery services are getting slimmer. Service providers have to take advantage of opportunities to provide new value-added content services for differentiation and additional revenue. Examples of such services include, but are not limited to, content filtering, content adaptation, dynamic and personalized content assembling, ad insertion and virus scanning.

This talk outlines the evolution from traditional web caching towards a flexible and open architecture to support a variety of content-oriented multimedia services. Enhancements include added support for streaming media, a component for global traffic redirection, and a set of protocols and interfaces for value-added features, such as compression, filtering, or transformation. Additional functionality can be integrated in different components, or be available as plug-ins. The talk will conclude with service examples currently being implemented on top of such a platform.

D. Shepherd et al. (Eds.): IDMS 2001, LNCS 2158, pp. 110-110, 2001.
© Springer-Verlag Berlin Heidelberg 2001

Design and Application of TOAST: An Adaptive Distributed Multimedia Middleware Platform

Tom Fitzpatrick[1], Julian Gallop[2], Gordon Blair[3], Christopher Cooper[2],
Geoff Coulson[1], David Duce[4] and Ian Johnson[2]

[1]Computing Department, Lancaster University, Lancaster, LA1 4YR UK.
{tf, geoff}@comp.lancs.ac.uk

[2]CLRC Rutherford Appleton Laboratory, Chilton, Didcot, Oxfordshire, OX11 0QX UK
{J.R.Gallop, C.S.Cooper, I.J.Johnson}@rl.ac.uk

[3]Department of Computer Science, University of Tromsø, 9037 Tromsø,
Norway (on leave from Lancaster University)
gordon@cs.uit.no

[4]Oxford Brookes University, Gipsy Lane, Oxford, OX3 0BP UK
daduce@brookes.ac.uk

Abstract. The rise of mobile computing and wireless network technology means that, increasingly, applications must adapt to their environment, in particular network connectivity and resource availability. This paper outlines the TOAST middleware platform which provides component-oriented CORBA support for adaptive distributed multimedia applications. In particular, the paper examines how the areas of reflection and open implementation have shaped the approach to adaptation support in TOAST. The paper then discusses novel ongoing research which is investigating middleware support for distributed cooperative visualization using TOAST as a base.

1 Introduction

The modern computer user is increasingly likely to be mobile. With the advent of powerful laptop computers, personal digital assistants (PDAs) and, more importantly, wireless networking technology, mobile computing is a fast-growing area. Understandably, the mobile computing user expects applications to function regardless of mobility issues, in the same way that cellular voice or fax services are (generally) expected to be available regardless of location. To achieve this ideal, there are, unsurprisingly, many challenges to be overcome.

Perhaps the greatest hurdle for mobile computing is that the Quality of Service (QoS) differences between mobile network types make transparent use of most networked applications impossible. Today, a mobile user may roam from a desktop scenario with a 10 or (more commonly) 100Mbit/s Ethernet connection, round a local site with 2-10Mbit/s Wireless LAN connectivity or in the wide-area with low-bandwidth GSM dialup or TETRA wireless link. In addition to connectivity changes, resource availability may also vary. For example, a laptop computer may reduce its processor power to increase battery life when mobile. In addition, PC-CARD devices such as media capture or compression cards may need to be removed to make room

D. Shepherd et al. (Eds.): IDMS 2001, LNCS 2158, pp. 111-123, 2001.
© Springer-Verlag Berlin Heidelberg 2001

for network interface cards, thereby reducing the capabilities of the system or placing a higher load on software.

In almost all cases, conventional applications with fixed QoS constraints simply cannot function correctly in this dynamic environment. As a result, a new class of application called *adaptive applications* has emerged [3, 7]. As their name implies, such applications *adapt* to QoS changes so that they remain functional in a mobile or changing environment. The TOAST multimedia middleware platform, developed in the Adapt Project [1] and being extended in the Visual Beans Project [25, 13], provides a component-oriented framework that supports the development of adaptive distributed multimedia applications.

This paper is structured as follows. Section 2 outlines the design of the TOAST middleware platform, while section 3 describes how TOAST supports adaptive applications. Section 4 presents some details about the current implementation of TOAST, while section 5 discusses how ongoing research is investigating the application of TOAST to the area of distributed cooperative visualization in the Visual Beans Project.

2   The Design of TOAST

2.1   Introduction

The *Toolkit for Open Adaptive Streaming Technologies* (TOAST) is a CORBA-based multimedia middleware platform. TOAST is an attempt to not only implement multimedia support in CORBA in an RM-ODP [2] inspired manner, but to do this in a way which provides the same plug-and-play component-based mechanism as common multimedia programming frameworks [16, 18, 5]. While basic CORBA multimedia streaming support exists [20], it does not truly follow the RM-ODP model, nor the concepts of component-orientation [24]. A key feature is that TOAST is entirely designed and specified in terms of CORBA IDL, allowing it transcend language and platform boundaries. While this section presents a brief overview of the design of the TOAST platform, a full discussion of the design and implementation of TOAST can be found in [10].

2.2   Component Model

The main abstraction in TOAST is that of a multimedia processing *component*; the basic unit from which applications are built. Examples of components include audio input/output components, video grabbers, network sources/sinks and filters. Following a dataflow or 'plug-n-play' model, components exchange continuous media and other data through *stream interfaces* and *flow interfaces*.

Flow interfaces are the fundamental endpoint for media interaction in TOAST and come in two varieties, input and output. Stream interfaces are a direct realization of the RM-ODP concept of a stream interface; an interface which groups one or more flow interfaces into a single composite interaction point, thus simplifying otherwise complicated connection processes. A commonly-used example of a stream interface is a (bi-directional) telephone handset with two unidirectional audio flows. An IDL definition of such a stream interface in TOAST is shown below:

```
interface Handset: TOAST::Stream     interface VideoHandset: Handset
{                                     {
        INFLOW audioIn;                      INFLOW videoIn;
        OUTFLOW audioOut;                    OUTFLOW videoOut;
};                                    };
```

Components can possess both flow and stream interfaces, allowing more traditional RM-ODP compliance using only stream interfaces, or a more low-level 'plug-n-play' multimedia programming framework approach with flow interfaces. An IDL definition of a component with both flow and stream interfaces appears below:

```
interface Phone: TOAST::Component
{
        STREAM handset;
        OUTFLOW recordChannelOut;
};
```

While components may statically declare their stream and flow interfaces as attributes of their main interface (INFLOW, OUTFLOW and STREAM are pre-processor macros), underlying mechanisms allow these to be discovered through a dynamic querying/enumeration process. Also, rather than use enriched IDL to (statically) declare a flow interface's media or information type, this information is always queried dynamically from the flow interface itself.

In addition to stream and flow interfaces, TOAST provides components with event-based interaction. This form of interaction is more asynchronous, dynamic and decoupled than traditional CORBA interaction, and is ideal for the type of application that TOAST is designed for. The programmer can enumerate and query which events a component supports at run-time, and indeed even be notified when new event types are made available by a component. Event-based interaction in TOAST is less ambitious and consequently more lightweight than the CORBA Event Service [19], and is seen as complementary to that service rather than as a replacement.

2.3 Basic Component Interaction

Local binding in TOAST is the process by which two *collocated* stream or flow interfaces are bound together to enable media data to flow between them. Since the local binding of stream interfaces is essentially a compound operation involving the local binding of all compatible pairs of flow interfaces, this section will only examine flow interface local binding.

Flow interface local binding is strictly typed, requiring both flow interfaces to agree on a single, common mediatype which they will exchange. The process of mediatype negotiation is an important one, since without it the programmer must ensure that all connections are meaningful, reducing extensibility and allowing inconsistency. This process of type-checking connections between multimedia processing components is found in DirectShow [5] but not in systems such as MASH [18] or the Berkeley CMT [16] where, for example, a video capture component could be connected to an audio renderer – presumably with painful results.

2.4 Distributed Component Interaction

Whereas collocated flow and stream interfaces can be directly locally bound, to allow distributed interaction requires a *binding object*, a concept defined by the RM-ODP. Binding objects (actually standard TOAST components, albeit complex ones) are essential to allow components to interact over a network, or between incompatible address spaces. Binding objects, or more simply *bindings*, are responsible for the complete end-to-end communications path between the components that they bind.

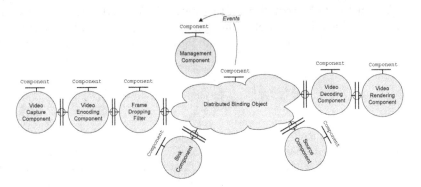

Figure 1. Complex binding with a binding object

Binding objects are created by a *binding factory* and are locally bound to their client components in a semi-recursive fashion. Note that bindings can be arbitrarily complex and are in fact special types of TOAST component. Fig. 1 presents an example of how both local and complex binding is used to build distributed applications.

Binding factories are a crucial part of the TOAST architecture, since they allow components to interact in a distributed manner by creating binding objects to fulfil a particular role. In addition, in combination with the provision of new component implementations via component factories, augmenting the range of available types of binding through the addition of new binding factories is the principal means of achieving extensibility in TOAST.

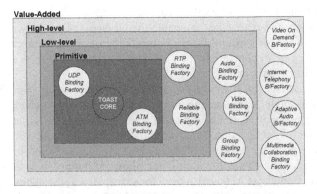

Figure 2. Hierarchy of binding factories for recursive binding

To encourage extensibility, it is intended that binding factories be available to the programmer as a set of distributed services available on the network. Furthermore, the process of creating a binding object is intended to be recursive; whereby higher-level binding factories call upon lower-level binding factories to aid their construction efforts (see Fig. 2). This process of *recursive binding* is explained in [2].

2.5 Component Factories

The dynamic capability discovery features of TOAST components are complemented by component factories which allow component instances to be created dynamically. Each TOAST application or process automatically possesses a component factory allowing components to be created in that process. A component factory exports a CORBA interface, thus allowing it to be accessed from anywhere in the network (permissions allowing). The TOAST API allows one to create components either in-process, on a given node or collocated with another component, with a single call. In addition, new component implementations may be added to factories at run-time.

3 Support for Adaptation in TOAST

3.1 Approach

TOAST adopts a framework approach to adaptation, in which specific algorithms and techniques are made possible through a generic support architecture. The benefits of this approach include extensibility with regard to adaptation techniques and mechanisms. This generic support architecture is heavily influenced by the concepts of *open implementation* and *reflection*.

3.2 Use of Open Implementation Techniques

Background. Open implementation [14] seeks to overcome the limitations of the 'black box' approach to software engineering by opening up key aspects of an implementation to the programmer. Reflection [22] is often used to provide a principled means of open implementation by separating the functionality provided by a system (its interface) from the underlying implementation. In a reflective system, a *meta-interface* allows one to manipulate a causally-connected self-representation of the system's implementation through *inspection* and *adaptation*. Open implementation and reflection were applied initially to programming languages [14, 26] but have also been used in windowing systems [22], operating systems [29] and CORBA [17, 23]. Complementary work at Lancaster investigates the use of reflection techniques in more generalized middleware in the OpenORB project [32].

Open Bindings. TOAST applies reflection and open implementation to supporting adaptation, for example for mobile computing environments. Bindings are responsible for the entire end-to-end communications process, including resource management, signalling, flow filtering/compression and scheduling. To support mobile computing it is crucial that the application be able to exert some control over binding objects [7]. Providing this control via a control interface on a binding has several drawbacks however. In particular, it is difficult if not impossible to design a *general* means of achieving adaptation, mainly due to the sheer proliferation of possible actions, for example in the mobile computing domain [12]. In addition, such an approach would neither be extensible nor dynamic, and would, for example, preclude the use of new adaptation techniques or components introduced during the lifetime of an application or binding.

Instead of a control interface, TOAST allows bindings to offer a meta-interface which operates on a causally-connected self-representation of the implementation of the binding object. This self-representation is modelled as a *component graph*; the nodes of the graph being the TOAST components that make up the binding's implementation; the arcs between them representing the local bindings between these components. Adaptation is achieved by directly inspecting and adapting this self-representation, as will be discussed in section 3.3.

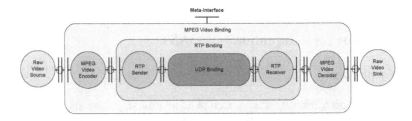

Figure 3. An open binding and its implementation graph

Bindings which expose their implementation in this way are called *open bindings*. An example of an open binding is shown in Fig. 3. Note the use of hierarchical open bindings in the example, where the various subordinate bindings resulting from a recursive binding process can also have their implementations accessed. This recursion is terminated by *primitive components* which do not expose their implementation, for example standard media processing/filtering components or UDP network bindings. TOAST uses *interface mapping* to associate flow interfaces on internal implementation components with a binding's externally visible interfaces in a principled manner.

3.3   Adaptation through Open Implementation

Introduction. As mentioned previously, adaptation is achieved in TOAST by inspecting and adapting the implementation of a binding via its meta-interface; effectively a *procedural* rather than *declarative* approach to QoS management [1]. This approach is the result of earlier work at Lancaster investigating the use of logic or QoS attributes to specify QoS requirements [6]. While valid for certain types of scenario, we have found that declarative techniques do not extend well to the mobile, adaptive environment targeted by TOAST. For example, in the face of greatly varying network connectivity. Achieving adaptation in TOAST is divided into two categories: *minor adaptation* and *major adaptation*, which will both be discussed next.

Minor Adaptation. This form of adaptation is the most basic supported by TOAST. This technique allows fine-grained changes or tweaks to be made to the operation of a binding while it is running. The intended use is to allow the programmer or adaptive agent (e.g. a control script or active object) to counteract slight changes in the environment, such as network QoS fluctuations or end-system resource availability.

The first step in minor adaptation is the identification and location of the appropriate components within a binding's implementation graph using the binding's meta-interface. Once located, these components may be interrogated, for example to determine the true state of QoS or performance. If desired, adaptation can then be achieved by accessing these components' control interfaces to alter their operation. An example of minor adaptation would be locating a primitive network binding component offered network QoS reports via its interface (e.g. through TOAST events), and using this information to change the encoding rate/quality of a video encoder component elsewhere in the implementation graph.

Figure 4. Restricting access to implementation-graph components

While such techniques can be used to good effect, it is also important to allow a meta-interface to maintain consistency in the face of adaptation. For example, one could easily access a network source component in a binding and change its destination address, thereby destroying the operation of the binding. For this reason, the meta-interface and implementation component graph refer to components using opaque IDs; to access a component's interface one must request it specifically. This allows a meta-interface to restrict access to certain 'safe' components, or, by way of TOAST COM-style multiple interface support, even to only certain interfaces on certain components (see Fig. 4).

Major Adaptation. The second, most drastic, form of adaptation supported by TOAST is major adaptation. Similarly to minor adaptation, one uses a binding's meta-interface to inspect its implementation; however major adaptation involves changing the structure of this implementation graph to alter the implementation of the binding. Since a binding's implementation is represented as a graph, the meta-interface provides methods to add and remove nodes and arcs (components and local bindings) to and from this graph. In addition, a number of higher-level or *compound* adaptation operations are provided. These include operations allowing the transparent hot-swapping of one side of a local binding and completely replacing one component with another 'similar' one.

Figure 5. Using major adaptation to reconfigure a binding

Perhaps the most common use for major adaptation is to alter the 'big-picture' strategy of a binding to adapt to an environmental change. This might involve replacing unsuitable components with newer ones, the insertion of extra components (e.g. QoS filters [28]) or the removal of redundant components. An example of major adaptation is shown in Fig. 5. Here, the meta-interface is being used to adapt a unidirectional video binding in the face of a network change from ~2Mbit/s WaveLAN to a <9.6Kbit/s GSM dialup link. In this case, the video compression type must be changed to match; consequently the motion-JPEG CODEC components are replaced with H.263 counterparts to provide a much lower-bitrate video channel.

In practice, while adaptation using such techniques does introduce transient 'glitches' into media streaming (e.g. while inserting filters), usually the benefits outweigh these costs. For example, one application developed at Lancaster used major adaptation techniques to alter the compression used in a music-on-demand streaming session from uncompressed CD quality (1.2Mbit/s) down as far as GSM compressed levels (13.2kbit/s) to match available network bandwidth. A slight (e.g. ~100ms) pause in audio was noticed during reconfiguration, however this was insignificant compared to the effect of *not* reconfiguring the application – namely severe packet loss and/or jitter.

Perhaps more so than with minor adaptation, the maintenance of consistency is extremely important with major adaptation, since once could quite easily remove all components from a binding's implementation, or alternatively break all local bindings, thereby preventing correct operation. Again, the meta-interface is responsible for consistency, and for determining, and vetoing, all major adaptation operations. The provision of compound adaptation operations, such as replacing components, is a direct result of lessons learned in this area; while the act of inserting/removing a filter component would be deemed acceptable by a meta-interface, the individual breaking/binding operations that make up this compound operation would not be. The compound operations therefore allow adaptation operations that would otherwise be unacceptable to the meta-interface. Additionally, since TOAST adopts a low-level graph-structured approach, it is ideally suited to the application of graph manipulation techniques such as those described in [30, 31].

4   Current Implementation

At present, TOAST has been implemented in C++ for the Win32 platform and Java for the JDK1.3 platform using the ORBacus [21] C++/Java CORBA system. A growing library of components exists for both C++ and Java, including video and audio capture, processing and playback. A number of demonstration applications showing the adaptive aspects of TOAST have been designed and implemented. Currently, ongoing research is investigating the uses for TOAST in the area of distributed co-operative visualisation (see Section 5).

To demonstrate that the design and specification of TOAST in CORBA does not introduce overhead making real-time media processing impractical, the remainder of this section presents some measurements from the current implementation[1]. Note that more detailed measurements, as well as a qualitative evaluation of TOAST, appear in [10].

Perhaps the simplest measurement of TOAST is the throughput, in terms of media data buffers per second, of a TOAST local binding between two flow interfaces in the same process. Compared to a C++ virtual function call which achieves about 11 million buffers (i.e. invocations) per second, a local binding achieves roughly half that figure at about 5.7 million per second. While TOAST obviously introduces significant overhead, the throughput is sufficient for almost all common media processing tasks; an example of the throughput in terms of buffers per second for some common media types is shown in Table 1.

Media Type	Throughput Required
Full Motion Video – all types (1 frame per buffer)	24, 25 or 30 bufs/sec
CD Quality Digital PCM Audio (1k buffers)	172 buffers/sec
CD Quality Digital PCM Audio (512 byte buffers)	345 buffers/sec
Telephone Quality PCM Audio (1k buffers)	16 buffers/sec
GSM Compressed Audio (1 frame per buffer)	50 buffers/sec
10Mbit/s Continuous Media (1k buffers)	10,240 buffers/sec

Table 1. Example media throughput requirements

To illustrate the overheads imposed by the TOAST component model, Figure 6 presents the throughput of *pipelines* of successive sizes made up of filter-style components. Two sets of measurements are presented; one for pipelines of non-threaded components, the other for pipelines made up of components which each have a worker thread handling their (null in this test case) processing. Contrasting these figures with raw local binding throughput, it is apparent that though throughput is

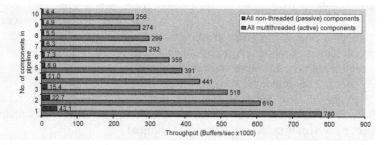

Figure 6. In-process component pipeline throughput

[1] All measurements were taken from the C++/Win32/ORBacus3.1 implementation of TOAST running on an Intel Pentium II 350MHz PC with 128Mb memory running Windows NT4.0 SP5. To reflect the target environment of TOAST, the machine was left connected to its Ethernet and ran all standard services.

greatly reduced by the overhead of the component model, it is still more than enough for most purposes. An interesting observation from Fig. 6 is that of the overhead imposed by multithreaded components; the context-switching and other thread synchronisation having a large impact on throughput values.

5   Application to Distributed Cooperative Visualization

The open adaptive streaming technology in TOAST is designed to support distributed multimedia applications and current work (within the Visual Beans project [25]) is investigating this by studying one particular field of applications, *distributed cooperative visualization* (DCV). Visualization is a key technology for many scientific, engineering, medical, geographical and social science applications and it is common for datasets to be large or complex or both. DCV aims to extend this so that groups of professionals can work at a distance, sharing visualization results, procedures and activities [3]. Various terminology has been used. *Distance visualization* [11] presents visualization on the Grid using dispersed resources and supporting dispersed end users. *Teleimmersion* [15] immerses a group of dispersed users in a single virtual world, which contains not only the focus of their common task but also virtual representatives of each user, referred to as avatars. In some sense the participants are not only looking at the focus of interest but are within it.

Experience of DCV [8, 27, 3] has revealed a number of directions and problems that require investigation. We outline here the ones that relate to component technology and TOAST in particular.

- Allowing the participants to access the visualization software actively, by contrast with previously prepared images on a distributed whiteboard, enables alternative plans to be tested ("What happens if I change this parameter?") and seen and optionally controlled by all. Different experts in a collaboration can offer expertise on different data sources, algorithms and phenomena. Thus, some variation of collaboration policy needs to be allowed, examples of which are to allow control to be centralized or devolved; to allow meeting styles to be controlled, such as peer-to-peer or lecturing format.
- Remote data archives or data archives local to one user need to be accessible to the collaboration. Although, for reasons of quantity and sensitivity, some data processing takes place logically close to the data, it is still necessary to accommodate large data transfer to all participants.
- Video communication amongst participants adds to the level of awareness of all concerned. However, far more critical for the collaboration is a sufficiently good quality of voice communication.
- Availability of Grid technology means that computational resources and data access will be dispersed without the location being known to the participants. A coherent local visualization environment is required.
- The use of the visualization system can itself result in the delivery of a movie to all participants. A good example is the study of time-varying phenomena. While these are being studied, explanation and discussion may continue. It can be important to know that the participants are looking at the same frame at the same

time. Whether an action replay is under the control of one person or controlled on an individual basis, synchronization may well be vital.

- Thus several types of information are required (for example voice, video, whiteboard, image, data, movie, web link), some of which each require a continuous flow of information.
- Some visualization processes may require intensive use of storage, computational or networking resources, which may therefore compete with the processing of continuous flows.
- A collaboration will involve a number of host computers of diverse power and network connectivity. Developments in mobile technology will increase the diversity of network connections in use and thus will increase the range of QoS changes to which the collaborative application will need to adapt.

  These can be summarised in the following major issues.

- The need to allow reconfiguration and coordination of audio, visual and visualization components to achieve the most effective meeting style in the remote collaboration.
- The need for resource management to control the competing demands of several continuous flows, transmission of data and low-latency distributed interaction.
- The need for adaptation to diverse and changing resources.

The Visual Beans project [25] is investigating the open adaptive streaming approach provided by TOAST to manage these problems. By merging a component based visualization system (specifically VisAD) [13], into the TOAST component model, visualization applications gain access to the adaptation and distribution support offered by TOAST. This approach allows visualization systems to benefit from existing TOAST continuous media support (e.g. pre-existing components) as well as providing an integrated approach to resource management.

6   Conclusions

This paper has outlined the design of the TOAST distributed multimedia middleware platform, in particular its component-oriented approach to multimedia systems. The architectural support for adaptation offered by TOAST was then described, along with some details of current implementation work. Finally, ongoing research was introduced that is using TOAST to investigate its application to distributed cooperative visualization.

Acknowledgements

The authors acknowledge the support to the Visual Beans Project provided by the (UK) Engineering and Physical Sciences Research Council (EPSRC) under grants GR/M81779 and GR/M82011.

References

1. Blair, G., Coulson, G., Davies, N., Robin, P. and Fitzpatrick, T., "Adaptive Middleware for Mobile Multimedia Applications", Proc. NOSSDAV'97, Missouri, USA, May 1997.
2. Blair, G. and Stefani, J., "Open Distributed Processing and Multimedia", Addison-Wesley, Harlow, England 1998.
3. Braden, R., Clark, D. and Shenker, S., "Integrated Services in the Internet Architecture: an Overview", IETF Request For Comments, RFC 1633, June 1994.
4. Brodlie, K.W., Duce, D.A., Gallop, J.R. and Wood, J.D., "Distributed Cooperative Visualization", Eurographics '98 State of the Art Reports, deSousa, A.A. and Hopgood, F.R.A. (Eds), pp27-60, 1998.
5. Chatterjee, A. and Maltz, A., "Microsoft DirectShow: A new media architecture", SMPTE Journal, December 1997, Vol.106, No.12, pp.865-871.
6. Coulson, G and Waddington, D.G., "A CORBA-compliant Real-time Multimedia Platform for Broadband Networks", Proc. TRENDS'96, Aachen, Germany, September 1996.
7. Davies, N., Friday, A., Blair, G. and Cheverst, K., "Distributed Systems Support for Adaptive Mobile Applications", ACM Mobile Networks and Applications, Special Issue on Mobile Computing System Services, Vol. 1, No. 4, 1996.
8. Duce, D.A., Gallop, J.R., Johnson, I.J., Robinson, K., Seelig, C.D., Cooper, C.S. : Distributed Cooperative Visualisation - Experiences and Issues from the MANICORAL Project, in *Proceedings of the Eurographics Workshop on Visualisation in Scientific Computing*, Eurographics Association, 1998.
9. Fitzpatrick, T., Blair, G., Coulson, G., Davies, N. and Robin, P., "A Software Architecture For Adaptive Distributed Multimedia Systems", IEE Proceedings – Software, Special Issue on Configurable Distributed Systems, 1998.
10. Fitzpatrick, T., "Open Component Oriented Multimedia Middleware for Adaptive Distributed Applications", PhD thesis, Lancaster University, May 2000.
11. Foster, I., Stevens, R. : Corridor One, An Integrated Distance Visualization Environment for SSI and ASCI Applications, DoE NGI Testbed Workshop, July 1999, http://www.itg.lbl.gov/NGI/Jul99/IFoster/index.htm
12. Friday, A., "Infrastructure Support for Adaptive Mobile Applications", Ph.D. Thesis, Computing Department, Lancaster University, Lancaster, England, September 1996.
13. Gallop, J., Cooper, C., Johnson, I., Duce, D., Blair, B., Coulson, G., and Fitzpatrick, T., "Structuring for Extensibility - Adapting the Past to Fit the Future", *In* Slagter, R.J., ter Hofte, G.H., and Stiemerling, O., (Eds.), *Proceedings of CBG2000, the CSCW2000 workshop on Component-Based Groupware, December 2, 2000, Philadelphia, USA*, Telematica Instituut, The Netherlands, ISBN 90-75176-24-4.
14. Kiczales, G., Des Rivieres, J. and Bobrow, D., "The Art of the Metaobject Protocol", MIT Press, 1991.
15. Leigh, J., Johnson, A.E., Brown, M., Sandin,D.J., DeFanti,T.A.: Visualization in Teleimmersive Environments, Computer, Vol 32, No 12, December 1999.
16. Mayer-Patel, K. and Rowe, L., "Design and Performance of the Berkeley Continuous Media Toolkit", in Multimedia Computing and Networking 1997, Freeman, Jardetzky and Vin (Eds), Proc. SPIE 3020, pp 194-206, 1997.
17. McAffer, J., "Meta-Level Architecture Support for Distributed Objects", Proc. Reflection'96, G. Kiczales (Ed.), pp39-62, San Francicso, USA, 1996.
18. McCanne, S., Brewer, E., Katz, R., Rowe, L., Amir, E., Chawathe, Y., Coopersmith, A., Mayer-Patel, K., Raman, S., Schuett, A., Simpson, D., Swan, A., Tung, T., Wu, D. and Smith, B, "Towards a Common Infrastructure for Multimedia-Networking Middleware", Proc. NOSSDAV'97, Missouri, US, 1997.

19. Object Management Group, "CORBA Event Management Service", OMG Document formal/97-12-11, Object Management Group, Framingham, MA, USA.
20. Object Management Group, "Control and Management of Audio/Video Streams", OMG Document formal/98-06-05, Object Management Group, Framingham, MA, USA.
21. Object Oriented Concepts Inc., "ORBacus for C++ and Java", Object Oriented Concepts Inc, Billerica, MA USA. Available on the Internet at http://www.ooc.com/ob/
22. Rao, R., "Implementational Reflection in Silica", Proc. ECOOP'91, Lecture Notes In Computer Science, P. America (Ed.), pp251-267, Springer-Verlag, 1991.
23. Singhai, A., Sane, A. and Campbell, R., "Reflective ORBs: Supporting Robust, Time-Critical Distribution", Proc. ECOOP'97 Workshop on Reflective Real-Time Object-Oriented Programming and Systems, Jyvaskyla, Finland, 1997.
24. Szyperski, C., "Component Software: Beyond Object-Oriented Programming", Addison-Wesley, Harlow, England 1998.
25. The Visual Beans Project web page: http://www.acu.rl.ac.uk/VisualBeans/
26. Watanabe, T. and Yonezawam A., "Reflection in an Object-Oriented Concurrent Language", Proc. OOPSLA'88, Vol. 23 of ACM SIGPLAN Notices, ACM Press, 1988.
27. Wood, J., Wright, H., Brodlie, K. : Collaborative Visualization, Proceedings of IEEE Visualization 97, pp 253-259, ACM Press, 1997
28. Yeadon, N., "QoS Filtering for Multipeer Communications", PhD Thesis, Lancaster University, September 1996.
29. Yokote, Y., "The Apertos Reflective Operating System: The Concept and Its Implementation", Proc. OOPSLA'92, Vol. 28 of ACM SIGPLAN Notices, pp414-434, ACM Press, 1992.
30. Le Metayer, "Describing software architecture styles using graph grammars", IEEE Transactions – Software Engineering 24(7), 1998.
31. Drira, K., "A coordination middleware for collaborative component-oriented distributed applications", Netnomics Journal, No. 2., pp85-89, 2000.
32. Blair, G.S., Coulson, G., Andersen, A., Blair, L., Clarke, M., Costa, F., Duran-Limon, H., Fitzpatrick, T., Johnston, L., Moreira, R., Parlavantzas, N., Saikoski, K., "The Design and Implementation of OpenORB v2", IEEE DS Online, Special Issue on Reflective Middleware, 2001.

QoS Management Middleware:
A Separable, Reusable Solution

Denise Ecklund[§1], Vera Goebel[1], Thomas Plagemann[1], Earl F. Ecklund Jr. [§1], Carsten Griwodz[1], Jan Øyvind Aagedal[2], Ketil Lund[3], Arne-Jørgen Berre[2]

[1] Department of Informatics, University of Oslo, Norway
{denisee, goebel, plageman, earle, griff}@ifi.uio.no

[2] SINTEF Telecom and Informatics, Oslo, Norway
{Jan-Oyvind.Aagedal, Arne.J.Berre}@informatics.sintef.no

[3] UniK - Center for Technology at Kjeller, University of Oslo, Norway
ketillu@unik.no

Abstract. Research in the area of end-to-end Quality of Service (QoS) has produced important results over the last years. However, most solutions are tailored for specific environments, assume layered system architectures, or integrate QoS management within the respective service components, such that the QoS management functionality is not easily reusable. Furthermore, proprietary QoS solutions are not interoperable and QoS management for logical objects is not supported. In this paper, we present a separable and reusable QoS management service for end-to-end QoS in a distributed environment. This QoS middleware extends the classical feedback controller with QoS-aware agents. We describe the resulting *seven-agent QoS manager*, a generic management protocol, and define interfaces between the agents, platform services, and QoS-aware application components. Wrappers can be used to interface the QoS middleware with all types of legacy distributed service components, both QoS-aware and QoS-unaware.

1 Introduction

Software development is - despite all recent advances in software engineering - still a (time) costly and error prone task. This is especially true for the development of distributed applications and systems, because distribution generally means that the software components must function well in heterogeneous environments. For example, application components can be written in different programming languages on different operating systems and communicate with each other over different kinds of networks. The main task of middleware is to mask out this heterogeneity and provide a transparent view onto distributed systems to enable developers to implement correct software components easier and faster. Heterogeneous components also have different

---

[§] At the time of this work these authors were senior guest researchers at UniK – Center for Technology at Kjeller, University of Oslo.

D. Shepherd et al. (Eds.): IDMS 2001, LNCS 2158, pp. 124-137, 2001.
© Springer-Verlag Berlin Heidelberg 2001

non-functional requirements, like performance aspects and error tolerance. In response, OSI defined the concept of QoS for communication services [38] in the late 70s. In the 90s, operating systems services were defined to enable end-to-end QoS [23, 28]. In the classic understanding of QoS, service users express their needs in the form of QoS specifications and negotiate a QoS contract with the service provider. The service provider uses QoS management services like QoS negotiation, monitoring, admission control, resource reservation and allocation, and adaptation to establish and fulfill the QoS contract. Considerable research on QoS management services has resulted in numerous proposals, standards, and implementations of mechanisms to perform these services, e.g., ODP framework [17], ISO QoS framework [16], TINA QoS framework [33]. In the OMODIS[1] project [10], we reviewed the state-of-the-art in QoS management in order to develop a QoS framework for multimedia database management systems (MMDBMS). We observed the following problems in related works:

- Most QoS works (see [2]) are based on layered system architectures: Communication sub-systems are traditionally structured in layers, e.g., physical, link, network, and transport layer. The current trend in distributed applications and other sub-systems is to structure them as a set of configurable components. In general, a *component* can be a system, service, or resource in a distributed environment. Component configurations are a generalization of layers in which (1) the semantics of service user and service provider are not predefined, and (2) there is no *a priori* knowledge about who will use the service of a component. Therefore, components require more generalized QoS management services than layered architectures.

- Most QoS works are tailored for specific environments: Domain-specific QoS management solutions limit the problem scope to reduce complexity, e.g., [21], or to improve performance, e.g., [11, 22]. Rather than providing a unifying solution, these single-use services simply increase the heterogeneity problem in distributed systems.

- QoS management is implemented as part of the service components themselves: Early works have integrated configurable QoS services into communication protocols and end-systems to meet new application requirements and to support end-to-end QoS guarantees, e.g., [5, 25, 37]. Others have proposed that all QoS service issues be managed by the application [34] or by end service systems [13, 33, 11, 15]. QoS mechanisms that handle concrete resources, like CPU time or disk bandwidth, must consider the particular properties of the resource. However, this typically results in QoS management techniques and mechanisms that are specific to that type of service and are thus not easily reusable.

• QoS management in Database Management Systems (DBMSs) and other complex services is an open problem: QoS work in file systems and storage systems has focused on scheduling disk bandwidth and allocating buffer space, e.g., [1, 32], leaving richer DBMS services unmanaged. For example, DBMS transactions must lock logical objects to assure data consistency. These objects must be regarded as logical resources and must be considered by QoS management services.

---

[1] The OMODIS project is funded by the Norwegian Research Council (NFR), Distributed IT Systems (DITS) program, 1996-2002.

Recent works have contributed positively to the state-of-the-art with feedback control based adaptation, e.g., [32, 30, 4], new solutions to QoS mapping, e.g., [12, 26, 36, 29], QoS negotiation and pricing [35], and generalized frameworks for object-oriented or component-based distributed systems [34, 6].

However, all current solutions propose a static architecture[2] comprised of a set of autonomous QoS managers. This is not effective because: (1) autonomous QoS managers can initiate conflicting adaptation strategies that are local in scope and that fail to achieve their collective QoS goals; and (2) static, pre-defined negotiation ordering among components can result in failure to reach a contract agreement. The problem of static QoS management architectures has also been identified within service-specific QoS management facilities [20]. To address the full set of identified problems, we have proposed a runtime-reconfigurable hierarchy of QoS managers [7]. Within the hierarchy, each application component is directly managed by one local QoS manager. Higher-level QoS managers direct the local managers, to co-ordinate adaptations and dynamically order QoS negotiations based on a broader view of the QoS tradeoffs among managed components and a hierarchy of QoS policies. Higher-level managers can accelerate negotiation convergence among local managers, thus reducing the cost of QoS management. Runtime adaptation includes modifying the management hierarchy by adding and removing QoS managers, updating QoS policies and strategies, and reorganizing manager relationships within the hierarchy. QoS managers are middleware services, separate and distinct from the application components they manage. Granularity of the managed component is defined by the component implementer. A local QoS manager should be associated with each separable service component that can efficiently support the minimal set of QoS management interfaces. Our scalable solution uses two types of reusable QoS managers. In this work, we focus on the local QoS manager, as a fundamental building block of our hierarchical, reconfigurable solution. We define the architecture of a local QoS manager and its interactions with a managed component. This architecture defines an abstraction over different component types and over different QoS management solutions. The primary contribution of this work is to provide a separable, reusable middleware solution that can manage any type of service component, use existing (legacy) QoS management solutions, and be organized in a dynamically configurable management hierarchy.

The remainder of this paper is organized as follows: We present the QoS management requirements for a distributed application. Based on these requirements, we describe the design of our reusable QoS manager. Then, we present the QoS-aware management agents within the QoS manager. Next, we demonstrate the feasibility of our approach in an example execution sequence. In the following section, we define the necessary interfaces between the QoS manager and a managed component. We conclude with a summary of the contributions of this work and an outline of our future work in this area.

---

[2] Note that a static architecture does not exclude the use of dynamic mechanisms like dynamic routing.

2 Requirements

We consider session-oriented applications in a distributed environment. Two popular system architectures supporting such applications are: the *N-tiered Server Architecture*, for synchronous multi-server applications, and the *Multi-agent Collaboration Architecture*, for mobile computations and asynchronous applications, such as workflow.

Fig 1 shows a simple, two-tiered server architecture, with six major components and seven QoS managers. Each component has a local QoS manager, and in this simple case, a single session-level QoS manager coordinates the local QoS managers. During a session, the client system submits requests to the application server over Net1. The application server requests data from a MMDBMS over Net1, and html pages from a web server over Net2. The application server performs post-processing on the data and sends the resulting data streams to the client system for presentation. The quality of service received by the client depends on the aggregate QoS provided by the three servers and the two networks.

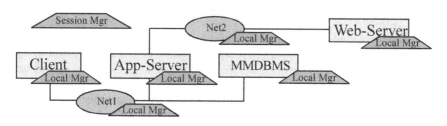

Fig. 1. Example two-tiered server architecture with six components
and seven QoS managers.

By controlling the characteristics that affect its QoS, a system can predictably and effectively deliver satisfactory performance to its users. Delivering QoS to a client (user) is managed by QoS contracts, each matching a QoS offer of a component with a QoS requirement of the client.

QoS management services are responsible for establishing, controlling, and maintaining QoS contracts for long-running sessions. Typical QoS management services include: negotiation of end-to-end QoS contracts, detection of QoS violations, initiation of service adaptation(s) to regain QoS conformance, and renegotiation of active QoS contracts when service adaptation is insufficient. In addition to the functional requirements for QoS management services, QoS management must provide a general, minimally-invasive, low overhead, reusable solution for all types of components.

3 Reusable QoS Manager

One of the major tasks of QoS management is to control components such that their cooperating services, i.e., observable behaviors, correspond to a client's QoS requirements. The traditional concept of feedback and closed-loop control theory defines models and mechanisms to perform such control tasks. Feedback control has been investigated as an approach to QoS management, but limited to layered services, domain-specific environments, or components with integrated controllers [32, 30, 4]. Even when applied in a general environment of interacting components, classical feedback control is not a complete solution for QoS management because it works best in fully deterministic environments. Therefore, we extend the traditional feedback controller [8] with QoS management agents that respond to the non-deterministic aspects of the runtime environment. In the following, we define the type of components we intend to manage, explain the deficiencies of the classical controller architecture, and introduce extensions to form a complete QoS manager for a general distributed environment.

3.1 Managed Components

In an open distributed system, a *Managed Component* (MC) is any system, service, or resource that presents itself as an atomic entity to a QoS manager. Components may be *QoS-aware* or *QoS-unaware*. Example QoS-aware components include: *Self-adapting components* [32], *QoS-mechanistic components* [25], and *QoS-managed subsystems* (such as QuO [34] for communications, command, and control applications, and QoS-A [5] for network services) in addition to QoS-support mechanisms.

QoS mechanisms contained in QoS-aware components are service-specific algorithms for maintaining QoS contracts held by that component. For example, a QoS-aware network service can implement flow filtering for multimedia streams, and channel sharing for specific types of network traffic. These mechanisms are not generic QoS management services, but a generic, reusable QoS manager can control such components using wrappers, that map portions of a common QoS management interface to such service-specific mechanisms.

3.2 Classical Feedback-Based Controllers

The classical closed-loop, feedback controller consists of four agents: *estimator*, *regulator*, *prober*, and *observer* [8]. The managed component is modeled by a *component state vector* that contains values for the state variables, capturing component state at a particular point in time. The estimator sets the values of the component state vector based on a pre-defined component model for the managed component and runtime input from the observer and the prober. The regulator uses the estimated state vector to generate effective input control values to the component.

The classical controller is not sufficient for QoS management. The primary deficiency arises from the fact that classical controllers are most effective in deterministic environments. An open environment of cooperating components is non-deterministic in several respects: some components cannot be predictably controlled, components do not have a deterministic workload, the migration of collaborating agents is based on runtime data, and components do not have dedicated access to external, shared resources in their base platforms. In addition, the classical controller monitors and controls a component based on attributes that summarize the component's state in general. These attributes may not relate directly to the QoS provided by the component. And the attributes do not support fine-grained control of QoS on a per-client basis. Also a highly complex component model may be needed to support the rapid and extreme forms of change required to adaptively support QoS in a non-deterministic environment.

3.3 Architecture of the QoS Manager

To address these shortcomings, we define a QoS manager consisting of seven QoS management agents: a *four-agent controller* and *three QoS-aware agents*. The QoS-aware agents create and maintain QoS contracts on behalf of a component. We also extend the traditional controller behavior as follows:

- Performance data gathered by the observer and the prober is partitioned and associated with specific component activities. A *component activity* is a separately identified unit of service performed by the component. An activity can correspond to one client or a set of related clients. QoS performance is monitored per component activity. Aggregate statistics may be computed over sets of activities.
- Estimator and regulator use a dynamically sized state vector to exert control on a per-activity basis. As activities are initiated and terminated, the subset of state variables used to control one activity are added to or deleted from the total component state vector.

The three QoS-aware management agents perform QoS-specific management services, including negotiation, admission control and reservation, and service adaptation. QoS management policies and QoS profiles for components are computed offline and periodically installed by system administrators. The QoS management agents use this pre-computed information as well as runtime information on QoS performance to manage QoS on behalf of components. The agents also make effective use of the classical controller by mapping between QoS goals (stated as QoS contracts) and the state vector, which the controller uses to control the component. The architecture of the seven-agent QoS manager is shown in Fig 2.

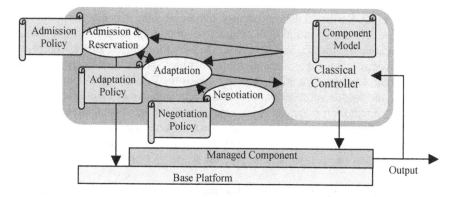

Fig. 2. Architecture of the seven agent QoS Manager.

4 QoS-Aware Management Agents and Platform Services

4.1 Negotiation, Renegotiation Agent

The *QoS Negotiation Agent (QNA)* implements a general negotiation protocol [12, 19] between two QoS managers, to construct an acceptable QoS contract between two parties, one acting as a client and the other as a server. To carry out a successful external negotiation, the QNA uses the services of the local QoS agents and operates on pre-computed, component-specific information, such as: *QoS profiles of the local component*, which can be defined offline and modified at runtime using an interpreted QoS specification language [24, 3]; *QoS mapping functions*, which define a many-to-many mapping of QoS characteristics between a client's QoS requirements and a server's QoS offers; and *QoS negotiation policy*, which governs how QoS requirements and QoS offers can be modified during the negotiation process, and includes the policy for translating actual costs into offered prices when agents of separate domains negotiate [18, 35].

Before committing to a QoS contract, the QNA uses the local QoS adaptation agent (QAA) and the admission control and reservation agent (ACRA) to analyze resource requirements and reserve the necessary local resources. The QAA proposes component configurations each of which could support the client's QoS requirements and determines the resource requirements of those various configurations. The ACRA admits or rejects a proposed configuration. If admitted, the ACRA reserves the required resources. A later section presents a detailed example of local interactions during negotiation.

4.2 Adaptation Agent

The *QoS Adaptation Agent (QAA)* is responsible for defining *quality-based configurations* of the local component. Quality configurations are derived from component configurations that support the functional requirements of a client request. Each quality configuration should be able to support the contracted level of QoS, possibly at a different cost. Traditionally, localized adaptation has been proposed as a mechanism to maintain QoS when violations occur within an ongoing session. Adaptation can also be applied: (1) during initial QoS contract negotiation to achieve an optimum, initial component configuration, and (2) across QoS-conformant sessions to compensate for other sessions that are experiencing QoS violations. To define a quality configuration from a functional configuration, the QAA needs the following pre-computed information: *Local component description*, which documents component structure and functionality; *Adaptation policies*, which control how the local component can be reconfigured; *Adaptation strategies*, which transform one component configuration into another configuration that should better meet specific QoS requirements; and *Adaptation evaluation metrics*, which compute the worth of a proposed component configuration.

The QAA obtains the current component state from the estimator agent and uses this as additional input to the configuration evaluation process. Once an adapted configuration has been approved for use, the QAA must represent that configuration in the form of a component state vector that can be used by the regulator to make the component conform to the adapted configuration. The QAA updates only the subset of the component state vector associated with the affected activities. If the QAA is unable to define an acceptable quality-based configuration, the QAA returns a list of unachievable QoS requirements and the specific reasons for failure. Example failure conditions include: transient or permanent resource insufficiency, inadmissible client requester, minimum cost exceeds client's price limits, etc. Ultimately, the session-level QoS manager uses this information to direct contract re-negotiation or to reject the end-client request.

4.3 Admission Control and Reservation Agent

The *Admission Control and Reservation Agent (ACRA)* admits client requests based on component-specific admission policies and resource availability, and reserves all required resources. To accomplish these tasks, the ACRA needs the following component-specific and request-specific information: *Raw resource requirements*, expressed as a runtime-computed resource schedule for the admitted request; *Raw resource status*, expressed as a runtime-computed aggregate resource schedule over all clients on the local base platform, and the cost to reserve and use those resources; and precomputed, but updateable, *Admission policies*, which define conditions for admitting a client request for service by the local component.

If the admission policy allows the request to be served and platform resources are available, then the ACRA reserves the required resources. If the request cannot be admitted, the ACRA rejects the request and returns the reasons for the rejection. The session-level QoS manager uses this information to direct contract re-negotiation or to reject the end-client request.

4.4 Platform Resource Management

Components consume platform resources in order to provide their services. The quality of that service depends on the sufficiency of available resources and the ability to use resources according to a schedule. Local resources are managed by one or more local *Platform Resource Managers* (PRMs).

Distributed applications operate on logical data objects, such as video clips, audio sound tracks, web pages, data folders, and geographical maps. In many applications (such as updating multimedia objects stored in a MMDBMS), a client must obtain a lock before accessing the object. Once locked, the client has exclusive access to the logical object. Physical resources are required to carry out operations on a logical object. Clearly physical resources should not be reserved for a client prior to obtaining the required set of logical locks. A logical lock has an application-specific semantic. Hence, this defines a strict ordering between a component setting logical locks on objects and a QoS manager reserving physical resources on behalf of the component that will access and manipulate those objects.

5   Example Execution Among Local QoS Agents

The following example illustrates local interactions among the QNA, QAA, and ACRA in support of contract negotiation between two QoS managers. Fig 3 shows process flow among the agents and the corresponding agent activity is described below.

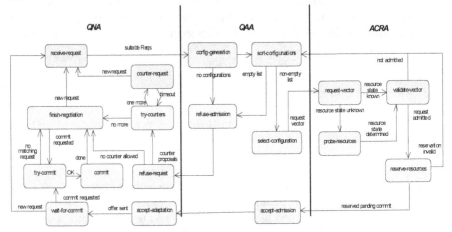

Fig 3. Process flow among local QoS agents supporting contract negotiation.

Receive-request. The QNA receives a set of QoS requirements defined by the requesting application and other service components involved in the application configuration. Based on the requested data and services, the QNA selects, from the list of QoS requirements, the requirements involving the QoS characteristic types that can be served by the component for this specific request.

Config-generation. The QAA receives a subset of QoS requirements. Using an Architecture Definition Language tool [9] or another runtime tool, the QAA obtains component configurations that meet the functional requirements of the request. The QAA matches the QoS requirements to the possible configurations and selects potential component configurations.

Sort-configurations. The QAA sorts the potential component configurations according to the preference of the adaptation policy. If the QAA has received reasons for the refusal of a previously checked configuration, the policy may take this into account and change the order, or the policy may not change the existing order at all.

Select-config. The QAA removes the preferred component configuration from the sorted list and translates it into a component state vector for the configuration. This state vector ("request vector") represents the impact of serving the new request at the requested QoS levels on an unloaded system.

Request-vector. The ACRA receives the request vector. The ACRA estimates the future state of the component, if the request was served at the requested level of QoS.

Probe-resources. The ACRA probes PRMs to obtain information on the current state of raw platform resources. (Raw platform resources are related to component state, but they are not identical. They include the resource usage of all QoS-managed and QoS-unmanaged components executing on the platform).

Validate-vector. The ACRA examines the predicted future state vector and consults the local admission control policy to determine whether to admit the new request. If the admission policy rejects the state vector, a notification of the refusal including an explanation is sent to the QAA.

Reserve-resources. The ACRA tries to reserve the resources specified in the accepted state vector from the PRMs. If the future state is supported by the PRMs and the requested QoS maintenance mode requires resource reservations, then the resources are reserved, the component state vector is updated, and a notification of acceptance is sent to the QAA. Otherwise, the ACRA sends a notification of the refusal including an explanation to the QAA.

Accept-admission. The QAA has received a positive response. The response is forwarded by the QAA to the QNA.

Accept-adaptation. The QNA informs the caller (application or remote QNA) about the success. It includes two QoS statements in the notification. The first is the QoS offer specifying the level of QoS that the local component has agreed to provide. The second is the QoS requirement specifying the level of QoS required by the local component to ensure that it meets its contracted-level of QoS.

Wait-for-commitment. The caller's request has been answered positively. The QNA maintains all information about the ongoing negotiation.

Try-commit. The QNA validates that the request matches an existing pre-commitment. If the validation fails, the caller is informed about the error.

Commit. The QNA calls the QAA, which in turn calls the ACRA to commit the pre-committed resources. If the commitment fails, the caller is informed about the error.

Refuse-admission. All possible configurations were rejected by the ACRA. The QAA creates a response, including reasons for the refusal, and sends it to the QNA.

Refuse-request. The QNA receives a negative response. If the negotiation policy does not allow counter-proposals, the caller is informed about the refusal of the request.

Try-counter-request. If the number of negotiation attempts for a given end-user session has reached a policy-defined limit, the QNA informs the caller about the negotiation failure, including the reasons in the response.

Counter-request. The QNA updates the number of attempts and makes a counter-proposal to the caller. The counter-proposal contains QoS requirements that have been modified based on feedback from the QAA and local negotiation policy. The negotiations continue, and the QNA expects another proposal from the caller. A timer is started to discard the session if no response to the counter-proposal arrives within a policy-defined time.

Finish-negotiation. The caller's request has been answered. The QNA discards remaining information about the negotiation and waits for further requests.

6 Interface Specifications for QoS Management

Based on the execution flow, it is clear that the QoS management agents must interact with the managed component at specific times during the QoS negotiation process (and also when performing other QoS management services). For example, the ACRA cannot reserve resources on behalf of the component without knowing which types and amounts of resources are required to serve the request at the contracted QoS level. The four-agent classical controller must also interact with the component to probe for component state and to control component behavior. Controller interfaces are not QoS-specific, hence they are not presented here. Manager-to-manager interfaces are overviewed in [7]. Table 1 presents the QoS-support interfaces that must be implemented by a managed component or a wrapper encapsulating a managed component, and the QoS-support interfaces that must be implemented by a PRM.

Implementer Interfaces to Support Specified Service		
Caller	Interface Prototype	Functional Description
Managed Component Interfaces to Support QoS Negotiation and Renegotiation		
QAA	[ClientID, {FunctionalConfiguration}] = **ControlAndConfigure** (ClientRequest)	Obtain a set of component configurations that functionally support the client request.
QAA	[ResourceSchedule, CostEstimate] = **LockObjectsAndEstimateResources** (QualityConfig, ClientRequest)	The component sets logical locks and returns the resource schedule required to service the client request.
QNA	Status = **Process** (ClientID, "commit/abort", ReservationHandle)	Informs the component of the final outcome (commit/abort) of the distributed negotiation.
PRM Interfaces to Support QoS-based Admission and Resource Mgmt		
ACRA	{(Rsrc$_i$ID, Rsrc$_1$Schedule, Rsrc$_i$Cost)} = **ProbeResourceState** (DomainID, ResourceSchedule, ReservationHandle)	Gets the cost for a new or modified resource schedule and the PRM's current aggregate resource schedule.
ACRA	[ReservationHandle, CostEstimate, RejectionReasons] = **ReserveResources** (ActivityID, DomainID, ResourceSchedule, ReservationHandle)	Reserves a resource schedule for a new request or modifies an existing reservation. The reservation supports future allocations.
MC	[Status, {AllocationHandle$_i$}] = **AllocateResources** (ActivityID, ReservationHandle, {R$_i$Schedule})	Allocates resources for immediate scheduling or use. The reservation handle may be null.
MC	{(Rsrc$_i$ID, Rsrc$_1$Schedule, Rsrc$_i$Cost)} = **ReleaseResources** (ClientID, {AllocationHandle$_i$})	Releases one or more previously allocated resources and updates the resource schedule.
Managed Component Interfaces to Support QoS-motivated Adaptation		
QAA	[ResourceSchedule, CostEstimate] = **EstimateResources** (ClientID, AdaptedConfig)	Sets logical locks and estimates resource requirements to modify an executing client request.
QAA	Status = **MigrateService** (ClientID, "commit/abort")	Informs the component of the final outcome of the adaptation process.

Table 1. Summary of QoS management interfaces.

7 Conclusions

This work is motivated by the fact that each existing solution for end-to-end QoS management suffers from one or more of the following restrictions (or disadvantages): (1) it is tailored for specific environments, (2) it assumes layered system architectures, (3) it implements QoS management within the respective service components such that the QoS management functionality is not easily reusable, (4) it does not interoperate with other proprietary QoS solutions, and (5) it does not manage QoS for logical objects, which are used by complex components, such as a DBMS. The QoS management middleware described in this paper overcomes these problems. By separating QoS management services from the managed component and defining an interface between them, we have created a reusable, generic solution for QoS management of arbitrary components in open distributed and heterogeneous environments. Similar to other recent approaches, we use feedback control in our QoS management middleware. However, classical feedback control was not designed to manage components in a non-deterministic environment, nor to exert control on a per-client basis. Therefore, we have extended the classical four-agent controller architecture, with three QoS-aware agents supporting negotiation, admission control and reservation, and adaptation. We identified dependencies between the QoS agents, the managed component, and the basic platform services. A critical dependency is that components must obtain logical locks on data objects before using platform resources to manipulate those objects. We defined a set of component interfaces to support a reusable QoS manager. In addition, we defined interfaces between the QoS manager and a platform resource manager supporting reservations to a resource schedule.

For our ongoing and future work on components, we are implementing the QoS management interfaces as defined in this work. To integrate legacy components, we are investigating wrappers for specialized QoS managers, such as QuO [34] and MULTE [27], as well as for individual QoS-aware services, such as RSVP [14]. Each wrapper defines a model for estimating component state information that is not provided by the legacy system, and makes runtime estimations within acceptable time- and resource-cost. Experiments will be performed using QLinux [31], which provides QoS-aware resource management services in the base platform. We are also continuing our investigation of QoS manager interaction with, and QoS mechanisms within, a compound service component for management of persistent multimedia objects.

References

1. Aberer K., Hollfelder, S., Resource Prediction and Admission Control for Interactive Video, Proc. 8th IFIP 2.6 Working Conf. on Database Semantics - Semantic Issues in Multimedia Systems (DS-8), Rotorua, New Zealand, Kluwer, Jan. 1999, pp. 27-46
2. Aurrecoechea, C., Campbell, A.T. and L. Hauw, A Survey of QoS Architectures, ACM Springer Multimedia Systems Journal, Special Issue on QoS Architecture, Vol. 6, No. 3, May 1998, pp. 138-151
3. Becker, C., Geihs, K., Generic QoS Specifications for COBRA, Kommunikation in Verteilten Systemen, 1999, pp.184-195

4. Bergmans, L., van Halteren, A., Ferreira Pires, L., van Sinderen, M., Aksit, M., A QoS-Control Architecture for Object Middleware, 7th Intl. Workshop on Interactive Distributed Multimedia Systems and Telecommunication Services (IDMS 2000), Enschede, The Netherlands, Oct. 2000, LNCS 1905, pp.117-131

5. Campbell, A., Coulson, G., Hutchinson, D., A Quality of Service Architecture, ACM Computer Communications Review, Vol. 24, No. 2, April 1994, pp. 6-27

6. Daniel, J., Modica, O., Traverson, B., Vignes, S., Modeling and Enforcement of Quality of Service in Distributed Environments, 2nd Intl. Symp. on Distributed Objects and Applications (DOA '00), Antwerp, Belgium, Sept. 2000

7. Ecklund, D., Goebel, V., Plagemann, T., Ecklund Jr., E.F., A Dynamically-Configured, Strategic QoS Management Hierarchy for Distributed Multimedia Systems, Technical Report of the University of Oslo, Informatics Department, April 2001

8. Franklin, G. F., Powell, J. D., Emami-Naeini, A., Feedback Control of Dynamic Systems, Addison-Wesley Publishing Company, Aug. 1986

9. Proc. First Intl. Workshop on Architectures for Software Systems, D. Garlan Editor, Seattle, WA, April 1995

10. Goebel, V., Plagemann, T., Berre, A.-J., Nygård, M.: OMODIS - Object-Oriented Modeling and Database Support for Distributed Systems, Norsk Informatikk Konferanse (NIK'96), Alta, Norway, Nov. 1996

11. Gopalakrishna, G., Parulkar, G., A Real-time Upcall Facility for Protocol Processing with QoS Guarantees, 15th ACM Symp. on Operating Systems Principles (SOSP), Dec. 1995

12. Hafid, A., Bochmann, G. V., Quality-of-Service adaptation in distributed multimedia applications, Multimedia Systems, ACM Springer, Vol. 6, No. 5, 1998, pp. 299-315

13. Braden, R., Clark, D., Shenker, S., Integrated Services in the Internet Architecture: An Overview, IETF Internet RFC 1633, June 1994

14. Braden,R., Zhang, L., Berson, S., Herzog, S. Jamin, S., RFC 2205, Resource ReSerVation Protocol (RSVP) - Version 1 Functional Specification, IETF, Sept. 1997

15. Blake, S., Black, D., Carlson, M., Davies, E., Wang, W., Weiss, W., An Architecture for Differentiated Services, IETF Internet RFC 2475, Dec. 1998

16. QoS – Basic Framework, ISO, ISO/IEC JTC1/SC21 N9309, 1995

17. Working document on QoS in ODP, ISO, ISO/IEC JTC1/SC21 WG7, 1995

18. Karsten, M., Schmitt, J., Wolf, L., Steinmetz, R., Provider-Oriented Linear Price Calculation for Integrated Services, Proc. 7th IEEE/IFIP Intl. Workshop on Quality of Service (IWQoS'99), London, UK, June 1999, pp. 174-183

19. Koistinen, J., Seetharaman, A., Worth-Based Multi-Category Quality-of-Service Negotiation in Distributed Object Infrastructures, Hewlett Packard Software Technology Laboratory Technical Report HPL-98-51 (R.1), July 1998

20. Kristensen, T., Kalleberg, I.B., Plagemann, T., Implementing Configurable Signalling in the MULTE-ORB, To appear in Proc. 4th IEEE Conf. on Open Architectures and Network Programming, Anchorage, AK, April 2001

21. Lazar, A.A., Lim, K.-S., Marcocini, F., Realizing a Foundation for Programmability of ATM Networks with the Binding Architecture, IEEE Journal on Selected Areas in Communication, Vol. 14, No. 7, Sept. 1996, pp. 1214-1227

22. Lee, S.-B., Ahn, G.-S., Zhang, X., Campbell, A.T., INSIGNIA: An IP-Based Quality of Service Framework for Mobile ad Hoc Networks, Journal on Parallel and Distributed Computing, Academic Press, 60, 2000, pp. 374-406

23. Leslie, I.M., McAuley, D., Mullender, S.J., Pegasus – Operating Systems Support for Distributed Multimedia Systems, ACM Operating Systems Review, Vol. 27, No. 1, 1993

24. Loyall J.P., Schantz R.E., Zinky J.A., Bakken D.E., Specifying and Measuring Quality of Service in Distributed Object Systems. Proc. First Intl. Symp. on Object-Oriented Real-Time Distributed Computing (ISORC '98), 20-22 April 1998, Kyoto, Japan

25. Nahrstedt, K., Smith, J.M., Design, Implementation, and Experiences of the OMEGA End-Point Architecture, IEEE Journal on Selected Areas in Communications, Vol. 14, No. 7, Sept. 1996, pp. 1263-1279

26. Nahrstedt, K., Chu, H., Narayan, S., QoS-Aware Resource Management for Distributed Multimedia Applications, Journal on High-Speed Networking, Special Issue on Multimedia Networking, Vol. 7(3,4), Spring 1999, pp. 229-258

27. Plagemann, T., Eliassen, E., Hafskjold, B., Kristensen, T., Macdonald, R. H., Rafaelsen, H.O.: Flexible and Extensible QoS Management for Adaptable Middleware, Intl. Workshop on Protocols for Multimedia Systems (PROMS 2000) Cracow, Poland, Oct. 2000

28. Saltzer, J, Reed, D, Clark, D, End-to-end Arguments in System Design, ACM Trans. on Computer Systems, Vol. 2, No. 4, Nov. 1984, pp. 277-288

29. Siqueira, F. Quartz: A QoS Architecture for Open Systems, Trinity College Dublin, TCD-CS-2000-05, Ph.D. Thesis, Feb. 2000

30. Steenkiste P., Adaptation Models for Network-Aware Distributed Computations, 3rd Workshop on Communication, Architecture, and Applications for Network-based Parallel Computing (CANPC99), Orlando, FL, IEEE Springer, Jan. 1999

31. Sundaram, V, Chandra, A, Goyal, P, Shenoy, P, Sahni, J, Vin, H, Application performance in the QLinux multimedia operating system, Proc. 8th Intl. Conf. on Multimedia, Marina del Rey, CA, Oct. 2000, pp. 127-136

32. Thimm H., Klas W., Walpole J., Pu C., Cowan C., Managing Adaptive Presentation Executions in Distributed Multimedia Database Systems, Proc. Intl. Workshop on Multimedia Database Management Systems, 1996

33. Quality of Service Framework, Telecommunications Information Networking Architecture Consortium (TINA-C), TP_MRK.001_1.0_94, 1994

34. Vanegas, R., Zinky, J., Loyall, J., Karr, D., Schantz, R., Bakken, D., QuO's Runtime Support for Quality of Service in Distributed Objects, Proc. IFIP Intl. Conf. on Distributed Systems Platforms and Open Distributed Processing (Middleware'98), The Lake District, England, Sept. 1998

35. Wang, X., Schulzrinne, H., An Integrated Resource Negotiation, Pricing, and QoS Adaptation Framework for Multimedia Applications, IEEE Journal on Selected Areas in Communications, Vol. 18, 2000

36. Witana, V., Fry, M., Antoniades, M., A Software Framework for Application Level QoS Management, Proc. 7th Intl. Workshop on Quality of Service (IEEE/IFIP IWQoS '99), June, 1999

37. Wolf, L.C., Resource Management for Distributed Multimedia Systems, Kluwer Academic Publishers, 1996

38. Zimmerman, H., OSI Reference Model – The ISO Model of Architecture for Open Systems Interconnection, IEEE Trans. on Communications (COM), Vol. 28, No. 4, April 1980, pp. 425-432

State Transmission Mechanisms for a Collaborative Virtual Environment Middleware Platform

João Orvalho[1], Pedro Ferreira[2] and Fernando Boavida[3]

Communications and Telematic Group
CISUC – Centre for Informatics and Systems of the University of Coimbra
Polo II, 3030 COIMBRA – PORTUGAL
Tel.: +351-239-790000, Fax: +351-239-701266
{orvalho, pmferr, boavida}@dei.uc.pt

Abstract. Collaborative virtual environments (CVE) require the use of specially designed mechanisms that allow for a consistent sharing of state among involved users. These mechanisms must, somehow, compensate for network latency and losses in such a way that all players have a single, coherent perception of the system state. Common middleware platforms have difficulty in guaranteeing this consistency, and this is the prime reason why the main research topic for CVEs is the efficient, scalable and reliable transmission of state information. This paper presents a state transmission framework developed for a middleware platform that was constructed by the authors in an earlier project [1]. This middleware platform, Augmented Reliable Multicast CORBA Event Service (ARMS), which already supported several QoS adaptation mechanisms and reliable transmission in multicast environments, was extended with CVE-oriented state transmission mechanisms. After an identification of key requirements of collaborative virtual environments, the relevant features of the proposed state transmission framework are presented. This framework has been integrated in the ARMS platform and was subject to a series of performance tests whose results are included and discussed in this paper. The paper ends with a summary of contributions and an identification of guidelines for further work

1 Introduction

One fundamental problem of collaborative virtual environments is the maintenance of a consistent shared state over interactive distributed media. The current state-of-the-art approach to achieve consistency in CVEs is to use dead reckoning [2, 3]. Nevertheless, in [3] it is demonstrated that traditional dead reckoning mechanisms may fail in ways that cause significant harm to the overall state of CVEs. Network latency and losses contribute to the difference between the predicted and the real system state, and this difference may significantly exceed the threshold that triggers state transmission, resulting in state inconsistencies. One of the main research topics

---

[1] College of Education, Polytechnic Institute of Coimbra

[2] Polytechnic Institute of Tomar

[3] Informatics Engineering Department of the University of Coimbra

D. Shepherd et al. (Eds.): IDMS 2001, LNCS 2158, pp. 138-153, 2001.

for CVEs, from a quality of service (QoS) point of view, is how to efficiently transmit update messages so as to provide scalability, minimized delay, consistency and reliability [4].

Mauve proposes the concept of *local lag* [5] to prevent inconsistencies, and the *timewarp* algorithm [3] to keep state consistency, possibly in combination with dead reckoning. The *local lag* is a simple mechanism: "instead of immediately executing an operation issued by a local user, the operation is delayed for a certain time before it is executed" [5]. The fixed amount of local lag constitutes a drawback of this method. In the *timewarp* method [6] each participant saves the state at certain moments in time. When an inconsistency occurs, the state is rolled back to the state that immediately preceded the operation that caused the inconsistency. After that, the medium is played (fast) forward until the current medium time is reached. This algorithm has a higher complexity than the dead reckoning algorithm, requiring a "strong" application to handle it [6], which renders it unfeasible in large CVEs.

The Georganas group introduces the original concept of "interaction streams" [4], "each consisting of a burst of update messages with a final and a critical update message". The concept is supported on a proprietary multicast transport protocol, the Synchronous Collaboration Transport Protocol (SCTP), which is ACK based and adapted to the transmission of key update messages. In this model, the mechanisms to achieve state consistency do not use synchronous information like, for instance, clock or time-stamping information, which main constrain its applicability to large CVEs.

There are other approaches to shared state consistency, based on synchronisation mechanisms. One of the more significant mechanisms is the bucket synchronization mechanism [7], which is used in the MiMaze multi-player game [7]. In this case, time is divided into fixed length sampling periods and a bucket is associated with each sampling period. All application data units (ADU) received by an application are stored in the bucket corresponding to the current interval. When the application has to deliver an updated global state, it computes all ADUs available in the current bucket [7]. This algorithm needs global clock mechanisms like NTP [8] and the synchronization delay is computed on ADU's reception. If the network delay is greater than a given threshold the ADU is dropped. MiMaze uses an unreliable communication system, based on RTP [9] over UDP/IP multicast [10].

This paper presents a set of state transmission mechanisms to be used in the ARMS middleware platform [1]. The objectives of the proposed mechanisms, hereafter referred to as state transmission framework (STF), are to extend the applicability of the platform to collaborative virtual environments maintaining, at the same time, the platform's QoS features. Section 2 identifies the main requirements of collaborative virtual environments. Section 3 presents, to a considerable extent, the proposed state transmission framework. Section 4 describes the performance tests made to STF and analyses their results. The conclusions and guidelines for further work are presented in Section 5.

2   CVE's Requirements

CVE applications have specific requirements in terms of scalability, interaction and consistency. The QoS characteristics that are relevant to these requirements are reliability, losses, delay and delay jitter. Additionally, application factors like data heterogeneity, frequency of events, synchronisation delay, number of participants and playout time (display frequency) [11] may play an important role in the behaviour of CVEs.

The following sub-sections briefly discuss some of these requirements and associated QoS characteristics. In turn, these have led to the development of several mechanisms that have been included in the ARMS middleware platform [1], which build on a set of extensions to the CORBA Event Service, providing native multicast communication, various reliability levels, congestion control and jitter suppression, with the aim to achieve QoS adaptability. These new mechanisms extend the ARMS platform with CVE-oriented QoS capabilities, and will be presented in Section 3.

2.1 Data Heterogeneity

Typically there are many different types of data exchanged in CVE's [2]: real-time audio and video data, scene description data, typical 2D data, control data and state or update data. In addition to dealing with various types of data, continuous distributed interactive media can change their state in response to user operations as well to the passage of time [5]. A broad variety of applications use this kind of media, such as multi-user virtual reality (VR), distributed simulations, networked games and computer-supported co-operative work (CSCW) applications.

2.2 State Synchronisation

All participants in a session must be synchronised in the same media state, i.e., the distributed shared state must be consistent. Different media have different state classifications and different state synchronisation needs. The state could be a simple change in a component. In the other extreme, it could be a bulk of data for latecomers or for re-synchronization. Some states may be essential and others may be redundant. State synchronisation must take the media type into consideration. Essentially, this is an issue for the applications' environment model, which must use the best solutions to deal with specific media.

2.3 Delay and Jitter

Regular collaborative update messages have stringent delay requirements in order to maintain the shared state of components. Some studies [12] suggest that CVEs must have an end-to-end delay less than 100 msec. Others [13] consider 200 msec as an acceptable delay. In addition to delay, delay jitter also affects update messages. As shown in [13], a session with 10 msec delay and considerable jitter results in a perceived quality that can be as bad as one with 200msec delay and no associated jitter.

2.4 Reliability

CVEs for distributed interactive media require that all participants must receive state changes. Due to their specificity there are some states that are time critical and described by small amounts of information, while others are generally non-time-critical and require large amounts of information for their description. Therefore, there is the need for different levels of reliability when exchanging these types of updates: minimal reliability (possibly with loss detection) for the former, and full reliability for the latter.

In a CVE, the last state of a shared object is the most crucial data [4]. These messages must be sent with a high reliability level, whilst regular messages can be sent with a different, lower reliability level as, for instance, best effort.

Basically, there are two forms of achieving reliability: by using a reliable transport protocol or by using network-aware applications. In the context of interactive media applications, loss detection and reliability become more complex since there is no longer a single linear namespace for objects and since some objects are persistent [14]. So, a single transport protocol is unlikely to be sufficient, as observed in [14]. Additionally, many authors [15, 16, 17, 18] have concluded that application level framing is a requirement too, in this application context.

Both approaches to achieve reliability should be usable with a framework like a framing protocol. This framework could be a middleware platform with a proper interface to the application level, which captures the common aspects of a media class, and provides access to reliable transport protocols.

2.5 Other Requirements

In [14], it is observed that many applications need structured application data unit (ADU) names, a simple mechanism for packet loss detection, a means of distinguishing different types of data, a means of identifying participants, and a time stamping mechanism.

All of these requirements add great complexity to the application level. Placing some of these capabilities in the middleware gives applications the ability to concentrate on specific functionalities, to enforce different adaptation policies and to interact with other components in the system in order to ensure fairness and other global properties.

3 ARMS State Transmission Mechanisms

The state transmission mechanisms presented in this paper were developed in the context of the Augmented Reliable Multicast CORBA Event Service (ARMS) middleware platform [1], that provides an end-to-end communication framework with QoS-matching capabilities. ARMS offers a set of QoS-related mechanisms for reliability guarantee in multicast environments, congestion control and jitter control. The QoS management process is supported on object-based monitoring and adaptation functions. The platform has specific objects for loss and jitter monitoring.

The general architecture of the ARMS platform (Figure 1) includes an ARMS QoS API that provides access to the QoS features of the reliable multicasting services, and to the standard CORBA Event Service. Additionally, the architecture includes the STF API, which will be described in the remaining part of this section.

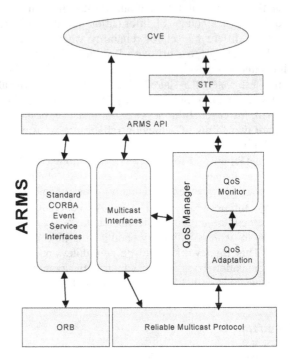

Figure 1 – ARMS architecture

3.1 State Transmission Framework

The STF API is a Java-based middleware especially designed for the transmission of state changes in virtual reality environments, which takes into account the requirements of state transmission in these types of applications. STF is an object-oriented framework integrated in the ARMS middleware platform (Figure 1) that supports state transmission and reception, a late join protocol – a process by which a client can join a ongoing interaction session and reconstruct the current global state, virtual world partitioning, and time synchronization. This paper discusses mainly the transmission and reception of states. The STF API comprehends a set of interfaces that expose methods that allow for the control various capabilities. Figure 2 illustrates the general architecture of STF, in UML.

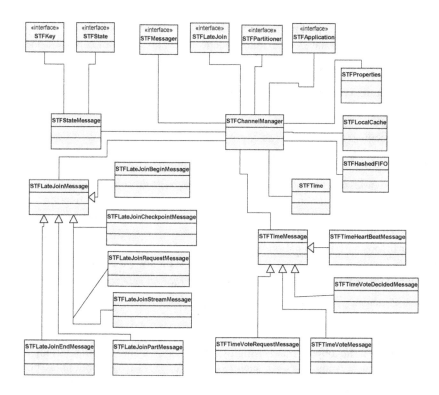

Figure 2 – Diagram of STF UML classes

3.2   State Categories

In STF, each state may be classified into various categories, according to the way it must be transmitted to and from the network and the way it must be treated with respect to the late join protocol. In terms of redundancy, a state may be classified as follows.

- Redundant state – A redundant state may fail to reach the destination, because it may be overwritten in the buffers by more recent states of the same stream. A stream made of redundant states always has the more recent states transmitted, in detriment of other, older states.
- Essential state – An essential state always reaches the destination. A stream made of essential states always has all its messages transmitted.

In terms of volatility, a state may be classified as follows.

- Volatile state – A volatile state may fail to reach the destination, even if it is not overwritten by any state in the buffers. A stream made of volatile states may have none of its states transmitted.
- Non-volatile state – A state that has not the volatile characteristic.

With respect to the late join protocol, a state may be classified as follows.

- Independent state – An independent state object completely describes the state of the object it refers to; thus, in a late join process it is sufficient to recover the last transmitted independent state.
- Cumulative state – A cumulative state object does not completely describe the state of the object it refers to, but only a state change. With this kind of states, it is necessary to recover a complete set of transmitted state objects to execute a late join process.

Excluding the late join classification as independent or cumulative, state categories lead to four possible combinations. Of these only three are meaningful:

- Essential and non-volatile – All states reach the destination
- Redundant and non-volatile – The latest state reaches the destination
- Redundant and volatile – The states are not guaranteed to reach the destination

The fourth possible combination, essential and volatile, must not be used, as it is obviously impossible to guarantee that a volatile state always reaches its destination, as required by essential states.

3.3 State Interaction Streams

What exactly is an object state is highly dependent on the specific virtual reality application that is using STF. As such, STF makes as few assumptions as possible about the state object. In fact, STF considers as state object any object that can be serialised and implements the STFState interface. This interface contains methods that permit STF to find out the special characteristics of each state object.

Similarly to the work presented in [4], the STF API divides the transmitted states into interaction streams, identified by a unique key that corresponds to a particular virtual world entity. Each interaction stream is made of state messages that include the state objects corresponding to that entity ordered by timestamp. Figure 3 illustrates this concept.

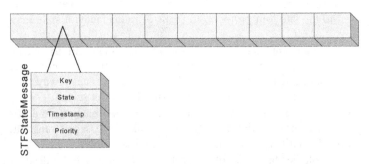

Figure 3 – State interaction streams

Using STF, applications can mix any types of states in the same stream, so we may have, for example, redundant states and some essential states in the middle, volatile and non-volatile states, etc. The streams are automatically generated by the API and are used to handle redundant and volatile states, so that STF may know which states to discard, if needed. A stream is made of *STFStateMessage* objects. Each of these objects is a message to be transmitted by the API, and includes the following information: the *key* object that identifies the virtual world entity to which the state refers that, by consequence, identifies the interaction stream to which this message belongs; the *state* object to be transmitted – an object of a class that must implement the *STFState* interface; message *timestamp* information – generated automatically by the STF API when the message is received from the application; and *priority* information of the message, which is a very important QoS property introduce in ARMS by STF, used when two or more messages from different streams are to be transmitted to the network. The *priority* information can take up one of five values:

- PRIORITY_LOWEST – The lowest priority possible
- PRIORITY_LOW – Low priority
- PRIORITY_MEDIUM – Medium priority
- PRIORITY_HIGH – High priority
- PRIORITY_HIGHEST – Highest priority possible

3.4 Transmission of State Messages

When the application wants to transmit a state object, it must construct an *STFStateMessage* object, containing the key – an object of a class that implements the *STFKey* interface, the state – an object of a class that implements the *STFState* interface, and the message priority information. The application then sends the message to be processed to the *STFChannelManager* using the *sendMessage* method of the *STFMessager* interface.

3.5 Reception of State Messages

The state messages – instances of *STFStateMessage* – are received by the application through the methods of the *STFApplication* interface. The method normally used for message reception is the *receive* method, with the *STFStateMessage* object as a parameter.

3.6 Reception Lag and Time Warp Avoidance

A time warp happens when a message that should have been received before some other message is received after it. This may cause an inconsistency in the virtual world and must be prevented. To prevent this from happening, STF orders all messages by timestamp and delivers them all in that order. However, when multiple conference nodes are transmitting messages about the same object, the underlying communication levels do not usually guarantee the total order of these messages. To circumvent this problem, STF makes it possible to enable a reception lag time. When enabled, reception lag causes a message to remain in the buffers for a specified minimal period of time since it has been passed to STF by the emitter application. In this way the buffers are used to order incoming out of order messages such that they do not cause a time warp.

The reception lag may degrade application performance, and even endanger virtual world consistency if not used wisely. So, this feature must be used with extra care. Reception lag is depicted in Figure 4.

3.7 Time Warp Detection

With or without reception lag, time warps are possible when transmitting data about the same entity in two or more conference nodes. When a time warp happens, STF detects this and delivers the time-warped message to the application using a special method of the *STFApplication* interface – *timeWarpReceive*. The application then has the chance to consider the message, ignore it or do whichever action it deems adequate to the situation.

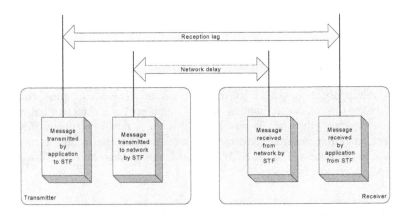

Figure 4 – Reception lag components

4   Tests Made to STF

In order to analyse the performance of the state transmission framework, a series of tests designed to evaluate the behaviour of this API were made, covering common situations in virtual reality applications. Due to the extension of the API, which comprises time synchronization, late join protocols, various transmission and reception options, and partitioning of virtual world entities it was, in practice, impossible to test all possible configurations. Thus, only tests related to common state transmission configurations were made, with the aim of discovering the limits of the API and assessing its behaviour under various circumstances.

4.1 The Testbed

The tests were made using three Pentium III 733Mhz-500Mhz computers (A-TEJO, B-CONCHA and C-SADO), with 128 MB RAM and Windows 2000 Professional, directly connected to a network switch by 100Mbit Ethernet full duplex links. All three computers had the Java Software Development Kit version 1.3, from Sun Microsystems [19], installed. The state transmission framework ran as part of the CONCHA conference controller system version 2.0 [20], which used Java 1.3, JSDT 2.0 [21] and ARMS 1.0 [20]. All three computers were synchronized using NTP through the installation of the NTPTime client for WindowsNT, adapted to work under Windows2000 [22]. All three computers used the same NTP server for time synchronization.

4.2 Tests Description

The objective of the tests was to measure the total message delay and also the message transmission throughput under different conditions, so as to conclude about STF's efficiency.

Two sets of tests were performed. The first set addressed the effect of increasing message transmission rate (increased throughput) on the total transmission delay and the redundant message discarding. These tests were used to conclude about the practical limits of STF under stress conditions.

The second set of tests addressed the effect of increasing message sizes (through the increase in state sizes) on the total transmission delay and the redundant message discarding, using a fixed message transmission rate. Both sets of tests used three different streams of states, with the purpose of simulating a simple but representative situation of mixed streams with different state characteristics:

- Stream 1: redundant, volatile and independent states;
- Stream 2: redundant, non-volatile and independent states;
- Stream 3: essential, non-volatile and independent states.

All state messages from all streams had the same priority – Highest.

The first set of tests – the message rate tests – used a state size of 22 bytes and a key size of 6 bytes, totalling 28 bytes. This is enough to transmit three-dimensional position and rotation information, which is sufficient for many applications, though not all. The test started by transmitting five messages per second (msg/s) in each stream. This was increased by 5 msg/s in each consecutive run. The test was set to stop at 400 msg/s for each stream, which amounted to a total of 1200 msg/s. Additionally, the test was programmed to stop as soon as the total message transmission delay – comprising the message transmission by the sending application to STF and the message delivery to the receiving application by STF – would reach one second, a value that was considered unacceptable. In the second set of tests, state messages of 22 bytes were first used, the state size being incremented by 100 bytes in each consecutive run. In both sets of tests, each individual test ran for 20 seconds.

4.3 The Test Application

A test application running as part of the CONCHA system version 2.0 [20,23] was created with the specific purpose of performing the STF API tests. The application enables the user to specify all properties of the STF session, such as underlying communication properties, transmission and reception lag control, late join protocol control, time synchronization settings and time warp detection. Figure 5 presents a screenshot of this application, where the setting of stream state transmission properties is visible.

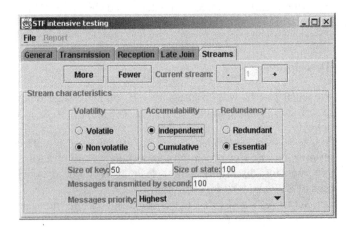

Figure 5 – Screenshot of the test application

This application allows for a completely automated testing process, through an option in the application's menu ("Start automatic testing") that executes the tests earlier discussed in this paper. It also allows for more specific testing of a large variety of situations under which STF may be used. With this application, it is possible to test most of STF's capacities without having to build a complete multiuser CVE. However, the authors plan to build such an environment in the near future in order to test and evaluate other STF's features that this application does not test properly, such as some of the features of the late join protocol.

4.4 Tests' Results and Analysis

Figure 6 identifies the four message probing points used to gather delay and throughput data. Point (A) corresponds to the sending application interface with STF. Messages passing through this point are shown in Figure 9 as *processed* messages. Point (B) is the sending STF interface with the communications layer. Messages passing through this point are shown in Figure 9 as *transmitted* messages.

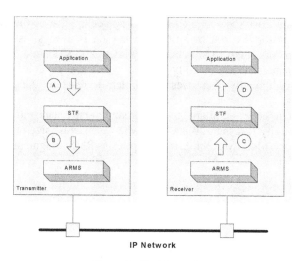

Figure 6 – Probing points

The obtained results have shown that these are the same as the messages that pass through the third message probing point (C), which correspond to the messages received by STF from the underlying communications layer at the receiving node. Thus, these messages are not represented in Figure 9, since the data are the same as the transmitted messages data. The fourth and final message probing point corresponds to the receiving application interface with STF (D). The corresponding messages are shown in the graphs as *received* messages.

The STF latency is the time that messages take since they travel from the probing point (A) to the probing point (D). Latency was measured as a function of message throughput (Figure 7) and as a function of message size (Figure 8).

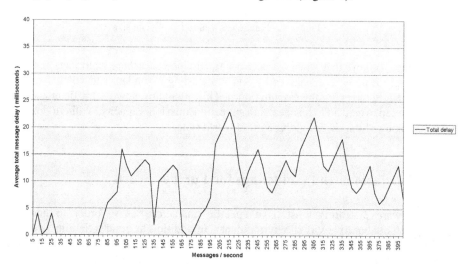

Figure 7 – Latency as a function of state rate

Figure 7 shows that the average total message delay, that is, the average latency is less than 20 ms for the vast majority of tests and is always less than 25 ms. It is noteworthy to say that this latency includes all STF and ARMS overheads (marshalling/demarshalling, encoding/decoding of the reliable multicast protocol packet, etc). Additionally, there was no problem in reaching the target value of 400 msg/s per flow.

Figure 8 shows that, similarly to the latency versus state rate case, the average latency is generally less than 20 ms even when the states' size is considerably high, well above the 1400-byte limit that implies ARMS fragmentation/reassembling overhead.

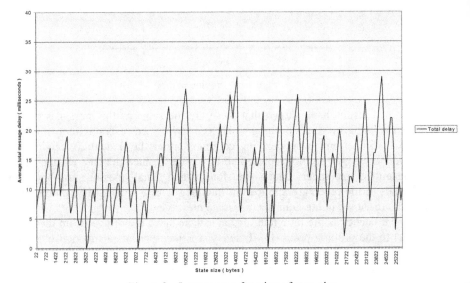

Figure 8 – Latency as a function of state size

Figure 9 shows that when the network traffic increases there is, in fact, an efficient utilization of network resources by STF, discarding redundant and volatile messages as needed, but keeping the essential ones. This maintains network traffic at acceptable levels even when STF reaches full state transmission capacity, without losing the consistency of the shared global virtual world state.

5   Conclusions and Guidelines for Further Work

Middleware platforms must have specific characteristics in order to adequately support collaborative virtual environments. In addition to good reliability, delay and jitter characteristics, it is essential that state synchronisation is efficiently guaranteed and maintained.

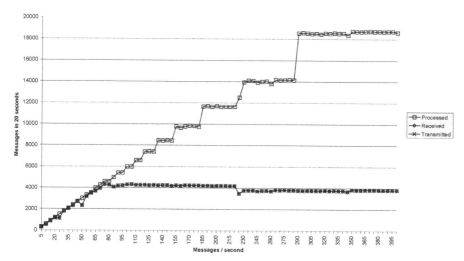

Figure 9 – Processed, transmitted and received messages as a function of state rate

In this paper, a proposal of a set of mechanisms that provide such synchronisation was made. These mechanisms, collectively referred to as a state transmission framework, were implemented and subject to functionality and performance testing in the context of a QoS-aware middleware platform named ARMS, developed by the authors in a previous project.

After a presentation of the main features of the framework, some of the tests' results were presented and discussed. In addition to validating concepts so important as the state redundancy and state volatility concepts, the tests have clearly shown that the implemented prototype has good performance in terms of throughput, latency and efficiency in the use of both processing and network resources.

Subsequent phases of this work will address further testing, namely scalability testing. Additionally, future work will try to optimise the integration with the ARMS platform, with emphasis on the exploration of some of its QoS capabilities such as multiple reliability levels.

Acknowledgements

This work was partially financed by the Portuguese Foundation for Science and Technology, FCT.

References

1.   João Orvalho, Fernando Boavida, "Augmented Reliable Multicast CORBA Event Service (ARMS): a QoS-Adaptive Middleware", in *Lecture Notes in Computer Science, Vol. 1905: Hans Scholten, Marten J. van Sinderen (editors), Interactive Distributed Multimedia Systems and Telecommunication Services*, Springer-Verlag,

Berlin Heidelberg, 2000, pp. 144-157. (Proceedings of IDMS 2000 – 7th International Workshop on Interactive Distributed Multimedia Systems and Telecommunication Services, CTIT / University of Twente, Enschede, The Netherlands, October 17-20, 2000).

2.   S. Singhal, M. Zyda. "Networked Virtual Environments Design and Implementation", ACM press, New York, 1999.

3.   Martin Mauve. "How to Keep a Dead Man from Shooting", in *Lecture Notes in Computer Science, Vol. 1905: Hans Scholten, Marten J. van Sinderen (editors), Interactive Distributed Multimedia Systems and Telecommunication Services,* Springer-Verlag, Berlin Heidelberg, 2000, pp. 144-157. (Proceedings of IDMS 2000 – 7th International Workshop on Interactive Distributed Multimedia Systems and Telecommunication Services, CTIT / University of Twente, Enschede, The Netherlands, October 17-20, 2000).

4.   Shervin Shirmohammadi and Nicolas D. Georganas. "An End-to-End Communication Architecture for Collaborative Virtual Environments", Computer Networks Journal, Vol.35, No.2-3, Febr. 2001, pp.351-367.

5.   Martin Mauve, "Consistency in Continuous Distributed Interactive media", Technical Report TR-9-99, Reihe Informatik, Department for Mathematics and Computer Science, University of Mannheim, November 1999.

6.   Martin Mauve, "Distributed Interactive Media", Ph.D. Thesis, University of Mannheim, Germany, September 2000.

7.   L. Gautier and C. Diot, "Design and evaluation of MiMaze, a Multiplayer Game on the Internet", IEEE Multimedia System Conference, Austin, June 28 - July 1, 1998.

8.   David L. Millis, "Network Time Protocol (version 3) specification, implementation", Request For Comments 1305, IETF, March 1992.

9.   Schulzrinne, Casner, Frederic, Jacobson, "RTP: A transport Protocol for Real-Time Applications", revision of RFC 1889, Internet-Draft (draft-ietf-avt-rtp-new-04.ps), June 25 1999.

10.   S. E. Deering, "Multicast Routing in Datagram Internetwork", Ph.D. dissertation, Standford University, December 1991.

11.   Dimitrios Makrakis, Abdelhakim Hafid, Farid Nait-Abdesselem, Anastasios Kasiolas, Lijia Qin, "Quality of Service Management in Distributed Interactive Virtual Environment", Progress Report of DIVE project.
http://www.mcrlab.uottawa.ca/research/QoS_DIVE_Report.html

12.   M. M. Wloka, "Lag in Multiprocessor VR", Presence: Teleoperators and Virtual Environments (MIT Press), Vol 4, N° 1, Spring 1995.

13.   K. S. Park And Robert V. Kenyon, "Effects of Network Characteristics on Human Performance Collaboration Virtual Environment", IEEE International Conference on Virtual Reality (VR '99), Houston, Texas, March 1999.

14.   Colin Perkins and Jon Crowcroft. "Notes on the use of RTP for shared workspace applications", ACM Computer Communication Review, Volume 30, Number 2, April 2000.

15.   J. Crowcroft, L. Vicisano, Z. Wang, A. Ghosh, M. Fuchs, C. Diot, and T. Turletti, "RMFP: A reliable multicast framing protocol", March 1998. Work in progress (Internet draft).

16.   B. DeCleene, S. Bhattacharaya, T. Friedman, M. Keaton, J. Kurose, D. Rubenstein, and D. Towsley, "Reliable multicast framework (RMF): A white paper", March 1997.

17.   S. Floyd, V. Jacobson, S. McCanne, C.-G. Liu, and L. Zhang., "A reliable multicast framework for light-weight sessions and applications level framing", *IEEE/ACM Transactions on Networking,* December 1997.

18.   M. Handley and J. Crowcroft, "Network text editor (NTE): A scalable shared text editor for the Mbone", In *Proceedings ACM SIGCOMM'97,* Cannes, France, September 1997.

19.   JavaSoft, www.javasoft.com
20.   João Orvalho, Luís Figueiredo, Tiago Andrade, Fernando Boavida, "A platform for the study of reliable multicasting extensions to CORBA Event Service", in *Lecture Notes in Computer Science, Vol. 1718: Michel Diaz, Philippe Owezarski and Patrick Sénac (editors), Interactive Distributed Multimedia Systems and Telecommunication Services*, Springer-Verlag, Berlin Heidelberg, 1999, pp. 107-120. (Proceedings of the 6th International Workshop on Interactive Distributed Multimedia Systems and Telecommunication Services, IDMS'99, IEEE, LAAS-CNRS, ENSICA, Toulouse, France, October 12-15, 1999).
21.   Java Shared Data Toolkit (JSDT), SUN Microsystems, JavaSoft Division, http://java.sun.com/people/richb/jsdt.
22.   The NTPTime client for the network time protocol, http://home.att.net/~Tom.Horsley/ntptime.html.
23.   João Orvalho, Tiago Andrade, Luís Figueiredo, Fernando Boavida, "CONCHA – CONference system based on java and corba event service CHAnnels", Proceedings of SPIES's symposium on Voice, Video, and Data Communications conference on Quality of Service Issues Related to Internet II, Boston, MA, USA, September 19-22, 1999.

A Stable and Flexible TCP-Friendly Congestion Control Protocol for Layered Multicast Transmission

Ibtissam El Khayat and Guy Leduc

Research Unit in Networking
University of Liège
Institut Montefiore - B28 - Sart Tilman
Liège 4000 - Belgique
elkhayat@run.montefiore.ulg.ac.be, leduc@montefiore.ulg.ac.be

Abstract. We propose an improvement of our RLS (Receiver-driven Layered multicast with Synchronization points) protocol, called CIFL for "Coding-Independent Fair Layered mulaticast", along two axes. In CIFL, each receiver of a layered multicast transmission will try and find the adequate number of layers to subscribe to, so that the associated throughput is fair towards TCP and stable in steady-state. The first improvement is that CIFL is not specific to any coding scheme. It can work as well with an exponentially distributed set of layers (where the throughput of each layer i equals the sum of the throughputs of all layers below i), or with layers of equal throughputs, or any other scheme. The second improvement is the excellent stability of the protocol which avoids useless join attempts by learning from its unsuccessful previous attempts in the same (or better) network conditions. Moreover, the protocol tries and reaches its ideal TCP-friendly as soon as possible by computing its target throughput in a clever way when an incipient congestion is confirmed.

1 Introduction

Contrary to the current compression standards (e.g. JPEG, MPEG-x, H.26x), wavelet-based compression techniques (e.g. JPEG 2000) allow for flexible and highly scalable (in resolution, time and quality) formats. Although inter-frame wavelet video coding is still an open research area, it will enable very scalable video transmission where the data stream can be split into several hierarchical layers whose bit contents (and thus throughputs) can be defined in a very flexible manner. Therefore, we believe that any congestion control protocol dedicated to video transmission to an heterogenous set of receivers should be independent from the relative and absolute throughputs of each layer. It should behave as well with an exponentially distributed set of layers (where the throughput of each layer i equals the sum of the throughputs of all layers below i), or with layers of equal throughputs, or any other scheme.

D. Shepherd et al. (Eds.): IDMS 2001, LNCS 2158, pp. 154–167, 2001.

A multicast congestion control protocol has to allow all receivers to reach their optimal level as quickly as possible. By optimal, we mean a fair share of the available bandwidth. We consider intra-session fairness (i.e. among receivers of the same session) and inter-session fairness (i.e. towards other sessions of the protocol or towards TCP connections).

A receiver-driven layered multicast (RLM) approach to solve the heterogeneity problem was first proposed by Mccanne in [8]. In RLM, every layer represents an IP multicast group and subscription to a layer implies subscription to all the lower layers. The receiver adds and drops layers according to the network state. This receiver-driven approach is probably the most elegant way to solve the multicast problem. It was later used in RLC [13], MLDA [12] and PLM [4]. The main concern of RLM was the intra-session fairness. To achieve it, a coordination mechanism between receivers has been designed. RLM was not designed to be TCP-friendly (i.e. fair towards TCP), nor to guarantee inter-session fairness. RLC was designed to be fair towards TCP connections whose round trip time (RTT) was close to one second, but not in general. RLC and MLDA support some form of inter-session fairness, in the sense that two competing RLC (MLDA) sessions will get the same number of layers in steady-state, which means that both sessions get the same throughput only in cases where the two sessions have partitioned their layers so that they have the same throughputs in all layers. This cannot be the case in general.

In an earlier work, we have proposed a protocol, called RLS [3], that provides intra-session and inter-session fairness guarantees. For example, for a large range of RTTs, the ratio of throughputs between RLS and TCP remains in the interval $[\frac{1}{3}, 3]$, which is excellent compared to RLM and RLC. However, we noted that RLS, though stable, still performed too many unsuccessful join experiments. Moreover, RLS was designed to work with exponentially distributed layers only. In this paper, we propose a better protocol, called CIFL, which improves RLS along the following lines:

- We make no hypothesis on the throughputs of the layers, they can have any value.
- The receivers reach the optimal level quickly.
- The stability is better, because the receivers learn from their past failures to join some layers under some conditions. This makes the received throughput very smooth, and improves fairness too.

The paper is organized as follows. We first remind some basic concepts in section 2. We explain the principles of CIFL in section 3, and show its simulated performance results in section 4.

2   Basic Concepts

2.1   TCP-Friendly

TCP is the most widespread traffic in the internet and any new congestion controlled protocol has to be designed to be TCP-friendly, which means that it gets an average share of the bandwidth (approximately) equal to the average share TCP would get in the same conditions. As TCP is unicast and we are considering multicast protocols, the definition should be refined as follows. A multicast protocol is TCP-friendly if each receiver gets an average share of the bandwidth equal to the average share a TCP connection, between that source and that receiver, would get.

In Best-effort networks, there is no reason to favour video transmission over TCP given the importance of the latter. In Integrated Services networks where receivers can reserve some (minimum) bandwidth for the video stream, one could let receivers get more bandwidth provided that this extra share is fairly allocated. In Differentiated Services networks where video stream can be aggregated with others and may, not be in the same class as TCP flows, inter-sessions fairness will be achieved if all video flows adopt the same definition of fairness (and TCP-friendliness may be a good candidate for that). So in all cases, TCP friendliness seems a good requirement to fulfill.

The throughput of TCP (in bps) in steady-state, when the loss ratio is below 16%, is roughly given by the following formula [6]:

$$B_{tcp} \approx \frac{C.s}{\sqrt{p}\overline{RTT}} \text{ with } C = \sqrt{\frac{3}{2}} = 1,22 \tag{1}$$

where s is the packet size (in bits), $\overline{RTT}$ is the mean round trip time (in sec) and p the packet loss ratio. A more precise formula that takes TCP timers into account can be found in [9].

The TCP cycle is the average delay between two packet losses in steady-state. So we have one packet loss per cycle, which can be formulated as:

$$p = \frac{s}{B_{tcp}.Cycle}, \tag{2}$$

where s is the packet size in bits and $Cycle$ the duration of the TCP cycle as described above. From (1) and (2), we derive:

$$Cycle = \frac{B_{tcp}.\overline{RTT}^2}{C^2 s} \tag{3}$$

2.2   Coordination of Receivers

It was pointed out in [8], that a multicast congestion control protocol cannot be effective if the subset of receivers behind the same router act without co-ordination. Indeed, if a receiver creates congestion on a link by requesting a new layer, another receiver (receiving less layers) might interpret its resulting losses as a consequence of its (too high) level of subscription and may end up dropping its highest layer unnecessarily (because this layer will continue to be received by other receivers). So coordination is necessary, RLM has proposed to use announcement messages, and RLC to use synchronization points (SPs). SPs are special packets in the data stream. Receivers can only join a new layer just after receiving an SP. In RLC, each layer has its own SPs, and the receiver can only join layer $i + 1$, when it receives an SP in layer i. [10] shows that the presence of SPs leads to a low redundancy and gives better fairness. That is the reason why RLS and CIFL build their coordination of receivers on the existence of SPs. The SPs will also contain information about the number of layers and their respective throughputs.

3   The CIFL Protocol

Our goal is to create a layered multicast congestion control protocol which is:

1. TCP-friendly.
2. Stable: as few unsuccessful join experiments as possible.
3. Generic: independent from the throughput of each layer. To achieve that CIFL will estimate the ideal throughput, and will join, or leave, one or several layers at once to reach a throughput which is close to the computed target, based on estimations of the RTT and the loss ratio.
4. Careful before adding layers at SPs, but quick at removing layers when an incipient congestion is confirmed. This is to be compared with the Additive Increase Multiplicative Decrease (AIMD) scheme of TCP.

3.1   Estimation of the Round Trip Time

Each receiver has to estimate its RTT to the source. The classical scheme is to ping the sender from time to time, e.g. each time the receiver joins or leave a layer, or more frequently. However, for large sessions, the sender can be flooded by ping requests. If routers are active, a solution based on [1] can be used, but we are looking for a solution that does not involve routers. If the sender knows the number r of receivers and the number p of ping requests it can process between two SPs, it can provide these numbers in the SPs.

Knowing these values, receivers can ping the sender with probability $\frac{p}{r}$.

We do not require that ping requests be immediately followed by a ping response from the sender. To achieve that, we implement a scheme similar to RTCP [11]. Suppose a receiver sends a ping request at time R_s which is received by the sender at time S_r. The sender stamps the ping request at its arrival, and when it is able to send a ping response, say at S_s, it stamps the response with that time value. If the sender is quick, S_s will be (almost) equal to S_r, but in any case the time spent at the sender can be computed as $S_s - S_r$. At R_r the receiver will get the ping response and perform the following operations:

$$Rec\_Send = (1 - g)Rec\_Send + g(S_r - R_s)$$
$$Send\_Rec = (1 - g)Send\_Rec + g(R_r - S_s)$$
$$RTT = Rec\_Send + Send\_Rec$$

If all the data packets are timestamped, the receiver can continuously estimate the $Send\_Rec$ value by using all the packets it receives. Between two pings, the Rec_Send can change without being noticed though, which requires that pings are not too distant from each other. This is also useful to compensate clock drift.

3.2 The Join

Synchronization Points. As said before, we use the SPs to co-ordinate the receivers. Contrary to RLC, SPs are only present in the first (base) layer and not in all of them. When a SP is received and if the decision to join is not taken, the receiver remains deaf to congestion during a deaf period T_d. This is necessary because this congestion can be induced by another receiver that has used that SP to get more layers. In practice the distance between SPs is at least 4 seconds. This distance is enough to be greater than any common deaf period (see next section). However, to avoid all kinds of synchronizations, the distance between SPs is randomized. It will vary between 4 and 16 seconds.

Increase of the Throughput. The receiver tries and estimates the bandwidth TCP would get in a similar situation. To do so, it will use formula (1) which requires to know its loss ratio. But the latter has a meaning only when it is computed over a duration close to a TCP cycle. Indeed, remember that formula (1) is only valid in steady-state. So, the receiver will refrain from using an SP to get more layers if it did not stay at least one TCP cycle at the current level. When it is the case, the receiver computes the bandwidth it can get as follows:

$$B_{next} = \frac{Cs}{RTT\sqrt{P_{cycle}}}.$$

with P_{cycle} the loss ratio computed over the last TCP cycle (see formula (3)). If there were no loss, the throughput can be doubled. That is smilar to TCP which would have doubled its window after a cycle. When the receiver has computed its optimal bandwidth, it joins the suitable number of layers to get the closest possible to the computed throughput. To do so, it is necessary that the SPs contain information about the throughputs of all the layers.

Stabilization. When the receiver has no good estimation of its RTT, e.g. because there is a large number of receivers and the pings are done less frequently, the estimated bandwidth can be overestimated. In this case, the receiver would join layers that it would leave soon after. These unsuccessful join experiments can be avoided if the receiver can learn something from past failures. To this end, the CIFL receiver will record the network state[1] as it was just before any unsuccessful join experiment. To do this, every receiver maintains a square matrix QD with one row (and one column) per layer. Each element $QD_{i,j}$ of the matrix represents the minimum queuing delay the receiver has ever monitored before any unsuccessful join experiment from level i to level j.

When a receiver at level *current* wants to join level *target*, it checks its matrix to see if it has already failed to join any layer below *target* with a queuing delay that was below the current queuing delay. It can be computed as follows:

---

[1] The network state is measured by the mean queuing delay computed over an equivalent TCP cycle

```
tested = current + 1
while (tested <= target &&
       current_queuing_delay < QD(current,tested))
     { join
       incr tested }
```

When the receiver has reached a stable level and is subjected to very few (or no) losses, it basically spends its time computing estimations of the RTT, the queuing delay and the loss rate, refraining from joining at SPs.

3.3   The Leave

If the decision to join layers can be done at (not so frequent) SPs and after a cycle has elapsed at the current level, the decision to abandon layers when congestion appears should be taken more quickly. So, when the receiver detects a potential incipient congestion by a packet loss, it will start monitoring the loss ratio P_{T_m} over a short interval (denoted T_m), and then the receiver will compute the number of layers it decides to abandon. We will discuss the value of T_m later, but we know it has to be short, say very few RTTs to fix ideas. The problem is that T_m is in general short compared to a TCP cycle, which makes it impossible to use equation [6] to compute a new (lower) target throughput. In order to propose another formula to compute that throughput, we will require that, when the suitable number of layers are abandoned, the receiver will not join any layer before a minimum amount of time (denoted T_c) has elapsed. Clearly, T_c should be larger than an equivalent TCP cycle, as before any join experiment, and should end at an SP. However, the distance between SPs being random, the future occurrences of SPs are unknown. In the calculation however, we will consider that all SPs are equally spaced out of 10 sec, which is the average spacing between SPs.

To derive our formula, we define

- T_m is the monitoring period starting at a probable incipient congestion detected by a packet loss in steady-state (or induced by a join experiment of the receiver).
- T_c (c for compensation) is the minimal period during which the receiver will have to stay at its new level before joining any layer. It is computed as described above.
- $B_{current}$ is the current throughput, which will remain so during T_m,
- B_{target} is the unknown throughput the receiver will request after leaving some layers, and will keep during at least T_c.

To compute B_{target}, we require that CIFL should get a TCP-friendly throughput over the $T_m + T_c$ interval.

Figure 1 shows the parameters we use, and illustrates also that T_c finishes at an SP arriving after the expiration of the cycle.

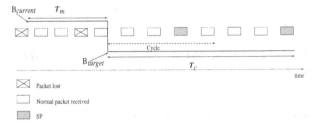

Fig. 1. A monitoring period followed by its compensation period

Let $\alpha = \frac{B_{current}}{B_{target}}$, the mean throughput of the receiver is:

$$\overline{B} = \frac{T_m B_{current} + T_c B_{target}}{T_m + T_c} = \frac{T_m \alpha + T_c}{\alpha(T_m + T_c)} B_{current}$$

We suppose that there is no loss during T_c, which means that the loss ratio p over $T_m + T_c$ is:

$$p = \frac{packets\ lost\ during\ (T_m + T_c)}{packets\ sent\ during\ (T_m + T_c)} = \frac{packets\ lost\ during\ T_m}{packets\ sent\ during\ (T_m + T_c)}$$

Whereas: $packets\ sent\ during\ (T_m + T_c) = (T_m + T_c)\overline{B}$

and: $packets\ lost\ during\ T_m = P_{T_m} T_m B_{current} = P_{T_m} T_m . \frac{\alpha(T_m + T_c)}{\alpha T_m + T_c} \overline{B}$

A simple replacement gives: $p = P_{T_m} \frac{\alpha T_m}{\alpha T_m + T_c}$,

TCP, which has a loss ratio equal to p, receives in average:

$$B_{tcp} = \frac{sC}{RTT \sqrt{P_{T_m} \frac{\alpha T_m}{\alpha T_m + T_c}}}$$

If we equate both throughputs, i.e. $\overline{B} = B_{tcp}$, we derive that:

$$\alpha = \frac{P_{T_m} T_m T_c}{(T_m + T_c)^2 \frac{C^2 s^2}{RTT^2 B_{current}^2} - T_m^2 P_{T_m}}$$

Recapitulation. When the receiver detects an incipient congestion, or just after joining a layer, it monitors the loss ratio during T_m and then computes α.

- If it is greater than 1 [2], the receiver leaves the suitable number of layers to get a throughput close to $\frac{B_{current}}{\alpha}$. Then the receiver ignores losses during the deaf period T_d, which is necessary to let the network reach its new state and monitor it. Initially, the deaf period is equal to $1\overline{RTT}$, but it is updated each time a layer is added or removed as follows. Knowing $time_{drop}$, the time at which layers were abandoned, and $time_{last}$, the reception time of the last packet belonging to one of the dropped layers, the receiver makes an exponential smoothing of T_d with the new value "$time_{last} - time_{drop}$".

---

[2] The development we have made is meaningless if α is less than 1.

– Else, it does nothing as it treats the losses as resulting from a small transient congestion.

Such a scheme would not be easily adapted to TCP itself because TCP may not receive enough segments during an RTT (when its window is small) to compute α accurately.

Note also that if a receiver is in a leave evaluation when an SP is received, and a deaf period is started, the leave evaluation is cancelled. Otherwise, the receiver may be falsely confused by a transient congestion due to a join experiment by another receiver.

The T_m Value. In this section, we briefly discuss the choice of T_m. We know that:

$$B_{tcp} = \frac{T_m B_{current} + T_c B_{target}}{T_m + T_c},$$

So, when T_m increases, B_{target} decreases and $\frac{B_{target}}{B_{tcp}}$ decreases too. If $B_{target} \ll B_{tcp}$ the receiver at the end of T_c will normally increase its bandwidth to reach B_{tcp}. To avoid this oscillation, we need $B_{target} \simeq B_{tcp}$. As T_c and α are fixed,

$$B_{target} \to B_{tcp} \quad \text{implies} \quad T_m \to 0$$

So T_m has to be short. However, as TCP takes decisions at every $\overline{RTT}$, if the CIFL receiver evaluates its loss ratio over a duration shorter than $\overline{RTT}$, it will get a bad estimation. For this reason, T_m has been fixed to $1\overline{RTT}$.

3.4   Start-Up Phase

We have explained how the CIFL receiver behaves in steady-state. However, this behaviour is unsuitable at the very beginning, because it tends to mimic TCP in congestion avoidance, instead of a TCP in the slow-start phase. Therefore, when TCP and CIFL start together, CIFL would not get its fair share, or only after a much longer period.

In this section, we describe the start-up phase of CIFL. In this phase, the receiver uses all the SPs to join new layers, so that it doubles its throughput at every SP. For a set of exponentially distributed layers, this would mean adding a layer (but only) at every SP. In other schemes, the receiver may join several layers at once. This mimics the exponential takeoff of TCP, which continues until the throughput of subscribed layers is greater than the peak throughput actually received. Once this state is reached, the receiver drops all layers above the maximum received throughput and exits the start-up phase.

Moreover, this more aggressive phase is used to estimate the bottleneck capacity by measuring the smallest delay between two received packets. Knowing this bottleneck capacity, the receiver will not attempt to join layers that would lead to a throughput above this value. This will reduce the number of unsuccessful joins, compared to other protocols like [13], [8], [12].

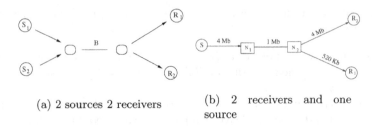

(a) 2 sources 2 receivers

(b) 2 receivers and one source

Fig. 2. Topologies

If, later during the session, packets happen to transit through another path with more bandwidth, or if the network is simply less congested, the receiver will discover it, because it will continue to estimate the bottleneck capacity as follows:

$$estimate\_bw_i = max(estimate\_bw_{i-1}, \frac{pktsize}{t\_recv_i - t\_recv_{i-1}})$$

On the other hand, if the traffic is routed to less provisioned or more congested links, it is not a real problem, because this estimated bottleneck capacity will just become overestimated, and thus a bit less useful to avoid unsuccessful join experiments.

3.5   Scalability

When the number of receivers is large, receivers will ping the source less frequently, which means that the RTT estimation may be less accurate. Note however, that the RTTs are still adjusted at every received packet by using the timestamping approach, but regular resynchronizations are also useful to compensate clock drift and delay variations on the return path as explained in section 3.1.

Note also that a less accurate estimation of the RTT will simply lead to a bandwidth target which is less TCP-Friendly (see formula (1)). Moreover, some experiences performed over internet have shown us that during 1 hour the ratio between the longest RTT and the shortest one is rarely greater than 2.

4   Simulations

For our simulations we use the network simulator NS ([7]). We will start by showing that the receiver, once at its optimal level, does not make unsuccessful join experiments. Then we will show that intra-session and inter-session fairness are fulfilled, both towards TCP and towards other CIFL sessions.

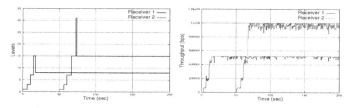

Fig. 3. Two different CIFL receivers beginning at different times

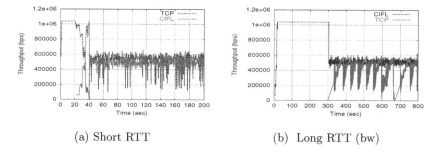

(a) Short RTT   (b) Long RTT (bw)

Fig. 4. Bottleneck sharing between TCP and CIFL

4.1 Several Receivers

In this section, we will show the importance of the deaf periods. To this end, we use the topology of Figure 3.5. We see on Figure 3 that when receiver R_2 starts, receiver R_1 has already reached its optimal throughput. The newcomer will create congestion on the $N_1 - N_2$ link and R_1 will be subjected to this congestion. Without deaf periods, receiver R_1 would react by leaving some layers. This decrease would be useless because the layers it would leave would continue to transit through the bottleneck. In section 4.4 of [3], we showed that without deaf periods and when the delay to R_1 is larger than the delay to R_2, R_1 loses its fair share. With deaf periods, receiver R_1 does not react to losses caused by R_2. We can see by the same occasion that the receivers reach quickly their optimal level thanks to the quick start-up phase. They also find that they cannot go over the bottleneck capacity. They leave some layers and maintain the optimal throughput until the end of the simulation.

4.2 TCP versus CIFL

Reminder. Previous studies ([5] and [2]) have shown that the most severe situations to get fairness towards TCP are the following:

– Either TCP begins before the multicast protocol, when the RTT is short,
– Or TCP begins after the multicast protocol, for long RTTs.

In the first case, TCP is so aggressive that it prevents the multicast protocol (RLM, RLC) to get a reasonable share of the capacity. In the second case, TCP is so slow and so vulnerable that it cannot get a reasonable throughput. This happens because TCP's clock is its RTT, which is not the case for the other multicast protocols. We will see that CIFL performs much better in the extreme cases.

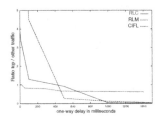

Fig. 5. RLM, RLC and CIFL according to the one way delay

Simulations. We use the topology of Figure 3.5 with one TCP source and one CIFL receiver to test the behaviour of both traffics. The parameter values are: $B_0 = 64$ kbps and $B_{i+1} = B_i + B_0$ i.e. $\forall i L_i = L_0 = B_0$.

Figure 4.2 shows the sharing in the first extreme case, i.e. a short RTT (1 ms) and TCP begins before CIFL. We see that CIFL is so aggressive in the beginning that it can take more bandwidth than TCP. After this, it decreases its throughput to get exactly what TCP gets. In the medium term, the sharing ratio, $\frac{rate_{TCP}}{rate_{CIFL}}$, is 1. For the second extreme case, the RTT is approximatively equal to 2 sec. Figure 4.2 illustrates this case and shows that when TCP begins, CIFL halves its throughput by leaving 8 layers, and does not perform any future attempt. TCP pays for its greediness. In fact, every time TCP wants to have more bandwidth than the optimum, it creates congestion and has to decrease its throughput. And since the RTT is large, TCP needs a long time to reach again its fair share of the bandwidth. That is why the ratio is around 0.6 for long RTTs, while it remains slightly below 1 for short RTTs.

To better illustrate the dependence of the sharing ratio according to the RTT, we carried out several experiments where we changed only the propagation delay. We have done it for RLM and RLC too (for more results concerning these two protocols, refer to [5]). The results are illustrated on Figure 5. The CIFL curve remains close to 1, contrary to RLM and RLC whose ratios converge to zero for long RTTs and are far above 1 for short RTTs.

Now we show that a CIFL receiver can find a better optimal level, when a competing TCP connection stops. We consider topology 3.5 with TCP and CIFL beginning simultaneously. After both protocols have reached their fair bandwidth, TCP stops. There are two possibilities:

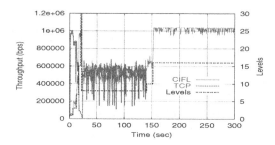

Fig. 6. The behaviour of the receiver when TCP disappears

1. If the next SP arrives more that a cycle after TCP has disappeared, the CIFL receiver is unlikely to have suffered loss during the last cycle. If so, it will double its bandwidth (limited to the bottleneck capacity it had computed).
2. If the next SP arrives less than a cycle after TCP has disappeared, the CIFL receiver can still have noticed some losses during the last cycle. This case is illustrated in Figure 6. The CIFL receiver computes its new estimated fair share and decides to join a certain number of layers (in our case, 2 layers). When the next SP arrives, the CIFL receiver behaves as in the previous case.

4.3   Fairness Towards Another CIFL Session

We will show that CIFL fulfills this requirement. This is so because all CIFL sessions try to be TCP-friendly. We use two different sessions, one with B_0^1 equal to 64 Kbps and the other one with B_0^2 equal to 124 Kbps. To be in a difficult case, the session with the smallest base layer begins when the other one has already reached its optimal level. Figure 7 illustrates the result. We see that both sessions get the same bandwidth, although these bandwidths correspond to different number of layers in the two sessions.

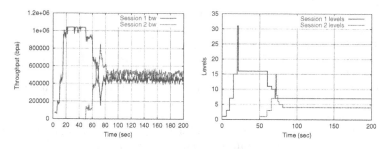

Fig. 7. Fairness between 2 different CIFL sessions

5   Conclusion

We have proposed a congestion control protocol for layered multicast transmission, called CIFL, that ensures:

- intra-session fairness,
- fairness towards TCP, the ratio $\frac{TCP}{CIFL}$ is close to 1
- fairness between sessions in terms of throughput (instead of levels),
- stability, the receiver uses its past failures to performs a sort of reinforcement learning.

We have simulated our protocol in different situations, and the obtained results show that intra- and inter-session fairness is fulfilled even when there are several TCPs and several CIFL in competition.

References

[1] A Basu and J. Golestani. Estimation of receiver round trip times in multicast communications. Technical report, Bell Laboratories, http://www.bell-labs.com/user/golestani/rtt.ps, 1999.

[2] Ibtissam El Khayat. Comparaison d'algorithmes de contrôle de congestion pour la vidéo multipoints en couches. Master's thesis, University of Liège, Belgium, June 2000.

[3] Ibtissam El Khayat and Guy Leduc. Congestion control for layered multicast transmission. *To appear in Networking and Information Systems*, 2000.

[4] A Legout and E. W. Biersack. PLM: Fast convergence for cumulative layered multicast transmission schemes. In *Proceedings of ACM SIGMETRICS'2000*, Santa Clara, CA, USA, June 2000.

[5] A Legout and W Biersack. Pathological behaviors for RLM and RLC. In *Proceedings of NOSSDAV'2000*, Chapel Hill, North Carolina, USA, June 2000.

[6] M. Mathis, J. Semke, Mahdavi, and T. Ott. The macroscopic behavior of the TCP congestion avoidance algorithm. *Computer Communication Review*, 27(3), July 1997.

[7] S McCanne and S Floyd. *The LBNL Network Simulator*. Lawrence Berkeley Laboratory, 1997.

[8] S McCanne, V Jacobson, and M Vetterli. Receiver-driven layered multicast. In *Proceedings of ACM SIGCOMM'95*, pages 117–130, Palo Alto, California, 1995.

[9] J. Padhye, V. Firoiu, D. Towsley, and J. Kurose. Modeling TCP reno performance: A simple model and its empirical validation. In *Proceedings of ACM SIGCOMM'2000*, August 2000.

[10] Dan Rubenstein, Jim Kurose, and Don Towsley. The impact of multicast layering on network fairness. In *Proceedings of ACM SIGCOMM'99*, Cambridge, MA, September 1999.

[11] Schulzrinne, Casner, Frederick, and Jacobson. RTP: A transport protocol for real-time applications. *Internet-Draft ietf-avt-rtp-new-01.txt (work inprogress)*, 1998.

[12] D Sisalem and A Wolisz. MLDA: A TCP-friendly congestion control framework for heterogenous multicast environments. In *Eighth International Workshop on Quality of Service (IWQoS 2000)*, Pittsburgh, June 2000.

[13] Lorenzo Vicisano, Jon Crowcroft, and Luigi Rizzo. TCP-like congestion control for layered multicast data transfer. In *Proceedings of IEEE INFOCOM'98*, San Francisco, CA, March 1998.

Content-Aware Quality Adaptation for IP Sessions with Multiple Streams[*]

Dimitrios Miras[1], Richard J. Jacobs[2], and Vicky Hardman[1]

[1] Department of Computer Science, University College London,
Gower St., London WC1E 6BT, UK.
{d.miras, v.hardman}@cs.ucl.ac.uk
[2] Prognet Lab, BTexact Technologies, Adastral Park, Ipswich IP5 3RE, UK.
richard.j.jacobs@bt.com

Abstract. While a considerable amount of research has been conducted
to address QoS issues for best-effort Internet multimedia applications by
utilising network-centric metrics (loss, delay, RTT, available bandwidth),
less attention has been paid to the quality that is perceived by the users
of the networked applications. Perceived quality of encoded multimedia
is highly dependent on the time-varying characteristics of the content.
We describe an approach for content-aware quality adaptation of multimedia sessions consisting of an ensemble of concurrent flows relevant
to the presentation scenario. Using a quality metric that is based on the
properties of the human visual perception process, we devise mechanisms
that improve the overall session quality by efficiently apportioning the
session bandwidth to the participating flows at appropriate adaptation
times. We discuss the approach, propose suitable adaptation time scales
and present results from trace-driven simulations that show the potential
of content-aware quality adaptation.

1   Introduction

In recent years, the Internet has been experiencing a proliferation in transmission
of real-time multimedia, mainly in the form of streamed live or stored audio-
visual content. While the stability of the Internet to date is owed to the sound
congestion avoidance and control principles present in TCP -the dominant IP
traffic type- the rapid explosion of unrestricted real-time traffic is threatening
its well-being [5]. As the use of real-time multimedia services over the Internet is
expected to proliferate, and Internet traffic patterns are continuously changing,
TCP-friendly congestion control for all kinds of Internet flows is regarded to
constitute a deployment baseline for such applications [6].

Furthermore, traditional forms of multimedia networking, like streaming and
conferencing, will be soon followed by content richer applications: Internet multi-
channel TV, complex immersive environments, etc. These applications will involve the transmission to the user of multiple continuous media flows relevant

---

[*] This work was supported by BTexact Technologies, UK

D. Shepherd et al. (Eds.): IDMS 2001, LNCS 2158, pp. 168–180, 2001.

to the presentation scenario. For applications that transmit multiple (TCP and UDP) flows between the sender-receiver pairs, as is the case for several current web-based applications, the benefits of integrated congestion control have recently been highlighted [6] [1]. Flows that belong to the same thematic presentation most probably traverse the same parts of the network to reach the receiver site, and will experience similar levels of service from the network. Such flows should be able to co-ordinate instead of competing for the available network resources. Integrated congestion management enables sharing of congestion control information among the flows and allows for collective adaptation decisions under varying network conditions. Coordinated congestion management enables the session bandwidth to be apportioned to the individual flows according to their dynamically varying utility and user preferences. While it is imperative that the user-perceived quality ultimately reflects the utility of an application, significant effort has not been put to integrating this factor together with conventional QoS measures (like congestion control and adaptation). Within a framework of integrated congestion control, the challenge is to devise efficient scheduling mechanisms to apportion the bandwidth available to the ensemble of flows and control the allocation to each stream based on the relative 'quality contribution' (or 'utility') of that stream to the session. So, it is important to introduce metrics to measure this contribution in a manner that precisely reflects the way humans perceive quality. The main reason for this is that the perceived quality of a flow is not only a function of the network resources allocated to it, but is also highly dependent on its time varying content features.

Our work relies on research in the area of human perception modeling. Using models of the human visual system, perceptual distortion metrics can be derived that are able to assess the quality of audiovisual content by objective means while being highly correlated to subjective quality assessment. Using an objective quality assessment model for video, we investigate efficient bandwidth sharing policies that maximise the 'perceived' session utility and propose suitable adaptation time scales to alleviate the impact of adaptation on the perceived presentation quality. In this way, we diverge from a model of adaptation that only considers network congestion signals for its operation to one that also accounts for the contribution of each flow to perceived quality.

While applications like those we anticipate in this work are realised by a number of concurrent media flows of different nature (audio, video, etc.), we here consider multi-flow sessions consisting only of video streams, for two of reasons. Firstly, because the audio part of a multimedia session usually requires less network resources to operate with acceptable quality than that of video, thus making adaptation of the video compartments more worthwhile and interesting. Secondly, the majority of users almost always prefer a constantly good audio quality in favour of a varying video quality.

The rest of the paper is structured as follows: we firstly present the motivation for our work and present related research (Section 2). We then (Section 3) describe a model for content-aware inter-stream bandwidth sharing, and discuss appropriate adaptation time scales. In Section 4 we present experimental results from trace-driven simulations. Section 5 concludes the paper.

2   Motivation and Related Work

The perceived quality of encoded multimedia (and especially video) is widely varying with different time scales. The main factors that influence the perceived quality are:

- The bit-rate assigned to a particular flow and the encoding method used (i.e., block-based DCT).
- Properties of the original visual content, like its spatio-temporal complexity, owing to the composition of its scenes, the video editing process, camera actions (like, zooming and panning), the scene's duration and features. These scene features change for different types of video (e.g., news, sports, movie, video-conferencing) but also change within the same video sequence as the visual content changes. Higher content complexity leads to greater impairment and distortions during the encoding process.
- Moreover, impairments may be introduced during transmission of encoded video over the Internet, due to packet loss and delay variation.

Since humans view the encoded material, in multi-stream presentations, we should strive to maximise the perceived quality given the current state of the network, by *stealing* bandwidth from some flows and *giving* to others that contribute more utility to the session. However, in order to perform this form of scheduling, a mechanism that measures the utility contribution (i.e., the perceived quality) has to be in place. The result of the measurement must be an accurate representations of the user's opinion on perceived quality. Subjective tests (like *MOS*) provide the most reliable scores as they reflect the opinion of human subjects. However, such tests are costly and time-consuming and cannot be applied to real-time monitoring and assessment of quality. Mohamed *et al.* [11] conducted a series of MOS tests to assess speech quality under various packet loss and encoding conditions. A neural network was then trained to accurately provide MOS-like scores in real-time. Those scores were used to make the adaptation decision (choice of encoding mechanism) that optimises quality under the given network conditions. The drawback of MOS for such cases is that it requires large numbers of MOS tests to cover all possible cases and achieve high consistency.

2.1   Objective Video Quality Assessment

Measurement of video quality by objective means offers a relatively easy way of obtaining consistent quality scores. The *Signal-to-Noise ratio* (SNR) is widely used to measure distortion due to its great simplicity of computation. However, SNR cannot catch all the artifacts of the encoding process and as a result it does not correlate well with subjective quality. Objective video quality techniques utilise models of the human visual system based on psycho-physiological research results on the sensitivity of the human eye in various dimensions (spatial and temporal resolution, colour). Objective quality assessment uses metrics that quantify the perceived video distortion and produces quality assessment scores highly correlated to those obtained by subjective assessment. Several proposed models (e.g., [24], [8], [20], [22], [23]) of video quality assessment are currently under an evaluation and standardisation process by the Video Quality Experts Group (VQEG) [19] and the ITU. These models can replace the costly and time-consuming process of subjective quality assessment and provide more consistent results.

For the purposes of accurate quality assessment of video material we implemented a perceptual model of video based on work by Wolf and Pinson (ITS video quality metric) [24]. The ITS quality metric is based on the extraction and statistical manipulation of scalar spatio-temporal features from the original and degraded video sequences to obtain a single measure of distortion. The extracted features are able to closely represent the perceived effect of various distortions introduced from the encoder and/or the transmission system. These distortions may be present in the spatial and the temporal dimensions. The most common spatial distortions appear in the form of blockiness (introduced by blocked-based DCT encoding), blurring or edge busyness (due to the absence of higher frequencies coefficients) and quantisation noise. Added motion energy may take the form of erroneous blocks that persist for a few frames, and lost motion energy (i.e., due to frame dropping) causing video to be jerky. The ITS model works on edge-enhanced versions of the original and distorted sequences (e.g., using Sobel filters) and gradient operators are used on the pixel domain to measure the magnitude and direction of the spatial gradient within spatio-temporal regions (S-T regions), usually $8 \times 8\, pixels \times 6\, frames$ large. The gradients give an indication of the type and size of the distortion. For example, larger horizontal and vertical gradients in the distorted image is an indication of blocking or tiling artifacts, where lost edge energy in the output frame, measured by loss of diagonal spatial activity, is caused by the blurring impairment. The perceptual impairments within each S-T region are calculated using functions that model human visual masking. These impairments are then pooled using spatial (average of worst 5% of measured distortions) and then temporal (average over the clip's duration) collapsing to obtain a single quality score for a video clip.

2.2   Integrated Congestion Control

Integrated congestion management allows flows that traverse the same network paths between a pair of hosts to cooperate rather than compete for time-varying networks resources, by sharing information about the levels of network service. Integrated congestion control handles all these relevant flows as an aggregate *macroflow*, and congestion control is applied to the macroflow. The server's total session rate remains the same as if the session was treated as an isolated TCP-friendly session and it is up to the server application to apportion it to its individual flows according to an appropriate policy. Such policies may involve features such as, user preferences for the individual flows and the flows' time-varying quality. Work in this area includes TCP control block independence [21], and TCP session [15] where a set of TCP sessions share the same control information. Our work is motivated by Balakrishnan et. al. and the Congestion Manager (CM) architecture [1], [2]. The CM integrates congestion management across an ensemble of concurrent unicast flows (TCP or UDP), maintains congestion control parameters and provides an API allowing applications to learn about network service levels and arrange for data transmissions accordingly. CM also features a TCP-friendly traffic shaping coupled with a lightweight protocol to elicit receivers' feedback, and a hierarchical round-robin scheduler for flow transmission scheduling. This scheduler is effectively apportioning the session nominal bandwidth among flows in proportion to pre-configured weights that may correspond to each flow's importance or based on receiver preference hints. We show later that this does not always provide the best aggregate perceived quality and that a scheduler based on the *quality-over-time* contribution of a flow is preferable.

3   Content-Aware Quality Adaptation Model

Figure 1 depicts the main components for content-aware inter-stream adaptation. The content analyser segments the video sequence into visually autonomous portions (i.e., scenes) and passes the information to the objective quality assessment module (OQAM) that calculates objective quality scores based on the model described in §2.1. A companion congestion control manager is continuously monitoring the nominal share of bandwidth for the session. This congestion manager may for example be as described in [2], or any other suitable congestion control protocol module. The set of all application flows form a macroflow. Based on quality profiles obtained by the OQAM, the inter-stream adaptation module (ISAM) apportions the session bandwidth by dictating the transmission rate of each flow.

In this work we assume that the participating flows are hierarchically encoded. With hierarchical encoding the original signal is stripped down to a number of complementary layers of increasing quality and the sender is transmitting as many layers as can be fitted into the given network bandwidth.

The frequency of inter-stream adaptation is very important to the efficiency of the mechanism. Running too frequently may cause undesirable quality fluctuations. On the other hand, reducing the frequency may result in bad responsiveness of the method and sub-optimal results. We propose the *video scene* boundaries as suitable adaptation points. A video scene is typically perceived as the number of consecutive frames within a video sequence that do not show significant changes in the video content. Within a video scene or shot the camera action may be fixed or may exhibit a number of relatively uniform changes like, panning, zooming tracking, etc. Shot transitions may be recognised by abrupt transitions of the camera action (usually due to the video editing process) or

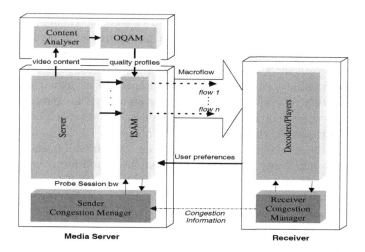

Fig. 1. Model schema of content-based inter-stream session bandwidth sharing archi-tecture. A media server transmits an ensemble of flows (macroflow) to a receiver. The Congestion Manager is probed at appropriate time intervals by the inter-stream adap-tation module (ISAM) to provide the nominal session bandwidth. The ISAM is using the objective quality profiles obtained from the Objective Quality assessment module (OQAM) for each stream to apportion the session bandwidth accordingly.

gradual transitions. Efficient techniques of scene boundary identification have been extensively investigated, like pixel differences, histograms, motion vector and block matching techniques [3]. Among them, of special interest are those that operate on the compressed sequence as they are less computational inten-sive and can operate in real-time [4], [9]. These methods have shown to produce quite accurate results.

From the above, it follows that scenes are the elementary building blocks of video. It is expected that under a given bit-rate allocation, the levels of per-ceived quality do not change considerably within a scene, but scene changes cause considerable changes in perceived quality, especially when the content fea-tures (spatial and motion energy) change a lot between subsequent scenes. As a consequence, there will also be a significant difference in the corresponding (objectively acquired) quality scores for those successive scenes that justifies a re-scheduling of the transmission bit-rates for the participating flows. For this reason, we choose the scene duration as the adaptation decision time scale, i.e., the inter-stream allocation operates when a scene cut occurs in any of the partic-ipating flows. This effectively emulates the process of a user continuously evalu-ating the perceived quality by means of a side slider; the user moves the slider up or down whenever a noticeable change in quality occurs. Characteristic time du-rations of video shots range from 2 to 10 sec or more, in typical video sequences (news, sports, movies, etc.). In several cases, however, the scene duration may be much shorter (e.g., in TV commercials or video clips where we observe rapid scene alternations), or much longer (like in video-conferencing applications). In the case of many successive short scenes an aggregation of numerous short scenes to a longer one and quality-assessment of that longer scene seems to be a rational approach as very short shots cannot have a great (positive or negative) impact on perceived quality, and in any case this impact (if negative) will be reflected in the quality score value of the aggregate scene by the spatial and temporal collapsing process. For longer duration scenes, the approach is to break them down to more scenes with duration 8-10 sec[1].

Besides the scene-based adaptation, the TCP-friendly session bandwidth share is also taken into consideration when there is either a need to drop the aggregate transmission rate, or when there is a bandwidth increase that could accommodate the addition of further layers. Thus, the inter-stream bandwidth adaptation process is triggered when any of the following holds:

1. The content analyser has detected a new scene boundary in any of the participating flows.
2. The nominal bandwidth available to the session is less than the total bandwidth consumption of all the currently transmitted layers of the flows. In this case, some layers need to be dropped, and the inter-stream adaptation will pick those that will minimise the effect on total quality.
3. The bandwidth available to the session is enough to add a new layer from (at least one of) the participating flows.

Obviously, (2) and (3) above follow an aggressive approach on dropping and adding layers, that may affect the smoothness of presentation. This can be tackled by more sophisticated transmission, add/drop mechanisms and receiver buffering (e.g., Rejaie's work on quality adaptation [17]).

Assume that the application consists of N different layered streams. For each stream, a *quality profile* exists in the form of 3-tuples $(t, l, Q(t, l))$, where t is the scene index in the video sequence, l means that the stream is encoded with l layers $(1, ..., l)$, and Q the corresponding objectively obtained quality score. We allow for the end-user to set a preference weight to each flow i of the application scenario, w_i, and $\sum_{i=1}^{N} w_i = 1$. Denote by B the aggregate nominal session bandwidth, provided by the companion congestion manager. The aim of the allocation is: for every flow i, calculate c_i that maximise total session utility: $\sum_{i=1}^{N} w_i Q_i(c_i)$, subject to: $\sum_{i=1}^{N} R_i(c_i) \leq B$, where $c_i = 0, 1, ..., L$ denotes the number of allocated layers for stream i, and R_i is the cumulative bandwidth requirement for c_i layers of stream i. This belongs to the general *knapsack problem*, where B is the knapsack size, R and Q the object's size and value respectively, and is solved by doing an exhaustive search on all (R_i, Q_i) pairs. This does not induce a significant computational burden as the number of pairs is usually restricted. When this number is high (i.e., when we have many participating flows), then a greedy, near-optimal solution was presented in [10] based on [16].

---

[1] This duration is proposed by video quality experts in order to alleviate the "recency effect" phenomenon in subjective quality evaluation, according to which, the quality levels of the recent past dominate the overall subjective score

4   Experimental Results

We tested our approach through a series of trace-driven simulations using the ns-2 network simulator [14]. In order to generate various source content dynamics between the participating flows, we used a number of different video sequences that cover a reasonably broad range of video content activities: head and shoulders, news, TV commercials, sports, movies, etc., that feature different levels of camera operations and spatio-temporal activity. Table 1 summarises the main features of the video sequences[2] used. Instead of using a scene cut detection algorithm, we manually processed the sequences for scenes in order to get an accurate detection of shot boundaries.

The video sequences were encoded to up to seven layers with cumulative bit-rates from 64 Kbps up to 2 Mbps using a H.263+ layered encoder [13]. Currently, the OQAM assesses the quality of the video material off-line; the encoded and original versions of these video sequences were processed off-line to generate the objective quality profiles.

Although the inter-stream adaptation mechanism is independent of the congestion control protocol used, from a number of available TCP-friendly protocols we chose the TFRC protocol [7] because its equation-based rate varies less aggressively than a strictly AIMD mechanism; continuous-media streams benefit when the available bit-rate varies more smoothly. The TFRC module in ns-2 was utilised to perform session-level congestion control. The network topology consists of a media server concurrently transmitting a number of video flows[3] to a receiver behind a single bottleneck link with 15 Mbps link capacity, 50 ms propagation delay, and drop-tail queue with size set to the bandwidth delay product. The flows share the bottleneck link with web-like (self-similar) background traffic, generated by using numerous Pareto ON/OFF CBR sources. The mean ON and OFF time is 1 sec and 2 sec respectively, and the average transmission rate 500 Kbps. The number of background connections is varied between 30 and 70. Each session flow in the simulation was realised by continuously selecting one of the video clips shown on Table 1 at random.

We compare the content-aware quality allocation mechanism we proposed with a proportional allocation, where within the session, each flow is allocated a bandwidth share proportional to its (user) preference weight. In order to highlight the benefits of integrated congestion control combined with content-based quality adaptation both in terms of improved perceived quality and proper congestion behaviour and consistency, we also calculate the total quality and aggregate bandwidth in the case where the individual streams of the session are transmitted as independent TCP-friendly (TFRC [7] in simulations) flows, as in the case of the current Internet. Each simulation ran for 360 sec. All the results presented are averages of 10 runs. Every simulation run corresponds to two dif-

---

[2] Some of these sequences can be found on the VQEG site, at http://www-ext.crc.ca/vqeg/frames.html

[3] In the experiments presented here, this number is four. The corresponding preference weights of these four flows were set to 0.2, 0.4, 0.2 and 0.2 respectively.

ferent simulations, one for integrated congestion control session and one where the session flows are transmitted independently.

Table 1. Video sequences used in simulations

Sequence	Frames	Features	No of scenes
TV commercial 1	770	Abrupt scene changes, modest motion	10
Claire	495	Head & shoulders, no background	1
Mobile & Calendar	125	Rich colours, some movement	1
F1 car	220	Fast movement, saturated colours	1
Fries	220	Movie, fast camera panning	2
Canoa valsesia	220	High details, movement in different directions	2
Jack&Box	145	Rich colours, partial motion	1
Miss America	150	Head & shoulders, no background	1
Why	1820	TV commercial, rapid scene changes, motion	53
Salesman	450	Head & shoulders, background	1

Figure 2 depicts the average quality gain over the simulation duration of the content-aware quality allocation against a proportionally weighted allocation and against the aggregate quality of independent TFRC flows for different levels of network load (different numbers of background connections). The error bars present the 0.1 and 0.9-quantiles. The graph shows that there is a consistent improvement in session quality when flows are scheduled based on their content and quality dynamics, as opposed to a proportional scheduling based only on the preference weights of the individual streams. However, the aggregate quality of the independent TCP-friendly set of flows outweighs that of content-aware allocation at higher network loads (shown by negative gain values). This is not surprising, because, as shown in Figure 3, the average aggregate throughput obtained by the independent TFRC flows is significantly larger than that of the integrated session, since the integrated session is actually behaving as a single TCP-friendly flow, and its increase and decrease coefficients are much smaller that a set of multiple flows, as mentioned in [1], to ensure that a group of connections between two hosts behave socially and less aggressively. The benefit of content-aware quality adaptation in this case is also depicted in Figure 3. Although the aggregate throughput of the independent flows is significantly higher, the aggregate quality gain percentage is not equally high; it is rather to the favour of the content-aware mechanism. The quality advantage of the content-aware mechanism is more evident at higher network loads; the mean aggregate quality gain of the independent flows is $\approx 7\%$ in comparison with the content-aware allocation, but at the expense of an average $\approx 33\%$ increased bandwidth.

4.1   Smoothness of Presentation Quality

Layered encoding provides a coarse-grain control on video quality: the original signal is split into cumulative layers, the sender transmits a subset of the layers so that the resource constraint is met. As the bit-rate available to the

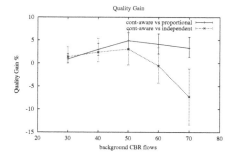
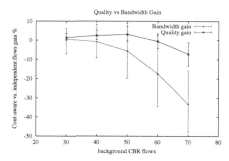

Fig. 2. Total average session quality gain for different levels of network load for the content-aware allocation vs. proportional allocation and aggregate quality of four independent TFRC flows. Error bars show the 0.1 and 0.9-quantiles. (Values below zero show a negative gain, that is explained in Figure 3)

Fig. 3. Average gain percentage for the aggregate session quality and session throughput for the content-aware vs. set of four independent TFRC flows. Error bars show the 0.1 and 0.9-quantiles. In comparison to the integrated session, the independent TFRC flows do not achieve an aggregate quality gain that is as high as their aggregate throughput gain percentage.

session is subject to significant variations the number of layers that are transmitted inevitably changes; this leads to quality fluctuations when layers are added/dropped. When layers are added/dropped frequently, the fluctuations in quality may become disturbing to the human viewer. Receiver buffering together with sophisticated transmission of the layers can alleviate the problem [12], [17]. As the content-aware adaptation mechanism described above involves an extra condition (when a scene cut occurs) for a re-assignment of the transmitted layers for the streams of the session, we try to identify its effect on the smoothness of the individual flows.

Figure 4 shows the coefficient of variance of the number of transmitted layers for each of the four streams of the session for the experiments described above. Clearly, the extra triggering condition for inter-stream adaptation when a scene cut appears in any of the participating flows, increases the number of layer changes for the content-aware mechanism. However, we believe that the frequency of layer changes is not always a representative measure of quality smoothness for a stream. We need to define a smoothness metric that is related to the objective quality of a flow, thus representative of the actual perceived quality. Figure 5 depicts the coefficient of variance of each stream's objective quality over different network loads for the four flows of the simulated session. In contrast to what conveyed from Figure 4, the fluctuation of quality for all the streams within the content-aware session is lower for most of the cases. This is a reward for accounting for the time-varying quality contribution of each stream and by also enabling integrated congestion control, thus allowing for co-operation and appropriate multiplexing among the participating flows.

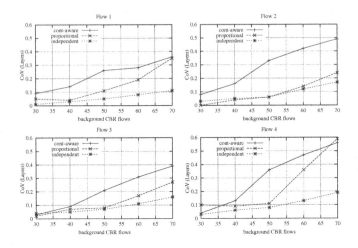

Fig. 4. Coefficient of variance of layer changes for each flow of the session for the content-aware allocation, weighted proportional allocation, and independent flows

5   Conclusion

In this paper we argued for the benefits of incorporating the perceived quality of encoded multimedia in the congestion adaptation process. The perceived quality of multimedia material can be quite accurately measured using objective quality assessment methods that employ properties of the human visual system. Significant research in this area has produced several proposals that demonstrate high correlation with subjective quality assessment. In this way the costly and inflexible process of subjective quality evaluation (like MOS) can by bypassed and replaced with consistent quality scoring mechanisms.

For content-rich Internet applications that involve the transmission of multiple concurrent unicast continuous media flows we outlined the benefits of integrated congestion management as it allows flows to co-operate rather than compete for network resources, and also offers the capability for efficient utilisation of the available bandwidth. We argued that multimedia quality is highly dependent on its content features and complexity and implemented an objective quality assessment metric based on the ITS-metric [24] to assess the quality of encoded video at the scene level. We introduced the video scene as a suitable adaptation time scale for our approach as it conveys interesting properties (such as relatively constant quality throughout its duration). We then described a mechanism that apportions the TCP-friendly bit rate budget of the session among its flows by considering the time-varying utility of each participating flow, measured by the objective metric deployed, so that the overall aggregate quality is maximised. We conducted several trace-driven simulations to compare the scheme with two alternatives: one that employs a proportional allocation based on user preference weights, within an integrated session and another where the participating flows are independent TCP-friendly flows. For both cases we showed that integrated

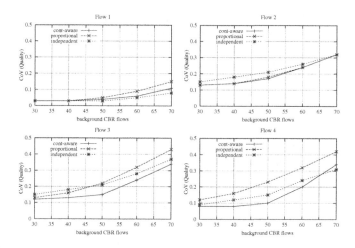

Fig. 5. Coefficient of variance of objective quality for each flow of the session for the content-aware allocation, weighted proportional allocation, and independent flows

congestion control together with an appropriate quality-based scheduling mechanism can result in improved quality and, more significantly, wiser utilisation of the session bandwidth. We also showed that flows within the content-aware session do not exhibit higher quality fluctuations, a usually disturbing phenomenon, despite the more frequent layer changes.

Our scene-based adaptation is based on the fact that the quality of encoded video does not change significantly within the duration of a scene. We plan to investigate whether considering successive scenes as independent entities for quality assessment, which is an assumption of our work, produces unbiased quality scores or if any potential interdependencies would invalidate the assumption.

References

1. Balakrishnan, H., Rahul, H S., and Seshan, S. An integrated congestion management architecture for Internet hosts. In Proc. of ACM SIGCOMM 99, Cambridge, MA. Sep. 1999.
2. Balakrishnan, H., and Seshan, S. The congestion manager. Internet draft, draft-balakrishnan-cm-04.txt, May 2001.
3. Boreczky, J., and Rowe, L. A. Comparison of video shot boundary detection techniques. In Storage and Retrieval for Image and Video Databases IV. I.K. Sethi and R. C. Jain, Editors, Proc. of SPIE 2670, pp. 170-179. 1996.
4. Feng, J., Lo, K.-T., and Mehpour, H. Scene change detection algorithm for MPEG video sequence. In Proc. of ICIP 96, vol. 2, pp 821-824. 1996.
5. Floyd, S., and Fall, K. Promoting the use of end-to-end congestion control in the Internet. In IEEE/ACM Trans. on Networking, 7(4), pp. 458-472. Aug. 1999.
6. Floyd, S. Congestion control principles. Internet draft, draft-floyd-cong-01.txt, Jan. 2000.

7. Floyd., S., Handley, M., a nd Padhye, J. Equation-based congestion control for unicast applications. In ACM SIGCOMM 2000. Stockholm, Sweden, Aug. 26 - Sep. 1, 2000.
8. Lambrecht, C., and Verscheure, O. Perceptual quality measure using a spatio-temporal model of the human visual system. In Proc. of SPIE Digital Video Compression: Algorithms and Technologies, vol. 2668, pp.450-461. San Jose. Feb. 1996.
9. Liu, H.-C., and Zick, G. Automatic determination of scene changes in MPEG compressed video. In IEEE Intl. Symposium on Circuits and Systems, vol. 1, pp. 764-767. Seattle, USA. 1995.
10. Miras, D., Jacobs, R., and Hardman, V. Utility based inter-stream adaptation of layered streams in a multiple-flow IP session. In IDMS 2000, LNCS 1905. Oct. 17-20, 2000, Eschede, The Netherlands.
11. Mohamed, S., Cervantes-Perez, F., and Afifi, H. Integrating network measurements and speech quality subjective scores for control purposes. In Proc. of IEEE Infocom 2001. Anchorage, Alaska, USA. April 24-26, 2001.
12. Nelakuditi, S., Harinath, R. R., Kusmierek, E., and Zhang, Z.-L. Providing smoother quality layered video stream. In Proc. of NOSSDAV 2000. Chaper Hill, North Caroline, USA. June 2000.
13. Nilsson, M., Dalby, D., and O'Donnell, J. Layered audio-visual coding for multicast distribution on IP networks. In 6th Intl. Conf. on Multimedia Computing and Systems. June 7-11, 1999.
14. -. UCB/LBNL/VINT network nimulator, ns-2. Available at http://www-mash.cs.berkeley.edu/ns/. 1998.
15. Padmanabhan, V. Coordinated congestion management and bandwidth sharing for heterogeneous data streams. In Proc. of NOSSDAV '99. Basking Ridge, NJ, June 1999.
16. Rajkumar, R., Lee, C., Lehoczky, J., and Siewiorek, D. A resource allocation model for QoS management. In Proc. of the IEEE Real-time Systems Symposium. Dec. 1997.
17. Rejaie, R. and Handley, M. Quality adaptation for congestion controlled video playback over the Internet. In Proc. of ACM SIGCOMM 99. Harvard Univ., Cambridge, MA, USA. Aug. 31-Sep. 3, 1999.
18. Rejaie, R., Handely, M., and Estrin, D. RAP: An end-to-end rate-based congestion control mechanism for real-time streams in the Internet. In Proceedings of IEEE Infocom'99 , New York, NY., March 1999.
19. Rohaly, A., Libert, J., Corriveau, P., and Webster, A. (eds.). Final Report from the Video Quality Experts Group on the Validation of Objective Models of Video Quality Assessment. Apr. 2000. Available at ftp://ftp.crc.ca/crc/vqeg
20. Tan, K. T., and Ghanbari, M. A multi-metric objective quality measurement model for MPEG video. In IEEE Trans. on Cicruits and Systems for Video Technology, vol. 10, no. 7, pp. 1208-1213. Oct. 2000.
21. Touch, J. TCP control block independence. RFC 2149, April 1997.
22. Webster, A., et al. An objective video quality assessment system based on human perception. In Proc. of SPIE Human Vision, Visual Processing and Digital Display, vol. 1913, pp. 15-26. San Jose, CA, 1993.
23. Winkler, S. Quality metric design: A closer look. In Proc. if SPIE Human Vision and Electronic Imaging, vol. 3644, pp. 175-184, San Jose, CA, 1999.
24. Wolf, S., and Pinson, M. Spatial-temporal distortion metrics for in-service quality monitoring of any digital video system. In SPIE International Symposium on Voice, Video and Data Communications. Boston, MA. Sep.1999.

The Minimal Buffering Requirements of Congestion Controlled Interactive Multimedia Applications

Kang Li[1], Charles Krasic[1], Jonathan Walpole[1], Molly H. Shor[2], and Calton Pu[3]

[1]Oregon Graduate Institute, Department of Computer Science and Engineering
{kangli, krasic, walpole}@cse.ogi.edu

[2]Oregon State University, Electrical and Computer Engineering Department
shor@ece.orst.edu

[3]Georgia Institute of Technology, College of Computing
calton@cc.gatech.edu

Abstract. This paper uses analysis and experiments to study the minimal buffering requirements of congestion controlled multimedia applications. Applications in the Internet must use congestion control protocols, which vary transmission rates according to network conditions. To produce a smooth perceptual quality, multimedia applications use buffering and rate adaptations to compensate these rate oscillations. While several adaptation policies are available, they require different amounts of buffering at end-hosts. We study the relationship between buffering requirements and adaptation policies. In particular, we focus on a widely pursued policy that adapts an application's sending rate exactly to the average available bandwidth to maximize throughput. Under this adaptation policy, at least a minimal amount of buffering is required to smooth the rate oscillation inherent in congestion control, and we view this minimal buffering requirement as a cost of maximizing throughput. We derive the minimal buffering requirement for this policy assuming that applications use an additive-increase-and-multiplicative-decrease (AIMD) algorithm for congestion control. The result shows the relationship between parameters of AIMD algorithms and the delay cost. We show that the buffering requirement is proportional to the parameters of the AIMD algorithm and quadratic to the application's sending rate and round-trip-time. We verify this relationship through experiments. Our results indicate that adaptation policies that maximize throughput are not suitable for interactive applications with high bit rates or long round-trip-times.

1 Introduction

Interactive multimedia applications, such as videoconferencing and IP telephony, are becoming important components of the Internet. Unlike traditional broadcast networks, the modern Internet is highly dynamic and is characterized by rapidly changing conditions. Applications must use congestion control protocols to react to the dynamics of the Internet in order to maintain its stability [1].

TCP is the de-facto standard transport protocol for bulk data transfer in the Internet. However, it does not work well for interactive multimedia applications. Its

D. Shepherd et al. (Eds.): IDMS 2001, LNCS 2158, pp. 181-192, 2001.

retransmissions and drastic rate adjustments can cause significant delays for applications. In recent years, researchers have proposed various TCP-friendly congestion control protocols, such as equation-based congestion control [2] and general *additive-increase-and-multiplicative-decrease (AIMD)* based congestion control [3]. These have significantly improved the performance of multimedia applications over the Internet [4], and flows of these protocols interact well with other TCP traffic. However, using TCP-friendly congestion control reduces but does not remove the oscillations in the transmission rate.

The rate oscillations of congestion control protocols are unavoidable because of the Internet dynamics and the nature of congestion control algorithms. The Internet dynamic is a result of the huge variation in applications, users, and usage patterns [5,6]. As a result, the Internet bandwidth share of an application varies with time. In addition, congestion control protocols must probe the network for available bandwidth. The process of probing for bandwidth and reacting to observed congestion induces oscillations in the achievable transmission rate, and is an integral part of the nature of all end-to-end congestion management algorithms.

Multimedia applications often use buffering at the receiver side to smooth these rate oscillations because users prefer smooth playback rates to the variable rate of the network transmission. In addition to buffering, multimedia applications adjust their playback quality based on the available transmission rate. This mechanism is known as quality-of-service (QoS) adaptation, which can be performed to adjust an application's sending rate (as well as playback rate) in a number of ways [7, 8,9].

In this paper, we study the buffering requirements of different *adaptation policies*. An adaptation policy is an application's way of estimating the network transmission rate and adjusting its transmission rate to match. Adaptation policies have significant impacts on buffering requirements. A sluggish adaptation policy that loosely tracks the network transmission rate requires a large amount of buffering to sustain the application's playback rate when the network transmission rate drops. On the other hand, an aggressive adaptation that tracks the network transmission rate closely requires less buffering.

We have noticed a trend of research toward adaptation policies that try to fully utilize the available bandwidth while preserves a smooth playback quality. Several existing papers [7, 10, 11] have described mechanisms, such as smart buffer management and fine-grained adaptation, to push the adaptation toward the direction of maximizing throughput. These works are mainly in the context of streaming media over the Internet, and aim to optimize bandwidth efficiency. Without inspecting the detailed effects of this adaptation policy, one might consider using it for interactive multimedia applications. However, we believe there is a cost associated with fully utilizing the achievable transmission rate. This cost is the buffering delay required to smooth the inherent rate oscillations of congestion control protocols. For interactive multimedia applications this cost may not be affordable.

In this paper, we derive the minimal buffering required to smooth the inherent rate oscillations of a congestion control protocol. We assume applications use general AIMD (GAIMD) based congestion control protocols. GAIMD congestion control protocols use TCP's AIMD algorithm but with an arbitrary pair of increase/decrease parameters (α, β). Throughout this paper, we use *AIMD(α, β)* to indicate a GAIMD-based congestion-controlled flow with (α,β) as parameters. For example, TCP's congestion control uses AIMD(1,1/2).

Our result shows that the minimal buffering requirement is proportional to the increment parameter α when the AIMD-based congestion control is TCP-friendly[1]. And more importantly, the buffering requirement increases quadratically with increases in rate and round-trip-time (RTT). This result indicates that using a small increment parameter α can reduce the buffering requirement, but the effect is limited as rate or RTT increases.

The rest of the paper is organized as follows. In Section 2, we describe the architecture of our target application, and explain how it adapts. In Section 3, we describe the general AIMD algorithm, and present an analytical derivation of its buffering requirement. In Section 4, we present our experimental architecture and results. Finally, Section 5 concludes the paper and outlines some future work.

2 Buffering and Adaptations

This section presents the structure of our target application, outlines how adaptation and buffering are used, and then describes the relationships between various adaptation policies and their minimal buffering requirements.

2.1 Application Structure

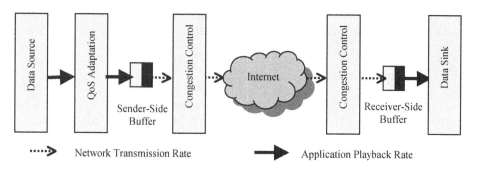

Fig.1. A QoS-Adaptive Application over the Internet

Figure 1 describes our target application's structure[1]. It includes a data source (e.g., a video camera) and a data sink (e.g., a display) connected via the Internet. The sender side generates data on the fly and sends data to the congestion control protocol through a buffer. Data is transmitted over the Internet, with transmission rate limited by the congestion control protocol, and is put into a receiver side buffer. The data sink fetches data from the buffer and presents it to users.

---

[1] We assume the application has only one-way traffic. A typical interactive application usually involves two-way traffic, which can be divided to two applications with one-way traffic but with tight dependency on each other.

The transmission rate over the Internet oscillates over time. To achieve a stable playback quality at the data sink, receiver-side buffering and a sender-side adaptation mechanism are used. For simplicity, we assume that a constant playback quality (in application terms) maps to a constant bit rate (CBR). Thus, the users' preference of constant playback quality maps to the preference of a constant draining rate from the receiver-side buffer.

The receiver delays the start of playback at the data sink side until enough data has been accumulated in the receiver-side buffer, to allow the sink to keep playing for a while even when the network transmission rate drops below the playback rate. As long as the network transmission rate can catch up before the receiver-side buffer reaches empty, the user would not perceive any network rate oscillation. Once the transmission rate is higher than the playback rate, the buffer will start to fill again.

Determining what data to send and how to fill the buffer is complex. Applications require smart buffer filling strategies so that all buffered data are useful to compensate for network rate reductions in the future. Since the buffer management is not the focus of our work, we simply assume that the application can fully utilize all the buffered data. Studies of smart buffer management strategies can be found in recent research work [10, 11].

To reduce the buffering requirements, the target application makes QoS adaptation to adjust its sending rate according to the network transmission rate. We assume that the adaptation is fine-grain layer-based, and the application can adapt its rate closely to the network transmission rate. Several research works have shown ways of matching application rates to network rates using fine-grained adaptations. For example, Jacobs et al. [7] adapt encoding parameters according to the available bandwidth, Krasic et al. [8] propose a priority-based encoding mechanism and make a scalable rate adjustment for video streams, and more recently, Byers et al. apply a fine-grained rate adaptation [9] to multicast environments.

2.2 Adaptation Policies

For layer-based adaptations, adaptation policies are rules determining when a layer should be added or removed. Buffering requirements are closely related to how the application adapts its rate. In this section, we use examples to show this relationship. Figure 2 shows four adaptation policies with the same saw-tooth shape transmission rate, which is typical of AIMD-based congestion control protocols.

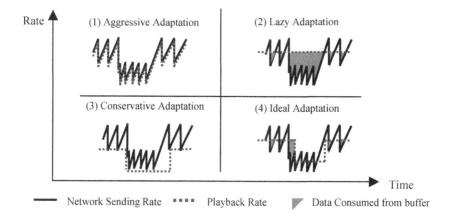

Fig. 2. Buffering Requirements of Different Backing-off Scenarios

Scenario (policy 1) shows an aggressive adaptation that closely tracks the network transmission rate: whenever the instant transmission rate is one layer higher than the current application sending rate, a layer is added; whenever the instant transmission rate is lower than the current application sending rate, a layer is dropped until the sending rate is equal to or lower than the network transmission rate. This adaptation policy does not require any receiver side buffering but results in frequent quality variations.

Scenario (2) illustrates an unresponsive (lazy) adaptation policy that is opposite to the aggressive one illustrated in scenario (1), and produces a very stable playback rate. The policy does not adjust the application's sending rate according to the available network bandwidth. However, it requires a large amount of buffered data to compensate for the network rate variations, even when it chooses a playback rate that is close to the average network transmission rate.

Scenario (3) shows a conservative adaptation policy that always sends data at a rate lower than or equal to the lowest transmission rate in the recent history. This policy makes a layer adjustment decision at every time the congestion control backs off its rate, and maintains a sending rate that equals the lowest rate of the recent saw-tooth shape. With this policy, applications require no receiver-side buffering, and give users a relatively stable playback rate. However, this policy doesn't let the application use all the achievable transmission capacity detected by the congestion control protocol.

Scenario (4) presents an ideal adaptation policy. It is called ideal because it assumes advance knowledge of the network behavior, one saw-tooth ahead of time. Since it has future knowledge, it can choose the average of the next saw-tooth as its sending rate. Therefore it achieves a stable quality (in the next saw-tooth period) and maximizes throughput. The buffering requirement for this ideal adaptation policy is the amount of data needed to smooth one saw-tooth of the network transmission rate.

2.3 Cost for the Ideal Adaptation

This ideal adaptation is not a realistic adaptation policy for applications. However, it presents an interesting case for studying buffering since it exposes the minimal buffering requirement for maximizing throughput. We give a derivation for this buffering requirement in Section 3.

3 Buffering Requirement for General AIMD Congestion Control

An AIMD-based congestion control protocol uses a General AIMD algorithm to limit its sending rate in order to avoid congesting the network. It is a window-based congestion control protocol. That is, it uses a congestion window to limit the maximum amount of data sent out by the application within one round-trip-time.

3.1 GAIMD Algorithm

GAIMD generalizes TCP's AIMD algorithm in the following way:

$$
\begin{cases}
\text{Additive Increase:} & W_{t+RTT} \leftarrow W_t + \alpha \times MSS; \quad \alpha > 0 \quad (1) \\
\text{Multiplicative Decrease:} & W_{t+\delta} \leftarrow \beta \times W_t; \quad\quad\quad 0 < \beta < 1 \quad (2)
\end{cases}
$$

in which W_t is the congestion control's window size (in bytes) at time t, RTT is the round-trip-time, and MSS is the packet size[2]. α and β are parameters of the AIMD algorithm which control the paces of the additive increase and multiplicative back off respectively. The rate behavior of the GAIMD algorithm is similar to the saw-tooth shape of TCP congestion control, which uses an AIMD(1, ½).

3.2 Minimal Buffering Requirement

To determine the buffering requirement for smoothing the rate oscillations, we need to describe how the rate of an AIMD-based protocol evolves over time. Figure 3 shows an AIMD flow with a playback rate R. For an AIMD flow, the achievable rate in a single RTT is its window size divided by the RTT. The window size is controlled by the GAIMD algorithm as follows. If the window size before a back off is W, the achievable network transmission rate for this flow periodically varies from $\beta*W$ / RTT to W/RTT.

---

[2] We assume the congestion control protocol uses a constant packet size and a constant RTT.

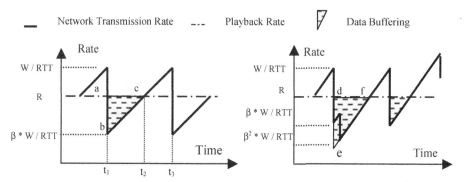

Fig. 3. Buffering Requirement for one Back-off

Fig. 4. Buffering Requirement for Two Continuous Back-offs

According to the ideal adaptation policy, R is the average of the achievable transmission rate. The application fetches data from the receiver-side buffer at this rate, but the network delivers data to the buffer at a rate of the saw-tooth shape. Therefore, the data buffering required to smooth the rate oscillations in one saw-tooth is equal to the area of triangle $\triangle abc$ in Figure 3, which is:

$$\triangle abc = \frac{1}{2\alpha MSS} \times (\frac{1-\beta}{1+\beta})^2 \times R^2 \times RTT^2 \tag{3}$$

The details of the derivation are in the technical report [12].

From Equation (3), we see the buffering requirement is related to the selection of AIMD parameters (α,β). More importantly, this buffering requirement is in proportion to the square of the rate and RTT, which is significant for high rate and long RTT applications. This result indicates that interactive applications might not want to fully utilize all the available bandwidth in order to avoid this buffering cost.

With the amount of buffering indicated by Equation (3), an application will have a stable playback quality within one saw-tooth period. If the bandwidth share is very stable and the saw-tooth shape is uniform over time, then the application keeps a stable quality all the time and utilizes its entire bandwidth share.

However, in the Internet, even a relatively stable bandwidth share would not produce a uniform saw-tooth shape. Very often, back-offs come closely to each other for a while, and spread sparsely for another while. With the ideal adaptation, the application changes its playback quality at every saw-tooth period. If the application prefers a more stable playback quality, it should buffer more data for the rate oscillations caused by closely spaced back-offs.

Figure 4 shows an example of two closely spaced back-offs. If an application wants to keep a stable playback quality when two back-offs happen continuously, the buffering requirement would be at most be the area of triangle $\triangle def$, which is

$$\triangle def = (1+2\beta)^2 \triangle abc = \frac{1}{2\alpha MSS} \times (\frac{1+\beta-2\beta^2}{1+\beta})^2 \times R^2 \times RTT^2 \cdot \tag{4}$$

Similar derivations can be applied to the buffering requirement that is used to smooth more than 2 continuous back-offs.

3.3 Buffering Requirement for AIMD-Based TCP-Friendly Congestion Control Protocols

Early research [13,3] has studied how to make AIMD-based congestion control friendly to TCP traffic in the Internet. A simplified result from the TCP-friendliness study can be expressed as a constraint on its α and β parameters: $\alpha = \dfrac{3(1-\beta)}{1+\beta}$. The derivation is available in [12]. With this α and β relationship, we can refine the buffering requirement in Equation (3) as:

$$\Delta abc = \frac{\alpha}{18MSS} \times R^2 \times RTT^2 \cdot \tag{5}$$

4 Experiments

We make several experiments to verify our derivation of minimal buffering requirements with various pairs of AIMD parameters. All these experiments are conducted in the ns simulator [14].

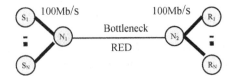

Fig. 5. Basic Experiment Topology

We use the simple topology shown in Figure 5, which has N nodes on each side of a bottleneck link. The bottleneck link uses RED queue management with ECN [15]. Every pair of nodes (S_i, R_i) corresponds to a flow which is either an ECN enabled AIMD-based flow or a UDP flow. The number of flows, the values of the bottleneck link bandwidth and its delay are stated within each experiment.

Each experiment includes two steps. First, we run a non-adaptive infinite source application over an AIMD flow to monitor available rate for the flow. Second, after we have the whole trace of the achievable rate by the AIMD congestion control, we simulate the application's adaptation behavior with this available bandwidth, and compare the buffering requirement of different adaptation policies. In this step, we use a simulated adaptive application, which is a fine-grain layer-encoded application with a rate range of 100Kbps to 1.5Mbps, in constantly spaced layers of 50Kbps.

4.1 Comparisons of Various Adaptation Policies

The first experiment we conducted illustrates the buffering requirements and bandwidth efficiency for various adaptation policies. In this experiment, the bottleneck link bandwidth is set to 1Mbps with 40ms delay. To produce regularly behaved saw-tooth rate shape we run a single AIMD(1,1/2) flow with a 256B packet size. Parallel with this AIMD(1,1/2) flow, a UDP flow runs through this bottleneck link. We adjust the UDP flow's rate to control the available bandwidth of the AIMD(1,1/2) flow. In this experiment, the UDP flow is set to 400Kbps CBR except for a short 10 seconds burst to 600Kbps.

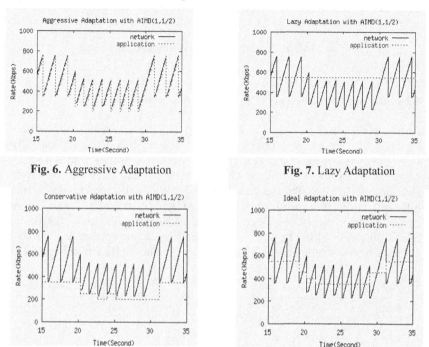

Fig. 6. Aggressive Adaptation   **Fig. 7.** Lazy Adaptation

Fig. 8. Conservative Adaptation   **Fig. 9.** Ideal Adaptation

Figures 6 – 9 show the application rate together with the network transmission rate for each adaptation policy. We summarize the result of this experiment in Table 1. For the buffering requirement, both aggressive and conservative adaptation policies keep the application's sending rate lower than the available network transmission rate, thus they don't need any receiver side buffering. The lazy adaptation has a relatively large buffering requirement, which is related to the duration of transmission rate degradation. In this experiment, a 300KB buffer is about 5 seconds delay for the application. For the ideal adaptation, it requires 7.8KB to smooth its saw-tooth size, which is about 100ms for the AIMD flow with a 600Kbps sending rate. Any other adaptation policy that maximizes the throughput would experience a delay between the delays of the ideal and lazy adaptation policies.

Table 1 also summarizes the bandwidth efficiency and number of rate adjustments that happened during the experiment period shown in Figures 6 – 9. Clearly the conservative adaptation has a relatively stable playback quality, but a low bandwidth efficiency. All the other three policies have a high bandwidth efficiency. The reason for not using 100% bandwidth is that the application is layer-encoded, and its sending rate can only approximate the available bandwidth with a sum of its existing layer rates.

Adaptation Policy	Minimal Buffer Requirement	Bandwidth Efficiency	Number of Quality Adjustments
Aggressive Adaptation	0	92%	105
Conservative Adaptation	0	58%	5
Lazy Adaptation	> 300KB	92%	0
Ideal Adaptation	7.8KB	92%	5

Table 1. Comparison of Various Adaptation Policies

4.2 Buffering Requirements of the Ideal Adaptation Policy

In this experiment, we verify the buffering requirement relationship described by Equation (3). We use only one AIMD flow with a 256B MSS, and one UDP CBR flow. First, we set the bottleneck link bandwidth to 1.5Mbps with a 40ms one-way delay. We vary the rate of the UDP flow to produce available bandwidth from 100Kbps to 1.5Mbps for the AIMD flow. We run this experiment 3 times with different AIMD flow parameters: (1,1/2), (1/3, 4/5), and (1/5, 7/8). The measured buffering requirements are plotted in Figure 10. Second, we give a 1.2Mbps available bandwidth to the AIMD flow and vary the bottleneck propagation delay from 10ms to 120ms. The result of the buffering requirement versus the RTT is in Figure 11.

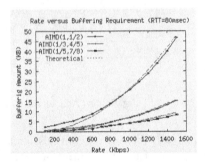
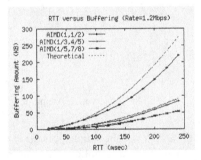

Fig. 10. Rate versus Buffering   **Fig. 11.** RTT versus Buffering

The experiment result shows AIMD parameters have an effect on the minimal buffering requirement. For example, a 1Mbps AIMD(1,1/2) flow on an 80ms RTT path requires more than 20KB buffering. This amount of buffering is equivalent to more than 160ms delay for this flow, which is too large for interactive applications [16]. Choosing a small AIMD parameter pair (α,β) allows the buffering delay experienced by the flow to be reduced. For example, by using AIMD (1/5,7/8), the buffering requirement can be reduced to 5KB, which maps to 40ms delay for this flow.

However, the experiment result also shows that the buffering requirement increases quadratically with rate and RTT, which is problematic for interactive applications with high rate and long RTT. In Figure 10, even with AIMD(1/5,7/8), the buffering delay becomes significant as the application's sending rate gets larger.

RTT has a similar effect on the buffering size as flow rate does, but the case is worse because a large RTT for interactive applications usually corresponds to a small buffering delay budget. For flows with a small RTT, for example 20ms, the resulting buffering delay is less than 10ms for a 1.2Mbps data rate. This indicates that the required minimal buffering is not significant for interactive applications on a metropolitan area network or even a WAN between cities not far away. However, it is problematic for interactive applications across oceans or between coasts within a continent (e.g. 80ms RTT in US). For example, for a flow with 100ms RTT and 1.2Mbps data rate, the required buffering delay is about 300ms, which is much more than most interactive applications can tolerant.

The buffering requirement results measured in this experiment slightly differ from the ones predicted by Equation (3). We believe one reason is that RTT is not constant as we assumed in Equation (3). Another reason is that the implementation of AIMD actually increases its rate sub-linearly rather than linearly, where the derivation of Equation (3) assumes that the additive part of the AIMD algorithm behaves linearly.

Even with this sub-linear increment, the buffering requirement is still quadratic to the application's rate and RTT. This result confirms our claim that interactive applications may not always prefer to maximize their throughputs, since they may come at the expense of unacceptable end-to-end delay.

5 Conclusion and Future Work

In this paper, we have addressed the minimal buffering requirements of adapting the application data rate to the average available bandwidth, which maximizes a multimedia application's throughput. The minimal buffering requirement is used to compensate for the rate oscillations of congestion control protocols. We derived the relationship between the minimal buffer requirements and congestion control's AIMD parameters, application rate, and RTT. Our result indicates that choosing an AIMD-based TCP-friendly congestion control with a small increment parameter can reduce the buffer requirement, because the buffer requirement is proportional to the increment parameter. However, the buffer requirement is also proportional to the square of the application's sending rate and round-trip-time. Thus, adapting application sending rate closely to the average available bandwidth is not a preferable adaptation policy for interactive applications with high rate and long RTT.

In this paper, we studied the buffering requirement of AIMD congestion control. Besides AIMD-based congestion control protocols, several other algorithms like binomial congestion control [17], Equation-based congestion control [2], and TCP emulation at receivers (TEAR) [18] have been proposed to reduce the oscillations in the application sending rate. Evaluation of the buffering requirements of multimedia applications using these protocols is one of our targets for future work.

References

1. Sally Floyd, and Kevin Fall. "Promoting the Use of End-to-End Congestion Control in the Internet" *IEEE/ACM Transactions on Networking*, August 1999.
2. Sally Floyd, Mark Handley, Jitendra Padhye, and Jorg Widmer. "Equation-based Congestion Control for Unicast Applications." In *Proceedings of ACM SIGCOMM 2000*, August 2000.
3. Yang Yang, and Simon Lam. "General AIMD Congestion Control" In *Proceedings of ICNP 2000*, Osaka, Japan, Nov 2000.
4. R. Rejaie, M. Handley, and D. Estrin. "An End-to-End Rate-Based Congestion Control Mechanism for Realtime Streams in the Internet". In *Proceedings of IEEE INFOCOM'99*, Mar, 1999.
5. Mark Allman, Vern Paxson. "On Estimating End-to-End Network Path Properties", In *Proceeding of SIGCOMM'99*, pp. 263-274, 1999.
6. K. Park, G. Kim, and M. Crovella. "On the Relatioinship Between File Sizes, Transport Protocols and Self-Similar Network Traffic". In *Proceedings of ICNP'1996*.
7. S. Jacobs and A. Eleftheriadis. "Providing Video Services over Networks without Quality of Sevice Guarantees". In *Proceedings of World Wide Web Consortium Workshop on Real-time Multimedia and the Web*, 1996.
8. Charles Krasic and Jonathan Walpole. "QoS Scalability for Streamed Media Delivery", OGI CSE Technical Report CSE-99-11, September, 1999
9. John Byers, Michael Luby, and Michael Mitzenmacher. "Fine-Grained Layered Multicast", In *Proceedings of IEEE INFOCOM 2001*, April 2001.
10. Charles Krasic, Jonathan Walpole, Kang Li, and Ashvin Goel. "The Case for Streaming Multimedia with TCP", OGI-Tech-Report 01-003, March, 2001.
11. R. Rejaie, M. Handley, and D. Estrin. "Quality Adaptation for Congestion Controlled Video Playback over the Internet". In *Proceedings of SIGCOMM'99*, Oct., 1999.
12. K. Li, C. Krasic, J. Walpole, M. H. Shor, and C. Pu, "The Minimal Buffering Requirements of Congestion Controlled Multimedia Applications", OGI-Tech-Report 01-008, June, 2001.
13. Sally Floyd, Mark Handley, and Jitendra Padhye. "A comparison of equation-based congestion control and AIMD-based congestion control." Under submission. Available at http://www.aciri.org/tfrc.
14. ns: UCB/LBNL/VINT Network Simulator, http://www-mash.cs.berkeley.edu/ns/ns.html
15. S. Floyd and V. Jacobson, "Random early detection gateways for congestion avoidance", *IEEE/ACM Transactions on Networking*, vol.1, pp.397-413, August 1993.
16. Stuart Cheshire. "Latency and the Quest for Interactivity". White paper for the Synchronous Person-to-Person Interactive Computing Environments Meeting, San Francisco, November 1996. Available at http://www.stuartcheshire.org.
17. D. Bansal and H. Balakrishnan. "Binomial Congestion Control Algorithms", In *Proceedings of INFOCOM 2001*, April 2001.
18. I. Rhee, V. Ozdemir, and Y. Yi. "TEAR: TCP emulation at receivers - flow control for multimedia streaming". http://www.csc.ncsu.edu/eos/users/r/rhee/WWW/export/tear_page.

Video Content Management
Using Logical Content

Nozomu Takahashi, Yuki Wakita, Shigeki Ouchi and Takayuki Kunieda

RICOH Company, Ltd., Image System Business Group, Software Research Center
{nozomu, yuki, shigeki, kunieda}@src.ricoh.co.jp

Abstract. A common video file format is generally used in video content management system composed of modules for archiving, retrieving, and video streaming on a network. However, the file format may not be suitable for these functions. This paper presents a new video content management that uses logical content. Logical content makes it possible to manage a system that may use files of differing formats to store the same content to be used by different modules. Using logical content makes it possible to access physical video files regardless of their formats, and to easily manage video content consisting of multiple physical files. Other modules are able to request the retrieval of a physical file by specifying a logical content ID and its range. Consequently, this system can be designed to be both modularized and extended. We also present an experimental video content management system that verifies the effectiveness of our video content management system.

1 Introduction

A general video content management system such as a video-on-demand system is capable of performing at least the following three functions: video registration, video clip searches, and video clip distribution [1][2][3][4]. Clients are able to register not only video files, but also simple information such as video titles and video duration. The system then generates an index using the information that can be used for retrieval. After receiving the required video clips the client requests the system to perform a search using the clip information as a query. The system returns a result list of video files and the clipped range for each video file. "Clipped range" is the term used to describe the starting and ending time of a video file. The clients choose a video file and its clipped range from the result list for viewing, and the system allows the chosen video clips to be streamed on the network.

Recently, an advanced video content management method using detailed metadata has been developed. The representative metadata is MPEG-7, and is used for retrieving multimedia including video. Work on MPEG-7 began in 1996 in ISO/IEC JTC1/SC29/WG11. It is referred to as a multimedia content description interface [5]. MPEG-7 can contain text information about a video, as well as hierarchically represent a video's structure [6][7], which is an aggregation of shots, scenes, and semantic video parts. For our purposes we will call the video metadata a content description.

D. Shepherd et al. (Eds.): IDMS 2001, LNCS 2158, pp. 193-198, 2001.
© Springer-Verlag Berlin Heidelberg 2001

Thanks to the growth of network technology, videos can now be transmitted over the Internet right into our own homes. There is rising demand for viewing high-quality video not only on LAN, but also over the Internet that makes remote viewing possible. This demand can be met by a system capable of managing files with two types of file formats. The first file format has a high bit-rate for quality, and the other can be streamed over the Internet, but is of lower quality. Because previous video content management systems were built on LAN, they have only been able to manage high-quality file formats. The popularization of digital video cameras and capturing applications ranging from analog video to digital video has simplified video file creation. Users would like to be able to have unnecessary images in videos remain unseen without having to edit the video by hand. Users may also want to manage multiple files as video content and allow each file to overlap. Overlapping occurs when files are recorded using two cameras. Before the tape in the first camera runs out, the second camera starts to record, much like the handing off of a baton in a relay race.

In this paper, we describe a new video content management system that uses logical content to meet the rising demand for advanced video content management systems. Logical content makes it possible to manage a system that may use files of differing formats to store the same content to be used by different modules. Video content is composed of a file or an aggregation of files, which represent a portion of the video content. By making logical content accessible by a logical content ID instead of a file name, our logical content video content management system simplifies the task of video management.

2 Logical Content

Regardless of the format used for storage, the conceptual content of a video can be described as a single "reality." Whether MPEG-1, MPEG-2, DV format or Motion JPEG, the object and the meaning of this reality are independent of the file format, the bit-rate, and the number of composition files, as an be seen in Fig.1. Take for example a video file in which the original format is MPEG-2. Even if we copy the file from the original file and convert the file format from the original file format, these three files still represent the same reality. It must be noted, however, that the converted MPEG-1 file is of lower video quality than the original MPEG-2 file. The concrete content can be called logical content. This logical content has the ability to maintain a content description about a reality.

We would now like to describe the three limitations of the previous video content management systems we mentioned in our introduction.

- It has been difficult for video content management systems to manage files of different format containing the same images. Even if a system is capable of managing multiple file formats of the same reality, they can be differentiated between using identification such as a file name. However, this causes a warp in which the reality has multiple content descriptions because each format file has its own content description.
- It has been impossible to leave extra parts in videos unseen without editing the video.

- Managing overlapping videos has been almost impossible. Methods for representing video content using multiple segmented files are well known, and Reference AVI is an example of one such method. However, this third limitation cannot be solved using the video content management systems currently available.

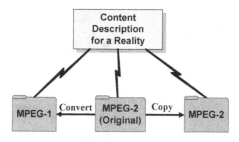

Fig. 1. Basic Concept

Figure 2 illustrates the structure of logical content. Logical content maintains both an ID and the original video content. The video content is composed of either one file or multiple files. Logical content can also maintain other formats for description or distribution over the Internet. The metadata of a reality, namely the content description, is included because it is independent of file format. If the video content is composed of multiple files, it has the each assignment range for the video content.

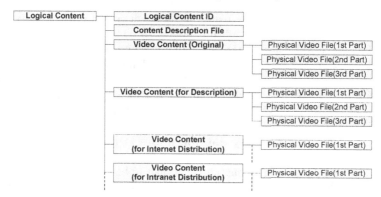

Fig. 2. Structure of Logical Content

Figure 3 illustrates a situation in which two files are assigned to a logical content. The logical content is composed of the first physical file from 00:04:00 to 00:26:00 and the second physical file from 00:02:00 to 00:30:00. The two files are assigned to a logical content with 00:00:00 and 00:22:00 as their respective start times. In this example, the first physical file from 00:00:00 to 00:04:00 and the second physical file from 00:30:00 to 00:32:00 are unseen because it is specified needless by register. The second physical file from 00:00:00 to 00:02:00 is unseen because it is overlapping. The logical content must manage three values of time for each physical file it is assigned. These values are the start time for logical content, the valid start time, and the valid duration.

Our logical content solves the three limitations found in previous video content management systems. The following is a description of the merits of using our new video content management system.

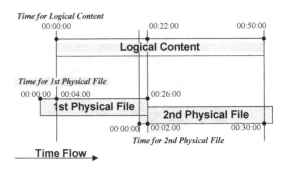

Fig. 3. Logical Content Composed of Two Files

With our system, video content management system developers can provide high modularization and extended design for each functional module. There are various video file formats, and each file format has its own specific features. Take for example video quality and the bit-rate of the file format. If our purpose is to archive videos, we should choose a high-quality video format. A digital video (DV) format, for example, has a video quality that is just as high as that of the quality of digital broadcasting images. On the other hand, if our purpose is to use a streaming format on the limited-bandwidth Internet, formats with a low bit-rate should be used. There are also other features. The DV format and the Motion JPEG without compression between frames provide an easy way to capture a frame image. MPEG-1 has an enormous number of past archives and applications. MPEG-2 is used for digital satellite broadcasting, and its archives are expected to increase in the future. Streaming media is showing rapid improvements in its video quality and implementation for QoS. Our system, which uses logical content, does not require restrictions on the functions or specifications of the file format as long as it is possible to convert from the original format to the format to be used. Even if new video file formats are developed in the future, the system will be capable of easily accepting them by using a converting module. Registration clients only need to specify three kinds time values for unseen, i.e. overlapping physical file parts rather than editing the extra physical file parts by hand. Clients can also execute overlapping parts rather than remove overlapping file parts.

Along with these merits also come a few demerits. One such demerit is the redundancy of multiple files representing the same reality. This influences the quantity of storage device use. Another demerit is that during the registration process a lot of time is spent converting each file format from the original file format. However, these are not serious problems because storage devices are expected to see a rapid reduction in price, as well as an increase in capacity, and we also expect that the conversion process can be made faster by execution the conversion and other processes simultaneously. So as you can see, the merits of our system far outweigh its demerits.

3   Experimental Video Content Management System

We developed an experimental video content management system that uses logical content. The framework for this system is shown in Fig. 4. We describe four functional modules: the content management sub-system, the content retrieval sub-system, the content distribution sub-system, and the content description tool.

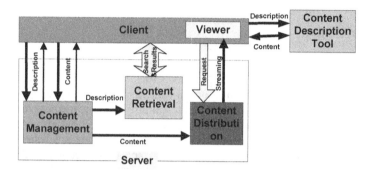

Fig. 4. Video Content Management Framework

Content Management Sub-system. This sub-system, which uses logical content, plays the role of a file server by managing physical video files and content description files. When the client requests that an original content be registered, the structure of the logical content and its ID are generated. At the same time, this sub-system converts the original files to other format files for other modules using the general format converter application products. These new converted files are then added to the structure. This sub-system can accept requests to retrieve physical files by using the logical content ID and a format-type name. If necessary, this can also be accomplished using the clipped range.

Content Retrieval Sub-system. This sub-system constructs a database with an index of the content descriptions registered by the content management sub-system, and this returns a result list of the logical content IDs and the clipping range to the client.

Content Distribution Sub-system. This sub-system can stream requested video clips by using the logical content ID and the clipped range. This sub-system requires that a video clip file format be streamed on a network. The adopted file format can be streamed at a transmission-rate of 64 kbps.

Content Description Tool. This tool is used to generate content descriptions. Users can input text describing a video's content, which is compliant with MPEG-7, while viewing the video. The video format is MPEG-1. This tool can also automatically extract the shot-changing points of the video structure.

This experimental system targets users who have access to the Internet. The video content used was about an acrobatic airplane show. We provided a Web server between the system and the client in the framework (Fig.4) for the Internet. We captured all master analog tapes and used them to generate MPEG-1 files as original video content. The content management sub-system needed to manage three files for the logical content. For registration, the content management sub-system automatically converted the original format to a streaming format.

4 Conclusion

We have described a new video content management system that uses logical content. Logical content structurally manages video files that have different formats or bit-rates, but are of the same content. Logical content makes it possible to access physical video files regardless of the format, and to simplify the management of video content consisting of multiple physical files not only providing QoS but also providing access to the appropriate format for applications. These functions are beneficial in actual infrastructure, where various formats exist and the acceptable format for the applications are limited. Other modules request retrieval of physical files by specifying a logical content ID and its range. Consequently, the system can be designed to be both modularized and extended. We have also discussed an experimental video content management system that verifies the effectiveness of our video content management system.

In the future, we plan to extend the use of logical content by:

- Automatically choosing a suitable format for network bandwidth using an intelligent distribution sub-system like QoS
- Enabling logical content to reference a physical file maintained by other logical content

References

1. J. Xia, J.S. Jin, "Internet video-on-demand e-commerce system based on multilevel video metadata," *Proceeding of SPIE Volume 4210*, Boston, USA, pp. 331-340, November 2000.
2. S.-Y. Lee, H.-M. Kao, "Video indexing: an approach based on moving object and track," *Proc. of SPIE Volume 1908*, San Jose, California, pp.25-36, February 1993.
3. B.V. Levinaise-Obadia, W.J. Christmas, J. Kittler, K. Messer, Y. Yusoff, "OVID: toward object-based video retrieval," *Proc. of SPIE Volume 3972*, San Jose, California, pp. 532-543, January 2000.
4. J.C.-L. Liu, D.H.C. Du, S.S.Y. Shim, J. Hsieh, M.-J. Lin, "Design and Evaluation of a Generic Software Architecture for on-Demand Video Servers," *IEEE Trans. on Knowledge and Data Engineering*, pp. 406-424, May/June, 1999.
5. Multimedia Description Schemes (MDS) Group, "Text of ISO/IEC 15938-5/CD Information Technology - Multimedia Content Description Interface - Part 5 Multimedia Description Schemes," *ISO/IEC JTC 1/SC 29/WG 11/N3966*, Singapore, March 2001.
6. H.J. Zhang, C.Y. Low, S.W. Smoliar, J.H. Wu, "Video Parsing, Retrieval and Browsing: An Integrated and Content-Based Solution," *Proc. ACM Multimedia '95*, San Francisco, pp. 15-24, 1995.
7. H. Ueda, T. Miyataka, "Automatic Scene Separation and Tree Structure GUI for Video Editing," *Proceeding ACM Multimedia '96*, Boston, pp. 405-406, 1996.

Adaptive Clustering Using Mobile Agents in Wireless Ad-Hoc Networks

Robert Sugar, Sandor Imre

Department of Telecommunications
Budapest University of Technology and Economics
H-1117. Pazmany Peter setany 1/D, Budapest, Hungary
{sugar,imre}@hit.bme.hu

Abstract. A Mobile ad-hoc network is a multihop wireless network, where nodes communicate with each other without any pre-deployed infrastructure. The most important problem on such dynamic networks is to find routing algorithms well performing in most cases. Cluster based algorithms are among the most effective and scaleable approaches. Up till now creation and maintenance clusters were mostly based on basic heuristic methods. Deploying mobile agents has several advantages in the ad-hoc environment due to their flexible, robust and autonomous nature, and their use seems promising for the clustering problem as well. In our proposed architecture every cluster has a clustering agent that is capable of making membership modification decisions, transferring nodes and splitting or merging clusters. Communication is used only between neighbouring agents to reduce the signalling overhead. Clustering decisions can be based on several network parameters modified by an adaptation mechanism to provide adequate performance even under dynamic conditions.

1 Introduction

Wireless ad-hoc networks (also known as MANETs) started to draw attention in the recent years. These networks require no fixed infrastructure and can be set up anytime anywhere. Network services are provided by hosts participating in the network, therefore every node acts as a packet forwarding router. MANETs can be very useful in ad-hoc conferencing, in deserted or arctic regions or in extending the coverage of base stations in sparsely populated areas. They may be the only way of communication in a catastrophe situation or in some military applications [1,2].

Several problems exist in MANETs that hinder effective communication. Bandwidth and radio resources are scarce, computing and battery capacity is limited, node mobility is high and link failures are much more frequent than in infrastructure environment. To overcome these problems new methods must be defined in order to allow the successful operation of these networks. The most important task is to find an appropriate routing algorithm that is adaptive, robust and introduces only a relatively small overhead. Several methods were presented and most of them fall into three basic categories [3,4].

D. Shepherd et al. (Eds.): IDMS 2001, LNCS 2158, pp. 199-204, 2001.
© Springer-Verlag Berlin Heidelberg 2001

Pro-active routing aims to maintain a route to every host by setting up and updating routing tables in each node. Examples for such algorithms are AODV (Ad-Hoc on Demand Distance Vector) [5] or WRP (Wireless Routing Protocol) [6]. Reactive or source routing discovers the path to a host only on demand. The source floods the network in search of the destination and chooses the path from which the first packet arrived to the target. Such algorithms are DSR (Dynamic Source Routing) [7] or LMR (Lightweight Mobile Routing) [8].

The third type is the hybrid or cluster based routing, which is a mixture of pro-active and reactive algorithms. The network is divided into several partitions, referred to as clusters or zones. The clusters can contain a special node, called the clusterhead, which routes the packets destined outside of the cluster. This, although creates a bottleneck at the clusterheads, reduces the number of control packets needed, because only the clusterheads have to be informed about changes outside the cluster. Clusters can be either distinct or overlapping. In the latter case the neighbouring clusters can have a common node, referred to as gateways [11]. Other algorithms can be superior to cluster based routing in special situations, but this solution is the most scaleable and adaptive, what is usually more important in such environment than finding optimal routes. Such algorithms are the ZRP (Zone Routing Protocol) [9], the CBRP (Cluster Based Routing Protocol) [10] or CGSR (Clusterhead-Gateway Switch Routing) [11]. During the rest of the paper we focus only on cluster based algorithms.

For the effective functioning of cluster based routing algorithms the size and the membership of the clusters must be chosen carefully. The most important requirement is to keep clusters as stable as possible, because dynamic membership changes need more communication between the clusters in order to provide up-to-date membership information. Long-lived clusters also reduce the probability that a packet will be routed to the previous cluster of the addressed node, thus causing more delay and overhead. Although for stability reasons larger clusters are desirable, large cluster size puts a heavy burden on clusterheads, and hinders the efficient communication within the cluster.

Previously, most of the focus was on the routing algorithms and simple heuristics were used for determining cluster size and membership. In [12,13] clusters are defined as "a set of nodes, where every node is at most two hops away from the others". Probably the most comprehensive study on this topic was the (α, t) clustering [14] that based clustering on user mobility and node availability focusing on selecting the most stable routes. An (α, t) cluster consists of nodes that can reach any other node in the cluster for a t time with at least the probability of α. These algorithms, although they are simple and need little signalling, lack the needed scalability and adaptability, and only use knowledge of one type of the network parameters, such as node connectivity or mobility.

Therefore, a more general, adaptive and scaleable clustering method should be designed that reduces the weaknesses and uses the strength of the previous methods. Since cluster membership changes are less frequent than routing packets, a slight overhead can be tolerated in order to maintain suitable clusters in all situations. In this paper a mobile agent based method is provided that can incorporate the previously defined requirements for effective clustering. Adaptivity is provided in a distributed manner by relatively simple entities showing intelligence as a system as in the case of swarm intelligence [16].

2   Mobile Agents

Mobile agents (MAs) are autonomous, intelligent programs that move through the network, performing actions on their creator's behalf [15]. Deploying mobile agents for network management tasks has several advantages over the traditional methods on large infrastructure networks, as presented in [17,18]. The usage of mobile agents in a wireless ad-hoc environment is even more appealing, because they easily fit into the distributed nature of MANETs, providing adaptivity, flexibility, robustness and even efficiency, which are prime requisites in such environment. Deploying mobile agents for clustering is mostly desirable because one fixed algorithm can rarely prove profitable in all situations.

2.1   Advantages of Agent Technology

The use of mobile agents, however, needs software architecture capable of hosting and executing agents at every node. As most MA platforms (such as Aglets [20] or Voyager [21]) work with Java code, it means that every host must contain a virtual machine and a mobile agent server listening on a specified port. This is not a heavy constraint, because as computational power increases, the overhead of the MA platform will be small enough, and for the equipment with limited capabilities, cheap JVM chips will be available in the near future. Most of the mobile hosts already have a JVM available, for example on the ones using the JINI [19] technology.

Agents can be quite bandwidth efficient due the code to the data phenomenon, which means that the agent arriving to a node can examine a larger portion of data for decision making, as opposed to the cluster-master that would have to retrieve all the data over the network. Java agents are relatively small in size, typically about several ten kilobytes and can be even smaller while migrating if their classes are cached on the targeted host, as in most of the cases. The agent based solution is also more dynamic, because the clustering algorithm is not hard-coded into the clusterheads or the nodes, can be decided at network set-up time and easily changed later on by replacing the agents with new ones or by changing their behaviour patterns.

2.2   Communication between Agents

As the location of agents is not known exactly an effective communication scheme between neighbouring agents must be achieved. In infrastructure networks mobile agent communication is usually facilitated by a directory service, often using CORBA, such as in [21]. It is rather effective, but it needs a centralised directory server, whom the agent must contact, every time it moves. In ad-hoc networks agents can use broadcast mechanisms to find a peer agent, which is relatively cheap due to the shared media. The broadcast can be limited to the target cluster, therefore the wide propagation of the searching packet can be avoided.

3 Agent Based Ad-Hoc Networking

The main purpose of a clustering agent is to collect statistics from its cluster and its neighbouring nodes in order to make correct decisions. It also communicates with neighbouring agents while performing cluster membership modifications, or gathering information about their own clusters. During network set-up many hosts on the network can generate agents to reach an acceptable initial clustering, and start the normal membership control process afterwards.

3.1 Controlling the Size of Clusters

In our scheme, four types of cluster state changes exist: Node transfer between neighbouring clusters, cluster division, cluster merging and node exploration.

Exploration process is very important during network set-up and also serves the robustness and fault tolerance in case of agent faults. It is needed when a host switches off with an agent residing on it, or leaves the connectivity range. When arriving to a host, agents can verify the neighbours of that host, especially the ones in different clusters, in order to check if a serving agent exists for that node, and analyse the timestamp that its agent had left there during the last visit. If it finds that the node has no serving agent or had not been visited for a longer period of time, it will consider the node free and starts the node discovery process either by sending out a new agent or by performing it by itself. In this way agents from the neighbouring clusters can soon repopulate the cluster of a broken agent. Furthermore, newly joined nodes can easily fit into the cluster structure, although they can initiate the node exploration by themselves at start-up as well.

Due to host mobility, changing network conditions or other reasons the agents can decide to move a node into a different cluster. The process can be started by any of the parties, but in most of the cases the previous agent of the node will begin the transfer. The actual decision rule possibilities will be covered in chapter III.B. The initiator of the transfer selects the new cluster of the node and communicates with the agent of that cluster, making a proposition that can be either accepted or rejected. If the answer was positive, the membership change takes effect. In case of rejection the agent can choose a different cluster or a different node for the next transfer attempt.

Dividing clusters may be necessary if the size of the cluster grows and neighbouring clusters refuse node transfers. The domain of the cluster will be separated into two – desirably equal – portions, a new agent will be spawned and new clusterheads will be elected. This procedure enables new clusters to emerge, because otherwise the number of clusters would be constant, as new clusters can exclusively be created by cluster divisions or through the exploration process.

Cluster merging is the contrary operator of cluster division. Both cluster agents can initiate it, but they have to agree on merging to bring the union into effect. The procedure is similar to node transfers, for the selected party must accept a merging proposition. If accepted, the two old clusters will form a new one, one of the agents will terminate and a joint clusterhead will be elected.

3.2 Decision Making Rules

Several network parameters must be taken into account in order to make correct clustering decisions. If the procedure is simple enough it could be solved with a rule based reactive agent. If the numbers of parameters are many, target oriented deliberative agents could be used, which can incorporate the needed intelligence to successfully react to unplanned situations. The parameters that could be taken into account during decision making can be the following: node connectivity, node mobility, node capability and link conditions, maximal and available bandwidth. The initial parameter set could be decided at network start-up time and can be changed by the self-adaptation procedures later on. Agents could define instant triggers, weights for performance evaluation and probabilities for certain actions.

Instant triggers are used if the situation demands immediate action, such as the loss of connectivity or the trashing of the clusterhead. Rules are defined, such as "Initiate the node transfer process with a given probability if the load of the clusterhead is significantly lower than the neighbour's" or "Prefer the highly mobile nodes over the static ones during transfers". When conditions of some rules are met, the defined action is performed with a certain probability. The limits and probabilities are influenced by the adaptation mechanism described in the next chapter .

3.3 Adaptivity

Adaptivity could be based on previous experiences of the agent and the estimated effect of its previous decisions. With the weights of certain network parameters (delays, number of errors or amount control packet flow) agents could construct a general "well-being" function evaluating the state of their cluster, used for feedback purposes. The agent could compare the well-being of its cluster before and after a certain decision. If the action was estimated to be successful, the agent encourages the given modification type (e.g. increase the probability of cluster division due to the danger of a cluster split), and if it was found to be ineffective, it discourages the further changes of the same kind. For adaptive behaviour, the probabilities are adjusted by a degradation parameter, thus recent events have more influence than elder ones.

4 Conclusions and Future Work

In this paper we presented a novel method of using mobile agents in wireless ad-hoc environment. Mobile agents harmonise with the basic principles of ad-hoc networks, their dynamic nature and the distributed architecture. They seem to be promising in the clustering problem due to their flexibility and adaptivity. We pointed out several advantages over the existing methods and proposed an architecture and framework for their operation. In the near future we will test agents in a simulated ad-hoc environment comparing them to the existing solutions. We will also evaluate rules and parameter sets for decision making and adaptation towards an effective clustering, and explore further usage of mobile agents in wireless ad-hoc networks.

The project is supported by Timber Hill Group LLC. and   OTKA F032268 (Hungarian Scientific Research Found).

References

1. C-K Toh. Wireless ATM and Ad-Hoc Networks. Kluwer Academic Publishers, 1997.
2. A. Alwan, R. Bagrodia, N. Bambos, M., L. Kleinrock, J. Short and J. Villasenor, "Adaptive mobile multimedia networks, IEEE Personal Communications, pp. 34-51, April 1996.
3. J. Broch, D. Maltz, D. Johnson, Y. Hu, and J. Jetcheva. A performance comparison of multi-hop wireless ad hoc routing protocols. In Proceedings of the Fourth Annual ACM/IEEE International Conference on Mobile Computing and Networking,October 1998.
4. S. Das, R. Castaneda, J. Yan, and R. Sengupta. Comparative performance evaluation of routing protocols for mobile, ad hoc networks. In Proceedings of 7th Annual ICCCN, October 1998.
5. Charles Perkins. Ad hoc On Demand Distance Vector (AODV) Routing. Internet draft, draft-ietf-manet-aodv-00.txt, 1997.
6. Murthy, S. , and Garcia-Luna-Aceves, J.J. A Routing Protocol for Packet Radio Networks. Proc. of ACM Mobile Computing and Networking Conference, MOBICOM'95, Nov. 14-15, 1995.
7. D. Johnson and D. Maltz. Dynamic source routing in ad hoc wireless networks. In T. Imielinski and eds. H. Korth, editors, Mobile Computing. Kluwer Academic Publications, 1996.
8. M.S. Corson and A. Ephremides. A distributed routing algorithm for mobile wireless networks. ACM-Baltzer Journal of Wireless Net-works,1:61-81, January 1995.
9. Z. J. Haas and M. Perlman. The performance of query control schemes for the zone routing protocol. In Proceedings of ACM Sigcomm'98, October 1998.
10. M. Jiang, J. Li and Y.C. Tay. Cluster-Based Routing Protocol (CBRP), Internet-Draft, draft-ietf-manet-zone-zrp-02.txt, August 1999.
11. C.-C. Chiang. Routing in Clustered Multihop, Mobile Wireless Networks with Fading Channel. Proc. IEEE SICON'97, Apr.1997, pp.197-211.
12. M. Gerla and J.T.-C. Tsai, "Multicluster, mobile, multimedia radio network," ACM-Baltzer Journal of *Wireless Networks,* Vol. 1, No. 3, pp. 255-265, 1995.
13. C. R. Lin and M. Gerla. Adaptive clustering for mobile wireless networks. IEEE Journal on Selected Areas in Communications, 15(7), September 1997.
14. A.B. McDonald and T.F. Znati. A mobility-based framework for adaptive clustering in wireless ad hoc networks, IEEE J. Selected Areas in Communications, 17, 8, August 1999, 1466-1487.
15. L. Ismail, D. Hagimont. A Performance Evaluation of the Mobile Agent Paradigm. Proc. Of the Communications of the ACM, Volume 41, Num. 10. ACM Press. October 1998. pp 44 - 52.
16 T. White, A. Bieszczad and B. Pagurek, Distributed Fault Location in Networks Using Mobile Agents. In Proceedings of the Second International Workshop on Agents in Telecommunications Applications (IATA '98), pp. 130-141, July 4th-7th, 1998.
17 A. Bieszczad, B. Pagurek, and T. White. Mobile Agents for Network Management. IEEE Communications Surveys, September 1998.
18. Robert Sugar, Sandor Imre. Dynamic Agent Domains in Mobile Agent Based Network Management. IEEE International Conference on Networking, 2001.
19. Sun Microsystems Inc. Jini connection technology. http://www.sun.com/jini/.
20. IBM Japan: Aglets Software Development Kit. http://www.trl.ibm.com/aglets/.
21. ObjectSpace: ObjectSpace Voyager Core Package Technical Overview. Tech. Repot. ObjectSpace Inc. Dallas, 1997.

Mobile 4-in-6: A Novel Mechanism for IPv4/v6 Transitioning

Joe Finney[1], Greg O'Shea[2]

[1] Distributed Multimedia Research Group, Lancaster University, UK
joe@comp.lancs.ac.uk
[2] Microsoft Research, Cambridge, UK
gregos@microsoft.com

Abstract. Mobility is indisputably one of the major drives promoting IPv6. Making the transition to IPv6 from IPv4, however, is one of the major stumbling blocks. It has recently come to light that Mobile IPv6 (the IETF routing protocol for IPv6 mobile hosts) may hold some of the keys to making this transition. This paper describes mobile 4-in-6, an extension to the Mobile IPv6 protocol that allows mobile nodes to transparently communicate with the IPv4 Internet irrespective of their current location on the IPv6 Internet. Furthermore, the protocol does not require the mobile node to hold an IPv4 address other than on its home network, and does not assume the availability of any Mobile IPv4 services.

1 Introduction

The current Mobile IPv6 (MIPv6) specification does not attempt to provide any support for IPv4 connectivity [1][5]. Even if a mobile node implements both an IPv4 and IPv6 stack, MIPv6 nodes roaming away from their home network have only one topologically correct address, namely an IPv6 care-of address. Consequently, it is likely that many mobile nodes would become disconnected from the IPv4 Internet while away from their home network(s). With the vast majority of today's Internet only accessible through IPv4, and with many of today's applications supporting only IPv4, this represents a major limitation in the utility of networks built around the Mobile IPv6 protocol.

Due to the increased address space provided by IPv6, it is likely that future mobile telecommunications networks will utilize IPv6 to address their mobile nodes. In fact, systems have already been demonstrated which prototype future mobile telecom services based on IPv6 [2][8]. If the growth of this industry continues at its present rate, it is likely that it will see large scale IPv6 deployment before today's Internet. We believe that this will result in the telecommunications networks 'leapfrogging' the current Internet in terms of IPv6 connectivity. This in turn will lead to the need for an IPv6 mobile routing protocol combined with a transitional mechanism to allow such nodes to converse with the 'legacy' IPv4 Internet.

Existing transitional mechanisms have been developed based upon the prediction that IPv6 networks will evolve slowly, out of the current IPv4 infrastructure, not rap-

D. Shepherd et al. (Eds.): IDMS 2001, LNCS 2158, pp. 205-212, 2001.

idly and independent of it. There are several proposed IPv4/v6 transitional mechanisms, ranging from the brute force solution of running both Mobile IPv4 and Mobile IPv6 protocols simultaneously, to more complex protocol translation mechanisms which allow IPv4 hosts to converse with IPv6 hosts [12][15]. Such schemes can incur costs of significant additional complexity in the end systems and networks, require the presence of specialized network servers, and often do not cope well with the dynamic nature of mobile environments [14]. Additionally, such systems have one thing in common – they view mobility as an additional problem to be solved by the v4/v6 transition mechanism. However, the very principles upon which Mobile IPv6 operates may help the IPv4/v6 transition, not hinder it.

The fundamental tenet of the Mobile IPv6 protocol is to provide location transparency by separating a network node's identifier (home address) from its routing information (care-of address), and manage the relationship between these two entities (bindings). If the bindings were made protocol independent, then this provides the basis for a powerful transitional mechanism. It is this mechanism that is exploited by mobile 4-in-6.

In this paper we introduce mobile 4-in-6 (m4-in-6), a new option that enables a MIPv6 mobile node to communicate with the IPv4 Internet while connected to any foreign network, even one with no IPv4 connectivity. In addition, it provides transparent host mobility for IPv4 applications through the Mobile IPv6 protocol. It achieves this without the need for any additional network servers, and supports optimal routing between pairs of m4-in-6 nodes.

The benefits of m4-in-6 are diverse, allowing every m4-in-6 mobile node to support host mobility for a suite of both IPv6 and IPv4 applications, without requiring any modification to application software. It also allows an m4-in-6 mobile node to exploit IPv4 versions of standard network services, such as DNS, for which IPv6 implementations may not (yet) exist. In these ways m4-in-6 facilitates both the rapid deployment of Mobile IPv6, and greatly improves its utility.

2 Background

Mobile IPv6 allows an IPv6 node to continue using an IPv6 address even when that address is topologically incorrect for the network to which the node is currently attached. It achieves this by allowing an IPv6 node to acquire and simultaneously use two IPv6 addresses: a *home address*, by which it is well known; and a temporary *care-of address*, which is automatically allocated on the network to which the node is currently attached [13]. Applications converse using home addresses, but packets are transmitted and received at the IP level using the care-of addresses so that they can be routed correctly and so that they can transit firewalls. An entity known as a *home agent* is responsible for forwarding packets to the care-of address of a mobile node that has left its home network. Central to MIPv6 is a *binding* between a pair of IPv6 addresses, used to map a home address onto a care-of address. MIPv6 nodes notify each other of their whereabouts using *Binding Update* messages, and each mobile node maintains a *Binding Update List* of destinations to which it has sent a Binding Update. Each node maintains a local *Binding Cache* of bindings known to it, so that packets can be routed directly to a mobile node's point of attachment thus avoiding the indirect route through the home agent.

A mobile node may have several IPv6 home addresses, but in m4-in-6 must have at least two: one IPv6 home address (as per the Mobile IPv6 specification) and an IPv6 address corresponding to the *IPv4-compatible* form of its IPv4 address [3]. An IPv4 compatible address is an IPv6 address generated by mapping an IPv4 address into the IPv6 address space. As IPv6 addresses are 128 bits in length, compared to the 32 bits of IPv4, it is simple to provide this mapping. IPv4 compatible addresses consist of a 32 bit IPv4 address prefixed by 96 binary zeros. IPv4-compatible addresses (and other conceptually similar addresses) are used by many IPv4/IPv6 transitional mechanisms.

The IETF NGTRANS working group has proposed an approach for encapsulating IPv4 packets in IPv6 packets which we employ in mobile 4-in-6 [15]. This allows us to route IPv4 packets to and from parts of the network where either no IPv4 connectivity exists, or for which the IPv4 addresses in the packets are topologically incorrect; without tunnels such packets might be lost or discarded by firewalls.

3 Operation of Mobile 4-in-6

In summary, m4/6 extends the Mobile IPv6 Home Agent to serve as an IPv4 proxy for a mobile node that is away from its home network, encapsulating any IPv4 traffic for the mobile node inside of IPv6 packets that are tunneled to and from the mobile node's IPv6 care-of address. In this way we avoid the need for the mobile node to acquire an IPv4 address other than on its home network. This approach is transparent to the entire community of IPv4 machines existing on the Internet today.

At the outset, in addition to obtaining the IPv6 home address required for Mobile IPv6, the mobile node also acquires an IPv4 home address on its home network, through any available mechanism. While connected to its home network, the mobile node uses its IPv4 address natively, as would any other IPv4 node. When the mobile node roams to a foreign network it forms an IPv6 care-of address, as per the MIPv6 standard, and in addition to transmitting the binding update to its home agent to provide a mapping between its IPv6 home address and its current IPv6 care-of address [5], it also sends a second binding update, mapping the IPv4-compatible IPv6 address corresponding to its IPv4 home address to its current IPv6 care-of address.

In m4-in-6 the MIPv6 home agent is extended to serve as an IPv4 proxy after the fashion of a simplified Mobile IPv4 home agent [10]. The home agent validates binding updates referring to IPv4 compatible home addresses, updates its binding cache and starts to act as an IPv4 proxy for the mobile node, in addition to the normal IPv6 proxy functionality.

While the mobile node is attached to a foreign network, an IPv4 packet sent to the mobile node's IPv4 address arrives on the home network and is intercepted by the m4-in-6 home agent. The home agent looks up the IPv4 compatible form of this address in its Mobile IPv6 binding cache to recover the IPv6 care-of address. It then encapsulates the IPv4 packet in an IPv6 packet, which it transmits to the mobile node. Upon reception, the mobile node decapsulates the IPv4 packet and injects it into its IPv4 stack.

When a mobile node is away from its home network, it cannot be assumed that it has any IPv4 connectivity. For this reason, any IPv4 traffic generated by a mobile node on a foreign network is encapsulated in IPv6, and reverse tunneled back to its home agent for distribution. Figure 1 shows the route taken by an IPv4 packet sent from a correspondent node to an m4-in-6 mobile node that is away from its home network. Traffic from the mobile node to the correspondent follows the same path but in the opposite direction.

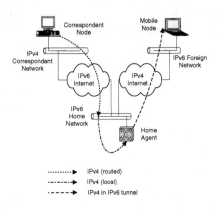

Fig. 1. IPv4 traffic from correspondent to m4-in-6 mobile node

When a m4-in-6 mobile node returns to its home link it sends a binding update to its home agent, and (re)starts its native IPv4 and IPv6 packet processing.

4   Implementation

Mobile 4-in-6 is currently being implemented on the Windows 2000 operating system, based around the Mobile IPv6 code developed as part of the LandMARC project [7]. The implementation operates by inserting thin layers of packet filtering and injection code into the ingress and egress points of the existing IPv4 and IPv6 stacks, in a similar way to the IETF 'Bump In the Stack' (BIS) mechanism [16]. Figure 2 illustrates the architecture.

When operating as a mobile m4-in-6 node away from its home link, a packet filter is installed at the egress of the IPv4 stack, which captures all outgoing IPv4 packets from the node, encapsulates them inside IPv6 and sends them to the mobile node's home agent for forwarding. This filter is removed when the mobile returns home, and thus allows the IPv4 packets to be transmitted directly. Conversely, when an IPv4-in-IPv6 encapsulated packet is received from the mobile node's home agent the IPv4 datagram is decapsulated and injected into the IPv4 stack for processing. Additional filters can be used for route optimization, as described in the following section.

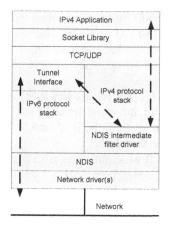

Fig. 2. Architecture and packet flow of a m4-in-6 node on a foreign network

5 Route Optimization

Routing all traffic through a mobile node's m4-in-6 home agent could result in all of the well-known problems of 'dogleg' routing in Mobile IP networks, namely increased traffic through the IPv4 and IPv6 internets, longer round-trip times, increased load on the home agent, increased load on the home network and more points of failure. In order to avoid these issues, m4-in-6 continues to utilize Mobile IPv6 primitives by allowing mobile m4-in-6 nodes to send binding updates pertaining to IPv4 compatible home addresses to correspondent nodes. The correspondent nodes can then tunnel traffic for a mobile node's IPv4 home address via its current IPv6 care-of address. A detailed description of this mechanism is beyond the scope of this positional paper.

6 Security

A detailed description of our security design is beyond the scope of this document. We are investigating a security design based on the use of IPSec AH Security Associations [6], as found in MIPv6, in combination with the CAM and LIKE protocols [9].

7 Evaluation

Mobile 4-in-6 provides transparent mobility for IPv4 applications over a Mobile IPv6 enabled network. It provides a transitional mechanism which requires no additional network servers, and as m4-in-6 uses the existing Mobile IPv6 and 6over4 protocols, does so with minimal modification to existing MIPv6 nodes. M4-in-6 enables the seamless coexistence of IPv4 and IPv6 applications on mobile nodes, greatly increases the number of applications available to a MIPv6 mobile node, relaxes the timescales in which applications need be upgraded to IPv6 and extends the useful lifetime of some IPv4-based applications.

Observe that m4-in-6 does not require any specialized servers outside of home networks, and neither does it require and special configuration of routing infrastructure. While m4-in-6 depends upon both the IPv4 and IPv6 routing infrastructures, it does not require that they be symmetrical.

The ability to support IPv4 applications without requiring any change to the IPv4 application software and network services is a major benefit of m4-in-6. We cannot enumerate all instances of important IPv4 applications, but with m4-in-6 we can provide for many of them, and perhaps forestall some ad hoc and inelegant patches.

While other mechanisms do exist which can be used to aid the IPv4/IPv6 transition, they require the presence of additional servers in the network, and often do not provide total transparency. For example, protocol translators cannot easily support applications that contain IPv4 address information in application layer data. Additionally, they do not directly provide support for mobility. M4-in-6 is unique in that it simultaneously provides mobility support and an IPv4/IPv6 transitional mechanism in one simple protocol.

One ongoing concern with M4-in-6 is with scalability. Although the protocol is highly distributed and results in little additional load on other network nodes, it does rely on each mobile device having a unique IPv4 address. This will become harder and harder to provide as the IPv4 address space becomes increasingly exhausted. One approach which reduces the number of required IPv4 addresses is to use short term address leasing in combination with site area IPv4 addresses which are not globally routable (e.g. 10.X.Y.Z). Such addresses are in common use today on sites where IPv4 addresses are scarce. Network Address Translators (NATs) are then used to dynamically translate publicly routable addresses onto these site area addresses on demand, as off site access is needed. Mobile 4-in-6 can work with such a scheme provided that them4-in-6 home agent is placed within the scope of the NAT, and that route optimization is not attempted by the mobile node. We are also investigating the other approaches to solving this problem.

An implementation of m4-in-6 is currently already underway. Our implementation is based on the Mobile IPv6 stack for Windows2000 developed in collaboration between Lancaster University and Microsoft Research, Cambridge, as part of the LandMARC project [7]. Experimental results will be published when they become available.

Our approach may result in additional load upon the m4-in-6 home agent and its local network (in the case where route optimization cannot be performed), but this is concentrated precisely where it is most predictable and where responsibility for its management resides. The managers of a home network can decide for themselves how large a population of mobile nodes they can (afford to) serve, and may provision their networks accordingly.

8 Concluding Remarks

In this paper we have described a way in which an MIPv6 mobile node can transparently support IPv4 applications even while roaming between IPv6 subnets which have no IPv4 connectivity, thus enabling a much faster roll out of IPv6 by providing a high level of backward compatibility with the existing IPv4 Internet.

We also briefly described a technique for providing route optimization for IPv4 traffic between IPv6 nodes.

Finally, we outline the benefits of m4-in-6, and its advantages over other similar technologies.

For future work, we plan to further investigate the benefits and drawbacks of Mobile 4-in-6 through evaluation of our ongoing implementation. Also, we intend to investigate how m4-in-6 interoperates with other v4/v6 transitional mechanisms, and how it behaves in a variety of mobile networking environments, including an evaluation of the impact of recent developments in IPv6 handoff optimizations on IPv4 multimedia applications.

We would like to thank Doug Shepherd, Andrew Scott, Stefan Schmid, Mike Roe, Dieter Gollman, Roger Needham, Tuomas Aura, Van Eden and Peter Key for their comments and suggestions upon an earlier draft of this paper.

References

1. S. Deering and R. Hinden, Internet Protocol, Version 6 (IPv6) Specification, RFC2460. December 1998.
2. Ericsson, SmarTone and BT stage world's first successful demonstration of end-to-end IPv6 in a mobile network. Ericsson Press Release, November 14th 2000. Available via the www at http://www.ericsson.se/press
3. R. Gilligan and E. Nordmark, Transition Mechanisms for IPv6 Hosts and Routers, RFC1933, April 1996.
4. C. Huitema, IPv6: The New Internet Protocol. Prentice Hall PTR, ISBN 0-13-850505-5, 1998, pp209-210.
5. D. B. Johnson, C. Perkins, Mobility Support in IPv6, <draft-ietf-mobileip-ipv6-13.txt>, 17 November 2000. Work in Progress.
6. S. Kent and R. Atkinson, Security Architecture for the Internet Protocol. RFC2401. November 1998.
7. The LandMARC project. http://www.LandMARC.net
8. Nokia demonstrates IPv6 live in the UK, Nokia Press Release, May 10th, 2000. Available via the www at http://press.nokia.com/pressreleases.html
9. G. O'Shea, M. Roe, Child-proof Authentication for MIPv6 (CAM), ACM Computer Communications Review, 31(2), Apr 2001.
10. C Perkins, IP Mobility Support for IPv4, Revised, Nokia Research Centre, draft-ietf-mobileip-rfc2002-bis-03.txt, 20 September 2000. Work in Progress.
11. S. Schmid, J. Finney, et al., Component-based Active Networks for Mobile Multimedia Systems, Proceedings of the 10th International Workshop on Network and Operating Systems Support for Digital Audio and Video (NOSSDAV), June 2000.
12. H. Soliman, E. Nordmark, Extensions to SIIT and DSTM for enhanced routing of inbound packets, <draft-soliman-siit-dstm-00.txt>, July 2000. Work in Progress.

13. S. Thomson and T. Narten, IPv6 Stateless Address Autoconfiguration. RFC2462. December 1998.
14. G. Tsirtsis and S. Corson, IPv4 over Mobile IPv6 for Dual Stack nodes, draft-tsirtsis-v4-over-mipv6-00.txt, August 2000. Work in Progress.
15. G. Tsirtsis, P. Srisuresh, Network Address Translation – Protocol Translation (NAT-PT), IETF RFC 2766, February 2000.
16. K. Tsuchiya, H. Higuchi, Y. Atarashi, Dual Stack Hosts using the "Bump-In-The-Stack" Technique (BIS), IETF RFC 2767, February 2000.

The Case for Streaming Multimedia with TCP

Charles Krasic, Kang Li, and Jonathan Walpole[*]

Oregon Graduate Institute, Beaverton OR 97206, USA,
{krasic,kangli,walpole}@cse.ogi.edu,
http://www.cse.ogi.edu/sysl/

Abstract. In this paper, we revisit and challenge the dogma that TCP is an undesirable choice for streaming multimedia, video in particular. For some time, the common view held that neither TCP nor UDP, the Internet's main transport protocols, are adequate for video applications. UDP's service model doesn't provide enough support to the application while TCP's provides too much. Consequently, numerous research works proposed new transport protocols with alternate service-models as more suitable for video. For example, such service models might provide higher reliability than UDP but not the full-reliability of TCP. More recently, study of Internet dynamics has shown that TCP's stature as the predominant protocol persists. Through some combination of accident and design, TCP's congestion avoidance mechanism seems essential to the Internet's scalability and stability. Research on modeling TCP dynamics in order to effectively define the notion of TCP-friendly congestion avoidance is very active. Meanwhile, proposals for video-oriented transport protocols continue to appear, but they now generally include TCP-friendly congestion avoidance. Our concern is over the marginal benefit of changing TCP's service model, given the presence of congestion avoidance. As a position paper, our contribution will not be in the form of final answers, but our hope is to convince the reader of the merit in re-examining the question: do applications need a replacement for TCP in order to do streaming video?

1 Introduction

The Internet's ubiquity has long made it an attractive platform for distributed multimedia applications. A particularly elusive goal has been effective streaming solutions. To prevent confusion, we clarify the distinction between streaming and other forms of distribution, namely download. We assume download is defined so that the transfer of the video must complete before the video is viewed. Transfer and viewing are temporally sequential. With this definition, it is a simple matter to employ quality-adaptive video. One algorithm would be to deliver the entire video in the order from low to high quality components. The user may terminate

---

[*] This work was partially supported by DARPA/ITO under the Information Technology Expeditions, Ubiquitous Computing, Quorum, and PCES programs and by Intel

D. Shepherd et al. (Eds.): IDMS 2001, LNCS 2158, pp. 213–218, 2001.

the download early, and the incomplete video will automatically have as high quality as was possible. Thus, quality-adaptive download can be implemented in an entirely best-effort, time-insensitive, fashion. On the other hand, we assume streaming means that the user views the video at the same time that the transfer occurs. Transfer and viewing are concurrent. There are timeliness requirements inherent in this definition, which can only be reconciled with best-effort delivery through a time-sensitive adaptive approach.

In considering TCP's viability for streaming video, our position has much in common with the recent proliferation of work on TCP-friendly streaming. For us, the important issue is whether TCP's service model need to change. Much of the TCP-friendly research does not involve changes to the programming interface, our position is concerned with proposals that do entail new service models.

2   Anti-TCP Dogma

Numerous works on streaming video have asserted that TCP is undesirable for multimedia streaming, yet propose alternate solutions compatible with the same best-effort IP infrastructure[3, 9, 17, 16]. In this section, we identify common objections to two of TCP's basic mechanisms, packet retransmissions and congestion control, that are at the root of this anti-TCP dogma.

2.1   Reliability through Retransmissions

One objection states that TCP's use of packet retransmissions introduces unacceptable end-to-end latency. The claim is that re-sending lost data is not appropriate because, given the real-time nature of video, the resent data would arrive at the receiver too late for display. Retransmissions can also be the result of packet re-ordering rather than loss, however the latency penalty for re-ordered packets will be small, since TCP will still accept an out of order packet when it arrives. We now consider the latency penalty for retransmission of lost packets. A TCP sender's earliest detection of lost packets occurs in response to duplicate ACKs from the receiver. TCP also uses timeouts, these should be rare for streams behaving as an infinite-source. An adaptive video streaming application will behave as such an infinite source, since it will attempt to use all the throughput TCP will provide. Therefore the typical time the re-transmission will arrive at the receiver is one full round-trip (RTT) after the lost data was originally sent, resulting in an end-to-end latency of 1.5 times RTT at the minimum[1]. Thus, the latency penalty for retransmission of lost packets will be on the order of one RTT. RTTs vary for numerous reasons on the wide-area internet, but the following is a rough taxonomy of RTT scales, and consequently the latency penalties resulting from TCP retransmission: 20ms between sites in the same region, 100ms for sites on the same continent, and about 200ms between sites

---

[1] There is no bound on TCP's contribution to end-to-end latency, since the underlying IP model implies that acknowledgments or packet retransmissions may be lost. However, retransmission-delay on the order of a single RTT is the normal case.

requiring oceanic crossings. We now consider how these latencies would relate to video applications.

For *purely-interactive* applications such as tele-conferencing or distributed gaming, users are highly sensitive to end-to-end delays of sub-second timescales, typically in the range of 150 to 200 milliseconds. This end-to-end delay requirement persists for the duration of these applications. Given the tight delay bounds, we think it is important to characterize various delay sources using the critical-path approach[12, 2]. The question is how much the retransmission-delay effects the mean and worst-case critical-paths for interactive applications. The critical path approach stresses the importance of interaction with other sources of delay. If congestion control is essential to the best-effort Internet, it may be that its delays dominate the critical path. For a deeper discussion of latency implications of congestion control, we refer to our separate work[10], which begins towards our goal understanding the critical path for latency.

Unlike purely-interactive applications, video on demand (VOD) has interactive requirements only for control events such as start, pause, fast-forward, etc., which are relatively infrequent compared to the normal streaming state. While streaming, the quality perceived by the user is not directly affected by end-to-end latency, as the interaction is strictly uni-directional. A VOD application may gradually increase buffering, hence end-to-end delay, by dividing its use of available bandwidth between servicing video play-out and buffer accumulation. After a time, the end-to-end delay will actually be quite large, but the user perceives it only indirectly, in the sense that quality during the buffer accumulation period might have been slightly decreased. In this way, we say that VOD does not have the inherent hard latency requirements of purely-interactive applications, and so TCP's packet-retransmissions are not a significant problem for VOD.

2.2 Congestion Control

The congestion control algorithms of TCP have been heavily studied and frequently discussed in the literature[4, 6, 14]. Briefly, the congestion algorithm is designed to probe available bandwidth, through deliberate manipulation of the transmission rate. In steady-state, TCP's congestion control converges on an average transmission rate close to a fair-share of available bandwidth[2]. When viewed over shorter time-scales, TCP's instantaneous transmission rate takes on a familiar *sawtooth* shape, where it cycles between periods of additive increase separated by multiplicative decrease (AIMD). This short-term rate sawtooth is the second major part of the common view that TCP is not a good selection for video applications.

Many TCP-friendly protocols with claims of better suitability for video have been proposed[3, 9, 17, 16, 18]. These protocols recognize the need for congestion control, but propose congestion control such that rate is smoother in the short-term than TCP's AIMD sawtooth. Discussion in the literature of the network

---

[2] Fairness under distributed control is necessarily somewhat subjective. TCP's control algorithm results in bias toward flows with shorter path RTTs.

implications in terms of efficiency, stability and scalability, continues. We now consider the implications from the perspective of a streaming video application, which are manifest in terms of relationship between rate variations and buffering.

An application's TCP flow experiences rate variations for two distinct reasons; the first being competing traffic in the network, and the second being the flow's own congestion control behavior[3]. Rate variations may be categorized by the application as either transient or persistent. The distinction between transient and persistent rate changes is whether the buffer capacity is large enough to smooth them out. The purpose of buffering is precisely to smooth out transient changes.

For any amount of buffering, competing traffic can have persistent effects on a stream's rate. Streaming video applications must deal with persistent rate changes, before the client-side buffers are overwhelmed. The usual way is to employ quality-adaptation, adjusting the basic quality-rate trade-off of the video[3, 9, 17]. The applications use a closed loop-feedback control between client and server, which monitors the transport's progress for persistent rate changes and actuates the stream's quality-rate trade-off in response. We call this the quality-adaptation control.

Conceptually, the cyclic nature of congestion control's increase and decrease phases, the TCP sawtooth, suggests it should be treated strictly as a source of transient rate changes. If the quality-adaptation control is intended only to adjust for persistent traffic changes, then it has the problem of masking out the TCP sawtooth by inference. Without direct information, the quality-adaptation control may be less than optimal in terms of responsiveness. However, from the perspective of the human viewer, frequent video-quality changes are annoying, so the quality-adaptation control should favor stability over responsiveness. Stable quality is a natural outcome of employing large client side buffers using methods like those described in section 2.1. On the other hand, for purely-interactive applications, it may not be possible to treat congestion-control adjustments as transient, since end-to-end latency and buffer capacity are constrained. In this case, the design of the quality-adaptation control will have to choose between having higher average quality, allowing quality to track the sawtooth, or smoother quality by imposing a rate-limit. New congestion controls may reduce the impact of these trade-offs, since they may spread the congestion control rate adjustments more evenly[16, 5].

3   Popularity and Momentum

Studies of traffic trends in the Internet suggest that applications based on TCP comprise most of the traffic[13]. Solutions that allow Infrastructure providers to improve network efficiency and application performance without changing the applications are naturally compelling, so there is a strong incentive to improve TCP. At the moment, video comprises a small minority of Internet usage, so

---

[3]   TCP's flow control may also contribute, but for our discussion we assume the client is not the limit.

video-only oriented transports have limited immediate appeal. Also, video-only transport proposals must struggle to overcome resistance based on their potential to disrupt existing majority of TCP based traffic. Meanwhile, improvements for TCP will move the performance target. We give two examples: Early Congestion Notification (ECN) and ATCP.

TCP's congestion control was predicated on the assumption that router buffer overflows were by far the most common source of packet losses. Accordingly, TCP's congestion control mechanism relies on packet losses to support probing for bandwidth and congestion detection, which implies a certain amount of deliberate waste. ECN is a proposal for extending IP and TCP so that active queue management at network nodes can pro-actively inform TCP of congestion before packet losses occur[15]. While the retransmission mechanism is still necessary for TCP's reliable service model, ECN allows TCP to perform congestion avoidance without packet losses. Performance evaluation of ECN shows that ECN-enabled TCP connections usually proceed with little or no retransmissions over their lifetime[1]. While this has immediate implications for interactive video, it also leads to solutions of another deficiency in TCP, namely its performance over the expanding component of the Internet consisting of wireless ad hoc networks. It is well known that Wireless links often suffer high bit error rates, which standard TCP will mis-interpret as congestion. Invoking congestion control for such errors impacts throughput more than is necessary, and is basically the wrong response. Liu and Singh[11] describe ATCP and show that with ECN it is possible to distinguish physical link losses from buffer overflows (congestion), and preserve TCP's throughput. While ECN and ATCP face deployment issues, the scope of change they propose is relatively modest, and yet they deliver comparable benefits to new protocols with video-centric service models.

4   Discussion

In this paper, we make the case that TCP is a viable and attractive choice for quality-adaptive video streaming. We discuss the main challenges for video applications using TCP, which are due to TCP retransmissions and congestion-control. For VOD applications, we describe how client side buffering can mitigate the effects of both. Further investigation is needed to understand how much interactivity is possible using TCP, and how much extra interactivity TCP alternatives make possible. We present initial study of TCP's relationship to interactivity in a separate work[10]. We have developed a video system prototype that supports tailorable fine-grained quality adaptation, of MPEG derived video, through priority packet dropping[7]. Based on our video system, we have developed a streaming algorithm over TCP, which we describe in an extended version of this report[8]. In future work, we will present measurements to illustrate the efficacy of our streaming system in supporting VOD over TCP, and explore further the issues of iteractivity.

References

[1] Uvaiz Ahmed and Jamai Hadi Salim. Performance evaluation of explicit congestion notification (ECN) in IP networks. IETF RFC 2884, July 2000.

[2] Paul Barford and Mark Crovella. Critical Path Analysis of TCP Transactions. In *In Proceedings of the 2000 ACM SIGCOMM Conference*, September 2000.

[3] Shanwei Cen and Jonathan Walpole. Flow and congestion control for internet streaming applications. In *Proceedings Multimedia Computing and Networking (MMCN98)*, 1998.

[4] Dah-Ming Chiu and Raj Jain. Analysis of the Increase and Decrease Algorithms for Congestion Avoidance in Computer Networks. *Computer Networks and ISDN Systems*, 17, 1989.

[5] Nick Feamster, Deepak Bansal, and Hari Balakrishnan. On the Interactions Between Layered Quality Adaptation and Congestion Control for Streaming Video. In *11th International Packet Video Workshop (PV2001)*, Kyongiu, Korea, April 2001.

[6] Van Jacobson and Michael J. Karels. Congestion Avoidance and Control. In *In Proceedings of ACM SIGCOMM'88*, pages pp. 79–88, August 1988.

[7] Charles Kasic and Jonathon Walpole. Qos scalability for streamed media delivery. CSE Technical Report CSE-99-011, Oregon Graduate Institute, September 1999.

[8] Charles Krasic, Jonathan Walpole, Kang Li, and Asvin Goel. The case for streaming multimedia with tcp. Technical report, Oregon Graduate Institute, CSE Technical Report 2001. CSE-01-003.

[9] J.R. Li, D. Dwyer, and V. Bharghavan. A transport protocol for heterogeneous packet flows. In *IEEE Infocom'99*, 1999.

[10] Kang Li, Charles Krasic, Jonathan Walpole, Molly H. Shor, and Calton Pu. The minimal buffering requirements of congestion controlled interactive multimedia applications. In *IDMS*, Lancaster, UK, September 2001.

[11] J. Liu and S. Singh. ATCP: TCP for Mobile Ad Hoc Networks, 2001.

[12] K. G. Lockyer. *Introduction to Critical Path Analysis*. Pitman Publishing Co., New York, N.Y., 1964.

[13] S. McCreary and K. Claffy. Trends in Wide Area IP Traffic Patterns: A View from Ames Internet Exchange.

[14] Jitendra Padhye, Victor Firoiu, Don Towsley, and Jim Kurose. Modeling TCP Throughput: A Simple Model and its Empirical Validation. In *In Proceedings of ACM SICOMM'98*, 1998.

[15] K. K. Ramakrishnan, Sally Floyd, and D. Black. The Addition of Explicit Congestion Notification (ECN) to IP. IETF Internet-Draft, January 2001.

[16] R. Rejaie, M. Handley, and D. Estrin. RAP: An end-to-end rate-based congestiong control mechanism for realtime streams in the internet. In *Proceeedings of IEEE Infocomm*, March 1999.

[17] Wai tan Tan and Avideh Zakhor. Internet video using error resilient scalable compression and cooperative transport prototocl. In *Proc. ICIP*, volume 1, pages 17–20, 1998.

[18] The TCP-friendly website. http://www.psc.edu/networking/tcp_friendly.html.

The MPEG-21 Standard: Why an Open Multimedia Framework?

Fernando Pereira

Instituto Superior Técnico - Instituto de Telecomunicações
Av. Rovisco Pais, 1049-001 Lisboa, PORTUGAL
fp@lx.it.pt

Abstract. MPEG [1] has been responsible for the successful MPEG-1 and MPEG-2 standards that have given rise to widely adopted commercial products and services, such as Video-CD, DVD, digital television, digital audio broadcasting (DAB) and MP3 (MPEG-1 Audio layer 3) players and recorders. More recently, the MPEG-4 standard [2] is aimed to define an audiovisual coding standard to address the emerging needs of the communication, interactive and broadcasting service models as well as of the mixed service models resulting from their technological convergence. The MPEG-4 object-based representation approach where a scene is modeled as a composition of objects, both natural and synthetic, with which the user may interact, is at the heart of the MPEG-4 technology. With this new coding approach, the MPEG-4 standard opens new frontiers in the way users will play with, create, re-use, access and consume audiovisual content. Following the same vision underpinning MPEG-4, MPEG initiated after another standardization project addressing the problem of describing multimedia content to allow the quick and efficient searching, processing and filtering of various types of multimedia material: MPEG-7 [3]. The need for a powerful solution for quickly and efficiently identifying, searching, filtering, etc., various types of multimedia content of interest to the user, human or machine, using also non text-based technologies, directly follows from the urge to efficiently use the available multimedia content and the difficulty of doing so.

The need for any standard comes from a very essential requirement relevant for all applications involving communication between two or more parts: *interoperability*. Interoperability is thus the requirement expressing the user's dream of exchanging any type of information without any technical barriers, in the simplest way. Without a standard way to perform some of the operations involved in the communication process and to structure the data exchanged, easy interoperability between the terminals involved would be impossible. Having said that, it is clear that a standard should specify the minimum number of tools to guarantee interoperability since it is important that as many as possible non-normative technical zones exist, to allow the incorporation of technical advances, and thus to increase the life time of the standard, as well as to stimulate the industrial technical competition. The existence of a standard has also important economical implications since it allows the sharing of costs and investments and the acceleration of applications' deployment.

Following the development of the standards mentioned above, MPEG acknowledged the lack of a "big picture" describing how the various elements building the infrastructure for the deployment of multimedia applications relate to each other or even if there are missing open standard specifications for some

D. Shepherd et al. (Eds.): IDMS 2001, LNCS 2158, pp. 219-220, 2001.

of these elements. To address this problem, MPEG started the MPEG-21 project [4], formally called "Multimedia framework" with the aim to understand if and how these various elements fit together, and to discuss which new standards may be required, if gaps in the infrastructure exist. Once this work has been carried out, new standards will be developed for the missing elements with the involvement of other bodies, where appropriate, and finally the existing and novel standards will be integrated in the MPEG-21 multimedia framework. The MPEG-21 vision is thus to define an open multimedia framework to enable the transparent and augmented delivery and consumption of multimedia resources across a wide range of networks and devices used by different communities. The MPEG-21 multimedia framework will identify and define the key elements needed to support the multimedia value and delivery chain, as well as the relationships between and the operations supported by them. This open framework guarantees all content creators and service providers equal opportunities in the MPEG-21 enabled open market. This will also be to the benefit of the content consumers who get access to a large variety of content in an interoperable manner.

This presentation will not only describe the technical objectives of the MPEG-21 standard but also its motivation and vision. Why it is important to have an open standard multimedia framework? To whom is essential this type of standard? What will be lost if MPEG-21 does not succeed?

References

1.   MPEG Home Page, http://www.cselt.it/mpeg/
2.   F. Pereira, "MPEG-4: why, what, how and when ?", Tutorial Issue on the MPEG-4 Standard, Signal Processing: Image Communication, vol. 15, n° 4-5, December 1999
3.   R. Koenen, F. Pereira, "MPEG-7: a standardised description of audio-visual content", Special Issue on MPEG-7 Technology, Signal Processing: Image Communication, vol. 16, n° 1-2, September 2000
4.   MPEG Requirements Group, "MPEG-21 overview", Doc. ISO/MPEG N4041, MPEG Singapore Meeting, March 2001

Selecting the QoS Parameters for Multicast Applications Based on User Profile and Device Capability

Khalil El-Khatib, Gregor v. Bochmann, and Yu Zhong

School of Information Technology & Engineering, University of Ottawa
161 Louis Pasteur St., Ottawa, Ont., K1N 6N5, Canada
{elkhatib, bochmann, yzhong}@site.uottawa.ca

Abstract. Most adaptive multimedia multicast applications require the source to select the number of streams to transmit as well as the QoS parameters for each stream. If the receivers have different bandwidth limits for their devices and have various preferences for the quality of the data, selecting the QoS parameters that generate the best average satisfaction for all receivers is a challenging problem. In this paper, we developed a selection algorithm that is based on the user profiles and the device capabilities. Receivers are required to send their profiles and the bandwidth limitation on their devices to the source once before the session starts. To avoid the implosion problem and have a constant running time for the selection algorithm, we partition the receivers according to the bandwidth limit of their devices into classes and use a virtual representative for each class of receivers.

1 Introduction

Multimedia broadcast applications like tele-teaching, teleconferencing, Internet TV, or remote presentation, are becoming valuable services for users of the Internet. These applications became possible due to advances in the capabilities of desktop machines and transport networks. At the level of transport, the most important advance that made these applications possible was the development of broadcast protocols, such as the Multicast Backbone (Mbone). The Mbone is an experimental virtual network imposed on the top of the Internet and has been used as a multicast test-bed. The Mbone consists of islands of multicast-capable networks, connected to each other by virtual links called "tunnels", and it shares the same transport infrastructure as the Internet.

Adaptive multicast applications require that the server solicit information from all its receivers in order to adjust the sending parameters as to provide the highest possible level of service to the receivers. When receivers are connected through variable bit rate connections (over the Internet or a Variable Bit Rate (VBR) ATM feed), receivers are usually required to periodically send feedback messages to the source in order to accommodate the changes in the available bandwidth along the path from the source to the receiver. Most of the works in the literature have focused on sending the data loss rate at the receiver as an indication of the congestion along the data path.

D. Shepherd et al. (Eds.): IDMS 2001, LNCS 2158, pp. 221-232, 2001.
© Springer-Verlag Berlin Heidelberg 2001

Based on the feedback reports, the source might adjust the sending rate [7,10,11] or keep the same sending rate and send more error-resilient data [1]. As the number of feedback messages scales with the number of receivers, with large numbers of receivers, the source might not be able to handle all these feedback reports, especially when these reports are sent periodically. This problem is known in the literature as implosion. Several approaches have been proposed to solve the implosion problem including back-off timers [2, 3], probabilistic polling [4], and network aggregation [5].

In our work, we simplify the problem of implosion by assuming that the receivers will only send one report before the session starts. Information in the report includes the preferences of the receiver for the QoS parameters such as frame rate and resolution and the bandwidth limit of the available local network access link. This information is used by the server to compute the QoS parameters for each stream to send. Our approach differs from other research work in that the selection of the QoS parameters is based on the user preferences (frame rate and resolution) and the limitation on the bandwidth of his device rather than the loss rate. Receivers are classified according to their bandwidth limit. Based on the capability of the source, our approach selects the number of streams as well as the QoS parameters of each stream. If the source has enough throughput limit to send a separate stream for each class of users, the source runs the selection algorithm for each class separately. If not, the source has to decide then on the number of streams to send as well as the QoS parameters for each stream. In both cases, the selected QoS parameters ensure the highest level of satisfaction of the receivers within their preferences, their device capability and the throughput limitation of the source. To avoid the scalability problem with the number of receivers, we introduced a way to select a virtual representative for each class, representing all receivers in the class. Receivers that haves the same bandwidth limit are more likely to have similar QoS preferences and adequately represented by one virtual receiver.

The rest of the paper is organized as follows: Section 2 gives a literature review of adaptive multicast applications. Section 3 introduces the user profiles and device capabilities used in the selection algorithm presented in Section 4. Based on the throughput limit of the source, Section 4 details two algorithms to select to QoS parameters for each stream to send. The use of group representatives is outlined in Section 5, and finally, a conclusion in Section 6.

2   Literature Review

Adaptive multicast applications are classified as either sender-driven or receiver-driven applications. In the sender-driven approach, the congestion feedback messages from the receivers and/or network are used to adapt the transmission rate at the source. In the receiver-driven approach, the source transmits the same data in different variants, and the receivers select the variant to receive depending on the congestion they encounter.

In [4], a single video stream is transmitted to all receivers, and congestion feedback is used to control the rate of the video stream. To prevent feedback implosion, a form of probabilistic feedback is used. In [6] the authors proposed an approach for the design of an available bit rate congestion control algorithm that maximizes inter-receiver fairness for multicast Available Bit Rate (ABR) sessions. Each receiver is assigned a weight value, and has an "isolated bandwidth" defined as the rate that would be achieved by the receiver when it is the only receiver in the multicast group. Every single receiver defines his maximum acceptable loss tolerance l and selects its own "receiver fairness function" that maps from the actual operating bandwidth value to a fairness value. The sender receives a feedback from each receiver including the isolated bandwidth and the receiver fairness function. The sender will then try to determine the sending rate that maximizes the weighted fairness among receivers. To achieve scalability, intermediate nodes are used to aggregate feedback messages from receivers according to their isolated rates. This approach was modified for use in the Internet [7]. The authors used the loss rate instead of the isolated rate to find the best sending parameters for the stream. The authors also suggested the use of two streams: a base stream with a constant data rate that can accommodate the receivers with the lowest connection rate, and another variable bit rate stream whose data rate can be modified based on feedback messages from receivers. Receivers with requests to lower the bit rate of the V-stream can always change to the base stream.

Layered encoding and group multicasting are combined in the receiver-driven approach. In the receiver-driven layered multicast (LRM) [8] approach, the video stream is decoded as a "basic" video stream, and a set of enhancement layers. Each layer is sent to a different multicast address. Receivers should receive the basic video stream and the enhancement layers that best suit their requirements. A receiver may use join-experiments to add more layers when there is extra capacity and release layers when the receiver experiences congestion. Thin Streams [9] reduces the congestion resulting from the join-experiments by dividing each layer further into "thin" layers.

The Destination Set Grouping (DSG)[10] is a hybrid between sender-driven and receiver-driven approaches. In this scheme, the source maintains a small number of video streams, broadcasting different variants of the same information. Receivers can tune to the stream with the quality they prefer. They can also send feedback messages to the source to adjust the quality of the stream to which they are tuning. The DSG protocol is composed of two components: an *intra-stream* protocol and an *inter-stream* protocol. Using the *intra-stream* protocol, receivers can determine their status as: LOADED, UNLOADED, and CONGESTED depending on the packet loss rate. Receivers are polled in a probabilistic manner in order to estimate the number of CONGESTED and UNLOADED receivers. Depending on the fraction of CONGESTED receivers, the source adjusts the sending rate in order to keep most of the receiver in the LOADED state.

The Source Adaptive Multi-Layered Multicast (SAMM)[11] is another hybrid algorithm that uses congestion feedback from the receivers to adjust the number of the generated layers as well as the encoding parameters of each layer. Two variations of the algorithm were proposed: a network based SAMM algorithm and an end-to-end SAMM algorithm. In the network-based algorithm, the source periodically generates a control packet called "forward feedback packet" and sends it to the multicast group. Each intermediate node updates the packet with the amount of bandwidth available for the transmission of the multicast flow. When the packet arrives at the receivers, it contains the bandwidth available on the path from the source to the receivers. Each receiver stores this value in a feedback message and sends it back to the source. Intermediate mergers combine feedback messages from downstream nodes and forward only one feedback message toward the source. If the number of requested rate values is higher than the maximum number of video layers allowed, then one or more rates must be discarded. The algorithm drops the layer with the smallest number of receivers and adds the number of receiver of that layer to the number of the preceding lower layer. The end-to-end algorithm is similar to the network-based algorithm, except that the receivers cannot determine their available bandwidth, and they only use an estimate based on the received video rate. Because the actual available bandwidth could be higher than the video arrival rate, the receiver might occasionally report a rate that is higher than the observed rate.

Active networks can also be used with adaptive multicast application [12]. In this approach, trans-coders are installed at intermediate nodes in the multicast distribution tree. The source sends only one high rate variant of the data, and intermediate nodes do the trans-coding depending on the requirements of down-stream receivers and network congestion. While this approach distributes the overhead of the source, saves bandwidth by sending only one variant of the data, and performs trans-coding only when necessary, the control and management of intermediate trans-coders is a complex problem.

3   User Profiles and Device Limitations

In earlier work [13], we used the DMIF session management protocol to develop a distributed QoS management framework for multicasting multimedia applications. The protocol aimed at distributing part of the QoS management process between source and receivers; each receiver process can make certain QoS decisions based on its local context. The QoS manager in the source node determines the list of potential stream variants for each logical multimedia stream, and informs all the receivers about these variants. Based on the user profile, the QoS agent at the receiver node selects the stream that gives the highest level of appreciation to the receiver. The QoS agent can request a certain stream from the QoS manager if the stream is not currently transmitted. We used the control-plane of DMIF for the session management and illustrated its usage for the management of a tele-teaching application including different QoS alternatives for the participating users.

In other work [14], we presented an architecture for personal telecommunication services, in which each user was required to have a profile that contains all his personal information. This information covers QoS preferences for multimedia communication in addition to the user policies for handling incoming and outgoing calls. Based on this information in the profile of all communicating parties in the session, and based on the limitations of their candidate devices, we presented a middleware architecture that can select the devices and QoS parameters for the session that best suit all the parties.

For the adaptive multicast applications discussed in this paper, we will restrict the user profile to the user's QoS preferences. As proposed in [15], we assume that each user specifies the *minimum acceptable* and the *ideal* value for each QoS parameter (such as frame rate and resolution). A satisfaction function that maps the actual QoS value of the user satisfaction onto a range between 0 and 1 is shown in figure 1. QoS parameters that are higher than the *ideal* values in the user's profile generate the same level of the satisfaction as the *ideal* values. The total satisfaction of the user is computed as the weighted average of satisfactions of individual QoS parameters (see [15] for more details).

Another important parameter is the bandwidth limit of the device that is used to receive the multicast stream. This value determines the class to which the receiver belongs (see Section 5 for more details).

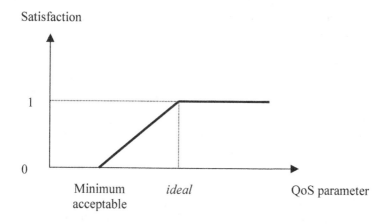

Figure 1. User satisfaction for a QoS parameter

The combination of user QoS preferences and the bandwidth limit of his device determine the possible parameters that the receivers can accept. Any accepted combination of QoS parameters must have each individual parameter higher than the *minimum accepted* parameter, and the combination must have bandwidth requirement less than the bandwidth limit of the device. A combination of QoS that requires a bandwidth limit higher than the bandwidth limit of the device will cause some packet loss and hence a zero (0) satisfaction value for the receiver.

4 Selecting QoS Parameters for Large Groups of Users

Traditional QoS parameter selection has been addressed in the context of small groups, mostly in two-party sessions or in a small group of users collaborating in a teleconference session. With such small group, it is feasible for group members to negotiate the QoS parameters that represent best the participants' preferences. However, the negotiation algorithms for small groups do not easily scale to large groups. The task of finding a common denominator for all participants in a large group can pose interesting and challenging technical problems.

An approach to find a common ground for all participants in a session is to send the preferences of all participants to one node, which tries to find the QoS parameter values that generate the maximum satisfaction among all participants. In our approach, we assume that this node is the multimedia server or any node that controls the sending parameters of the source. All candidate receivers are required to send their profiles to this node. Intermediate nodes may be used to aggregate the user profiles as explained in Section 5. As we mentioned earlier, each profile will include, in addition to the QoS preferences of the user, the available bandwidth to the receiver. We assume that this available bandwidth is known and remains constant throughout the session.

In our earlier work on QoS management for inter-personal communication [18], we have adopted the framework presented in [15] for selecting the QoS parameters that provide the highest satisfaction for the user. The user satisfaction for a single application QoS parameter (S_{Xi}) is computed based on the *minimum accepted* (M_{Xi}) and *ideal* (I_{Xi}) values defined by the user profile. The user satisfaction (S_{user}) for a combination of different QoS parameters is computed as a function of the satisfaction for the individual parameters. We have modified the framework to assign weights to individual parameters. In addition, we have extended the framework to consider the overall satisfaction obtained for a collection of several users participating in the application. The total satisfaction of all users (S_{total}) is also computed as a function of the satisfactions of all the users, including possibly weight factors. The functions used to calculate S_{user} and S_{total} share the property that their value becomes zero when one of the individual constituent satisfactions becomes zero. This property ensures that all participants in a session will obtain a quality that is better than the *minimum acceptable* value. We note that this property is not ensured in the case that a simple weighted average is used as the function to combine the individual satisfaction values. The definition of S_{Xi}, S_{user} and S_{total} is the following:

$$
S_{Xi}(x) = \begin{cases} 0 & \text{if } x < M_{Xi} \\ 1 & \text{if } x > I_{Xi} \\ \dfrac{x - M_{Xi}}{I_{Xi} - M_{Xi}} & \text{otherwise} \end{cases} \tag{1}
$$

$$
S_{user} = f_{comb}\left(s_{X1}, s_{X2}, s_{X3} \dots, s_{Xn}, w_1, w_2, w_3 \dots, w_n\right) = \frac{n\overline{w}}{\sum_{i=1}^{n} \dfrac{w_i}{s_{Xi}}} \tag{2}
$$

$$
S_{total} = f_{comb}\left(s_{user1}, s_{user2}, s_{user3} \dots, s_{userM}, w_{user1}, w_{user2}, w_{user3} \dots, w_{userM}\right) = \frac{M\overline{w}}{\sum_{i=1}^{m} \dfrac{w_{user\_i}}{s_{user\_i}}} \tag{3}
$$

In the case of multicasting, we found that this framework for computing the overall satisfaction is not appropriate, since with a large population of receivers, at least one of the receivers would have a zero value for his satisfaction for any combination of QoS parameters, and therefore the overall satisfaction would always be zero. Instead, we decided to use the simple weighted average to determine the overall satisfaction of all receivers. Candidate receivers that have a zero satisfaction for the select QoS parameters simply will not join the session. This function for S_{total} can be written as follows:

$$S_{total} = f_{comb}\left(S_{user1}, S_{user2}, S_{user3} \cdots, S_{userM}, W_{user1}, W_{user2}, W_{user3} \cdots, W_{userM}\right) = \frac{\sum\limits_{users} W_{user\_i} S_{user\_i}}{\sum\limits_{users} W_{user\_i}} \quad (4)$$

4.1   Selecting QoS Parameters with Unlimited Throughput in the Source

Before the session starts, all receivers are required to send their reports to the source. The source then classifies the receivers into separate classes according to their bandwidth limits. If the source has throughput limit higher than the sum of all bandwidth limits of the class, it tries to find the QoS parameters for each class separately. The next section deals with the case when the server has a throughput lower than the throughput required by all classes.

For each class, the source tries to find the combination of the QoS parameters that generates the highest average satisfaction of all receivers in the class. This combination must also require lower bandwidth than the bandwidth limit of the class. The source selects the QoS parameters for every class of receivers, based on the preferences of the receivers in the class and their bandwidth limit. The source sends after a multicast report to all receivers, informing them of the number of streams, the QoS parameters for each stream, and the multicast address for each stream. Each receiver determines the stream that best suits his preferences and tunes to the address of that stream, as described in our earlier work [13].

4.2   Selecting QoS Parameters with Limited Throughput in the Source

It is very possible that the source receives requests to deliver a number of streams that exceed its bandwidth throughput. In this case, the source has to decide on the number of streams to send, as well as the combination of the QoS parameters for each stream.

To do the selection, the source does not separate receivers into separate classes as in the case with unlimited throughput, but it keeps all receivers in one group. When using class representative as discussed in Section 5, receivers of the same class are represented as one virtual representative, and all class representatives are treated together in one group. The source then tries to select the combination of possible number of streams and the QoS parameters of each stream. The combination that generates the highest average satisfaction is the one adopted by the source.

We have done some experiments using the MATLAB Optimization Toolbox 2.1 to see how the average satisfaction of the receivers and the number of streams change as a function of the throughput limit of the server. We selected four bandwidth limits (128Kbps, 256Kbps, 512 Kbps and *unlimited*) on receivers (four classes), and we run the experiment with 1000 receivers. The user preferences (i.e. the *minimum accepted* (M_{Xi}) and *ideal* (I_{Xi}) values) were selected randomly with uniform distributions for M_{Xi} and I_{Xi} within certain ranges. These ranges were chosen in such a manner that the ideal quality for most users would correspond to a bandwidth beyond the bandwidth limit of that particular user (users are usually optimistic about the quality they might receive).

The results of these simulations are shown in figure 2. The graph shows clearly that as the bandwidth limit of the source increases, the number of streams and the average satisfaction increases until it reaches a maximum point. While the average satisfaction did not get to one (1), all users were receiving up to the maximum bandwidth of their devices. Figure 3 shows how the number of streams increased from one to four, leading to higher average satisfaction for all receivers.

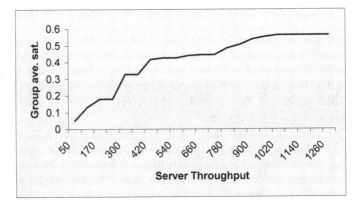

Figure 2. Server bandwidth limit vs. average satisfaction

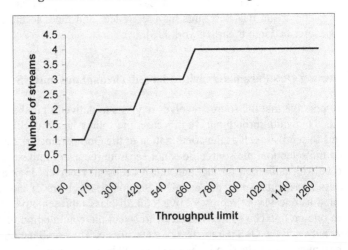

Figure 3. Server throughput limit vs. number of streams

5   Optimizing the Algorithm Using Receivers Partitioning

All adaptive multicast applications that require the server to solicit the receivers for feedback messages face the problem of feedback implosion, because the total number of feedback messages increases linearly with the number of receivers. Several approaches have been proposed to solve this problem including back-off timers [2, 3], probabilistic polling [4], and selecting group representative (or feedback aggregation) [5,16,17].

In our application, we avoided the implosion problem at two levels: first, we require that the receivers send their profiles and device limitations to the source only once, before the session starts, hence avoiding periodic feedbacks implosion. A problem with this approach is that it does not cover the variation over time of the bandwidth limit available for the receiver. To avoid this problem, users can use a conservative value for their bandwidth limit instead of the best all-time value.

To reduce further the implosion problem, we use class representation, where all receivers that have the same bandwidth limit are grouped together and are represented as one virtual receiver called the representative. The preferences of the representative are selected based on the preferences of the class members. The QoS selection algorithm would then select the QoS parameter for the class based on the QoS preferences of the representative. The decision to partition receivers according to their bandwidth limit is based on the fact that receivers that have the same bandwidth limit are more likely to have close preferences, and the values of their preferences is more likely to represent the preferences of individual receivers.

Even though receivers in the same class are more likely to have close preferences, there is still a range on the *minimum accepted* and *ideal* preference values for the class, and this gives several possibilities for selecting the preferences of the representative. Table 1 shows different variants for selecting the *minimum accepted* and *ideal* preference of the representative receiver based respectively on the *minimum accepted* and *ideal* value for all receivers in the class.

	minimum accepted value of the representative	**ideal value of the representative**
Variant 1	Average of the *minimum accepted* values for all receivers	Average of the *ideal* values for all receivers
Variant 2	Minimum of the *minimum accepted* values for all receivers	Minimum of the *ideal* values for all receivers
Variant 3	Minimum of the *minimum accepted* values for all receivers	Maximum of the *ideal* values for all receivers
Variant 4	Maximum of the *minimum accepted* values for all receivers	Minimum of the *ideal* values for all receivers
Variant 5	Maximum of the *minimum accepted* values for all receivers	Maximum of the *ideal* values for all receivers

Table 1. Variants of the preferences selection for the group representative

To evaluate the adequacy of the class representation, we selected one class of receivers, and run the selection algorithm once with all receivers directly considered by the source for the selection of the QoS parameters of the broadcast stream (no grouping) and another time with only the preferences of the class representative considered. We compared the average satisfaction of all the receivers in these two cases. Simulation results are shown in figure 4.

The graph in figure 4 shows clearly that variant 2 and 4 resulted in the worse average satisfaction for the group, even though the satisfaction of the representative with its selected parameters was one (1). This is basically due to the fact that the *ideal* preference for the group representative is the minimum of the *ideal* preferences of all receivers, reflecting hence the preferences of the most conservative receiver for the *ideal* preferences. The best variant for group representation is variant 5, where the *minimum accepted* value for the preferences of the representative is the maximum of the *minimum accepted* values for all receivers, and the *ideal* value for the representative is the maximum of all *ideal* values for all receivers. This variant avoids the conservative choice of the *minimum accepted* preference, and explores the optimism on the *ideal* preferences of all receivers.

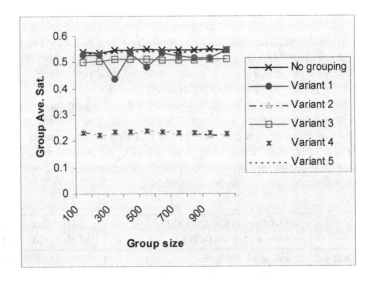

Figure 4. Average satisfaction with different variants of grouping.

6 Conclusion

In this paper, we have proposed an end-to-end rate-based mechanism for the selection of the optimum QoS for media broadcast that relies on the knowledge of the user preferences and bandwidth limitations of all receivers. Based on this information, the source will select the number of QoS variants for the given media stream and the QoS parameters for each of these variants. To limit the problem of feedback implosion from the receivers, we use a virtual representative for all receivers within a given group of receivers. Receivers are grouped according to the bandwidth limit of their device. We have considered several algorithms to determine the QoS preferences of the group representatives. Simulation results showed that not all of these algorithm lead to effective group representation. Simulation results also showed, as expected, that the average satisfaction of the receivers increases with an increase of the throughput of the source, which may limit the number and bandwidth of the available stream variants.

Acknowledgements

The authors would like to thank Dr. Dwight Makaroff for his help and comments on this work.

References

1. XU, X. R., Myers, A. C., Zhang, H. and Yavatkar, R., "Resilient multicast support for continuous-media applications," *Proceedings of NOSSDAV'97*.
2. S. Floyd, V. Jacobson, S. McCanne, C. Liu, and L. Zhang, "A Reliable multicast framework for light-weight sessions and application level framing," *in Proceeding of SIGCOMM*, 1995.
3. M. Grossglausser "Optimal deterministic timeouts for reliable scalable multicast," IEEE Journal on Selected Area in Communications, vol. 15, no.3, 1997.
4. J. Bolot, T. Turletti, and I. Wakeman, "Scalable feedback control for multicast video distribution in the Internet," in *Proc. Of ACM SIGCOMM*, pp. 58-67, August 1994.
5. R. Yavatkar, J. Griffoen, and M. Sudan, " A reliable dissemination protocol for interactive collaborative applications," in *Proceedings of INFOCOM*, 1991.
6. T. Jiang, M. Ammar, E. Zegura, "Inter-Receiver fairness: A Novel performance measure for Multicast ABR sessions," in *Proceedings of ACM SIGMETRICS'98* , Madison, Wisconsin, June 1998.
7. T. Jiang, E. Zegura, M. Ammar, "Inter-Receiver Fair Multicast Communication over the Internet," in *Proc. of NOSSDAV 99*, June 1999.
8. S. McCanne, V. Jacobson, and M. Vetterli, "Receiver-driven layered multicast," in *Proc. of ACM SIGCOMM*, pp. 117-130, August 1996.
9. L. Wu, R. Sharma and B. Smith, "Thin streams: An architecture for multicasting layered video," in *Proc. of NOSSDAV'97*, St.Louise,Missouri, May 1997.
10. S. Yan Cheung, Mostafa H. Ammar, and Xue Li , "On the use of destination set grouping to improve fairness in multicast video distribution," in *Proc. of IEEE INFOCOM'96*, March 1996.
11. Brett J. Vickers, Célio Albuquerque and Tatsuya Suda, "Source-adaptive multi-layered multicast algorithms for real-time video distribution," in *IEEE/ACM Transactions on Networking*, 1999.
12. P. Assunção and M. Ghanbari, "Multi-Casting of MPEG-2 Video with Multiple Bandwidth Constraints," in *Proc. of the 7th Int'l Workshop on Packet Video*, pp. 235-238, March 1996.

13. G. v. Bochmann and Z. Yang, "Quality of service management for teleteaching applications using the MPEG-4/DMIF," in *Intern. Workshop on Interactive Distr. Multimedia Systems and Telecom. Services*, Toulouse, Oct. 1999.

14. K. Elkhatib, G. v. Bochmann, "Selecting communication quality for mobile users based on device capabilities and user preferences," Technical report. U of Ottawa, Canada, 2001.

15. A. Richards, G. Rogers, V. Witana, and M. Antoniades, "Mapping user level QoS from a single parameter," in *Second IFIP/IEEE International Conference on Management of Multimedia Networks and Services*, Versailles, November

16. Michael J. Donahoo and Sunila R. Ainapure, "Scalable multicast representative member selection", *INFOCOM 2001*.

17. D. DeLucia, K. Obraczka, "Multicast feedback suppression using representatives," in *Proceedings of IEEE Infocom'97*.

18. K. El-Khatib, X. He, G. v. Bochmann, "*Quality of service negotiation based on device capabilities and user preferences*," Technical report. U. of Ottawa, Canada. May 2000.

A Novel Group Integrity Concept
for Multimedia Multicasting

Andreas Meissner [1], Lars Wolf [1,2], Ralf Steinmetz [1,3]

[1] GMD - German National Research Center for Information Technology, Institute IPSI,
Dolivostr. 15, 64293 Darmstadt, Germany
Andreas.Meissner@gmd.de

[2] University of Karlsruhe, Zirkel 2, 76128 Karlsruhe, Germany
Lars.Wolf@uni-karlsruhe.de

[3] Darmstadt Technical University, KOM, Merckstr. 25, 64283 Darmstadt, Germany
Ralf.Steinmetz@KOM.tu-darmstadt.de

Abstract. Multimedia multicasting brings together two technologies considered to be cornerstones of the future Internet, where rich media content will be distributed to a mass audience. It is obvious that unicasting will not be adequate for such content distribution due to the unacceptable stress imposed on network resources. Multicasting is a solution to this problem, and thus multicast routing and group management are now receiving high attention. However, so far, conditions on the *composition* of multicast groups have been kept rather simple. Requirements on group *membership*, member *roles* and group *organization*, commonly referred to as *group integrity conditions*, are rarely addressed or even enforced. Furthermore, the traditional multicasting model has been *flat*, with no finer granularity than a group, lacking any *inter-group relationships*. In our work, we address both issues that we see as shortcomings of current models. Our framework allows us to subdivide multicast groups into *subgroups* (e.g. for high and low quality versions of a media stream) and to form and manage *meta groups* from groups, integrating inter-related "multi" media groups. On all three levels, we specify a variety of *integrity conditions* as part of our comprehensive policy framework, including integrity on *state* and *state transition*, as well as group management *action* and *transition policies*.

1   Introduction

Recent work on group management protocols for Internet multicasting has focused on mechanisms supporting *source specific* multicasting, thus allowing a user to receive only data sent to a multicast group by a specific sender [2] [3] [18]. However, little effort has been spent on overcoming a major shortcoming of existing multicast group management approaches: Their limitation to simple user-initiated join and leave operations, to be evaluated locally, if at all, based on network-level conditions. For any further criteria to be applied during the join admission process, interaction with the application is required [20], and it is not obvious how control on group composition should be accomplished without a coordinating group manager.

D. Shepherd et al. (Eds.): IDMS 2001, LNCS 2158, pp. 233–244, 2001.

No comprehensive framework has yet been presented that provides a rich set of group integrity conditions for multimedia multicasting. In order to support multimedia multicasting, we use in our work three hierarchy levels: We propose to establish separate multicast *groups* for each medium, e.g. one group for video and another group for audio. We subdivide these groups into *subgroups* for actual data transfer, thus conceptually integrating e.g. different coding formats (such as audio streams of different quality levels) into one group. Observing that the data transmitted in several subgroups of a group will often be semantically identical, we identify a relation "*can be generated out of*" between subgroups, so *transformers* are introduced that feed one subgroup with re-coded data obtained from another subgroup. Finally, *meta groups* are formed by inter-related "multi" media groups.

We devise a framework for specifying, on all three hierarchy levels, *integrity conditions*, i.e. requirements imposed on subgroups, groups and meta groups that describe valid *states* and *state transitions* with regard to membership set, member roles, organization and topology, e.g. a minimum number of members or mandatory members. We also suggest integrity conditions on user data *traffic*. In addition to these conditions, our policy set includes *action policies*, specifying how a group manager should re-establish integrity in case it has been found violated, and *transition policies*, stating how to handle (potentially conflicting) requests received from members before advancing to the next state.

Paper Outline. After this introduction, we explain our basic concepts in section 2. Sections 3, 4 and 5 describe policies on subgroup, group and meta group level, respectively. A brief outline of related work is given in section 6. Section 7 concludes.

2   Basic Concepts: Subgroups, Groups, Managers, Transformers

We first introduce the basic concepts of our framework in the context of *monomedia multicasting,* i.e. multicast transmission of *one* medium, e.g. audio, from any number of senders to any number of receivers who are members of a multicast group. We thus employ, unless otherwise mentioned, the general *m:n* topology model; our framework is applied on top of any suitable network-level multicast protocol. In this paper we deal with *closed* groups, so only members may participate in the communication. Groups are also *determined*, thus all members are known, and *dynamic*, i.e. membership may change during the lifetime of the group. We denote groups by G_1, G_2, ... A central application-layer *group manager*, denoted $M(G_i)$, is responsible for managing its group's properties and members, their roles, rights and duties within the group [10], and for controlling group *integrity* according to a set of *policies*. We call any user data sent by a group member a *stream*, including non-continuous media data.

In our framework, a group is composed of zero or more *subgroups*, all controlled by the same group manager. If a group G_i has n subgroups, they are denoted G_i^0, G_i^1, ..., G_i^{n-1} and by definition $M(G_i) \equiv M(G_i^j)$ for j=0..n-1. This allows us to conceptually integrate into one group several formats used for transmission of one medium, such as a high quality audio subgroup (✧✧✧ in figure 1), a medium quality (✧✧) and a low quality (✧) subgroup, preferred for low-bandwidth receivers. A similar concept is employed in the context of *receiver oriented congestion control* [16].

We say that a subgroup G_i^j *mirrors* a subgroup G_i^k if the data transmitted in G_i^j is, apart from format differences, semantically the same as the G_i^k data.[1] A subgroup G_i^j is said to *super-mirror* a subgroup G_i^k if G_i^j mirrors G_i^k and is allowed to include *additional* data. Transfer of user data traffic always occurs in subgroups, not groups.

We employ the term *user* for a communication entity that is a *member* of zero or more subgroups; after a user U_k has joined G_i^j (which implicitly includes a join to G_i), U_k is called a member of G_i^j and G_i. A member U_k may have different *roles*: If U_k sends data, he is called a data *source*, if U_k receives data, he is a *sink* (figure 1). If U_k is a sink (source) in any G_i^j, he is called a sink (source) in G_i. Users are identified by their permanent *user ID* (as opposed to the current network address), and group managers maintain a current mapping for their members since most underlying multicasting protocols are built on network addresses. User ID assignment is out-of-band in our framework. Users lacking a permanent ID (as checked against a *user directory*) or users failing to authenticate themselves are, depending on group or subgroup policy, denied access or admitted only on a limited-rights basis and, e.g. by selective data encryption, excluded from sensible data exchange. User authentication is accomplished by a public/private key challenge-response mechanism initiated by the group manager during join request evaluation.

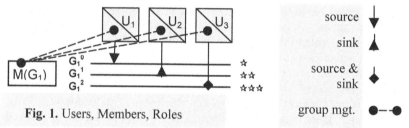

Fig. 1. Users, Members, Roles

Individual members may have specific *rights* and *duties* (selected from a set defined during subgroup, group or meta group establishment) on subgroup, group or meta group level, such as the right to modify policies or the duty to report observed integrity violations (see section 3). Group or subgroup policy may state that certain users are considered non-admissible or mandatory members, e.g. if they have some VIP status like the professor in a multicast lecture. As we will see later, it is the task of the group manager to evaluate any join or leave request against the applicable set of policies and the user properties. For example, if, according to property data looked up by the manager in the user directory, the right *"may initiate a voting among members"* is granted in group G_i to member U_k, we write $InitiateVoting(G_i, U_k) =$ true. Moreover, if *InitiateVoting* is the right known by the consecutive number 1, we alternatively write $R_1(G_i, U_k) =$ true. Granted rights and imposed duties may be further characterized or limited for individual members by *attributes*. For a possible extension to a more semantically rich specification of rights and duties see [5].

Each user has a *user controller* that interacts with a group manager and locally enforces instructions received by the manager of any group the user is a member of. We generally assume that user controllers always successfully enforce group manager orders locally and that externals (i.e. non-members such as users who were forcefully removed from a subgroup) cannot disturb communication within the subgroup. As we

---

[1] The exact definition of mirroring has to be made individually for each pair of formats.

do not intend to modify existing lower-layer group management protocols such as IGMP in this framework, it is obvious that non-complying users can bypass any user controller and simply join a group manually. In the presence of such "bad guys" we employ data encryption in order to leave them with unusable data unless they interact with the group manager, who in this case also performs key management.

With m the total number of users and n the number of subgroups of G_i, we write:

U: set of users $\{U_1, ..., U_m\}$

$P(G_i^j)$, sink(G_i^j), source(G_i^j): Set of members, sinks, sources of G_i^j, respectively

$P(G_i) = \cup_{j=0..n-1} P(G_i^j)$, sink$(G_i)$, source$(G_i)$: Set of members, sinks, sources of G_i, resp.

Note that groups and subgroups are *not* identical to the set of their members (i.e. $G_i \not\equiv P(G_i)$), as we will see later, when we further characterize them by a set of policies.

If group organization policy states that all subgroups mirror each other, a straightforward way to guarantee a proper data feed in all subgroups is to require any user who is a source for one subgroup to also act as a source for all other subgroups. This might, however, easily overload a source's CPU and, if clusters of sinks for certain (e.g. "low quality") subgroups exist only in isolated geographical regions, result in waste of bandwidth on long-distance network links due to the fact that redundant data is transmitted in the subgroups. As an alternative, we propose that a source be only mandated to feed a subgroup with a data format out of which all other subgroups' data formats can be computed. (If it cannot do that, the group manager has to deny it the source role in the first place.) The job of transforming one format into another is then accomplished by special members called *transformers*. We denote a transformer that generates the data format of G_i^j out of the format of G_i^k as $T(G_i^k, G_i^j)$. $T(G_i^k, G_i^j)$ may be located anywhere in the data tree for G_i^k; it is a sink for G_i^k and a source for G_i^j. If transformers are deployed to overcome the bandwidth waste issue in the above example, there may have to be several $T(G_i^k, G_i^j)$ in G_i if G_i^j is allowed to be partitioned and the transformers only serve a limited (geographical) region. Each partition of G_i^j may have its own data tree with a $T(G_i^k, G_i^j)$ as root. It is the responsibility of $M(G_i)$ to admit members only if the subgroup they want to join as a sink can be made available in their region, e.g. by activating a proper transformer.

While subgroups are not conceptually required to be *ordered* within a group, transformers allow us to introduce a *coding hierarchy*. For example, if we assume that the data in group G_i can be scaled along one or more dimensions, we introduce among its subgroups a relation "*can be generated out of*". We write $G_i^j \rightarrow G_i^k$ if it is possible to transform the data format in G_i^k into the data format in G_i^j. This does not imply that a transformer $T(G_i^k, G_i^j)$ is actually operational or even available in G_i. In some (multimedia) cases, we might have a relation $G_b^j \rightarrow G_a^k$, $a \neq b$, e.g. if annotations or subtitles can in some way be generated from a video in G_a^k and made available in subgroup G_b^j of a separate "text" group G_b. Therefore, we also allow transformers $T(G_a^k, G_b^j)$ with $a \neq b$, noting however that, due to the extra inter-group dependency, the deployment of such transformers should be carefully weighed against the benefits. We will come back to such dependencies when we discuss meta group integrity. Unlike some *layered multicasting schemes*, we do not assume that a user has to listen to several subgroups in parallel in order to re-construct a meaningful data stream.

A special type of transformers referred to as *mixers* aggregate data streams received from different sources in G_i^k into *one* data stream in G_i^j (such as audio mixers or video "thumbnail" generators). We denote a mixer as $T^m(G_i^k, G_i^j)$, generating *one aggregated* output stream, as opposed to $T(G_i^k, G_i^j)$ which means that multiple input streams in G_i^k are transformed into *multiple* output streams in G_i^j [11]. For a mixer $T^m(G_i^k, G_i^j)$, we do not require j≠k. Furthermore, if G_i^* is a set of subgroups of G_i, we extend the concept of mixers to the form $T^m(G_i^*, G_i^j)$, so to have a mixer feeding a "comprehensive" subgroup G_i^j from the data in other subgroups.

3   Subgroup Policies

In general, policies set forth for a subgroup describe rules according to which valid subgroup states and state transitions are determined, and actions the group manager takes to maintain or re-establish subgroup integrity. In our discrete model, a subgroup advances from one state i to the next state i+1. A state is described by membership set, member roles, rights and duties, and topology. In a simplified example, leaving out topology for the moment and assuming that "source-only" users exist, state i might be described as "Sources: U_1. Sinks: U_2, U_3", and state i+1 as "Sources: U_2. Sinks: U_3, U_4". We impose integrity conditions on *states* and on *state transitions*. For a subgroup G_j^k, the following is a sample integrity condition on state:

$$| \text{ source}(G_j^k) \, | = 1 \text{ and } | \text{ sink}(G_j^k) \, | \geq 2, \tag{S1}$$

i.e., at all times, there must be exactly one source and at least two sinks in G_j^k.

Now denoting the set of members of G_j^k during state i as ${}^iP(G_j^k)$, an integrity condition on state transition (that expresses some limit on member fluctuation) is:

$$| \, {}^iP(G_j^k) \cap {}^{i+1}P(G_j^k) \, | \geq 2 \tag{S2}$$

In our above example, condition S1 is met for state i and state i+1; the transition from state i to state i+1 fulfills condition S2.

The group manager has to control and maintain integrity within each subgroup according to subgroup policies kept in a dynamic *policy repository*. Before advancing from one state to the next, the group manager checks if all integrity conditions on state and state transitions would be met. If so (possibly after conflict resolution), it advances the subgroup to the next state. In the above example, $M(G_j^k)$ would have received, during state i, the following requests:

from U_1: "leave subgroup G_j^{k}"

from U_2: "switch role from sink to source in G_j^{k}"[2]

from U_4: "join subgroup G_j^k as sink"

It determined that, combined, these requests did not violate conditions S1 and S2, and therefore it committed them. *Group* policy states when the manager should proceed from *collecting* requests to *evaluating* them [19], e.g. after pre-defined time intervals, upon a manual trigger signal by a member holding a respective right, or (in the simple, non-scalable case) immediately after having received any single request.

In addition to the *membership and role related integrity conditions* introduced above, we use *topology related integrity conditions* on subgroup states. Such conditions may, for example, allow partitioning or limit the scope of the subgroup by applying the concepts of administrative or TTL scope. Such conditions can reflect the availability of transformers for feeding subgroups in certain regions. The condition:

---

[2] A *switch* is an atomic operation and guarantees successful *join-as-source* after *leave-as-sink*.

scope(G_j^k) = national   [S3]

results in denial of join requests from "foreign" (with respect to the manager) users.

Extending the above example, if U_1 had failed to complete the requested leave, state i+1 would violate condition S1 due to the number of sources being two. In such a case, the group manager has to know what action to take in order to re-establish integrity. Therefore, our policy set additionally includes *action policies* according to which the group manager reacts on observed integrity failures. A simple (yet not always feasible) action policy, applicable to any type of integrity violation observed in state i+1, requires a roll-back to the previous state i. Another general-purpose type of action policy is checking back with existing members, e.g. by having the manager initiate a *voting* [7] among members on whether or not condition S1 should be temporarily disabled, or if a subgroup suspension or even termination is desired. Changes in the policy repository trigger a re-evaluation of the current state according to the new set of integrity conditions. More specifically tailored to the above situation, we might apply (using source^L(G_j^k) to denote the source having joined most recently):

if | source(G_j^k) | > 1 then
{ perform forced-leave for source^L(G_j^k); commit }   [AS1]

where "commit" means that an immediate transition to the next state is required. We observe that subgroup integrity can be violated by unexpected events. The group manager detects this (e.g. by missing confirmations) and, according to action policies, takes action to re-establish integrity by advancing to a new state in which integrity conditions are met. It is thus possible to have such "emergency" state transitions.

Another type of subgroup policies are integrity conditions on *traffic*. While integrity conditions on state and state transitions, as previously introduced, are *discrete* conditions, traffic integrity conditions are *continuous*, i.e. they have to be evaluated continuously. They specify what requirements the data traffic in the subgroup has to meet, e.g. adherence to a certain data format, conditions on QoS or acceptable error rate, and conditions on security, such as mandatory encryption by all sources. Since the group manager is not necessarily involved in user data traffic (or for another reason, such as CPU power, unable to monitor all user data traffic), it may deploy members as trusted *agents* who carry the *duty* to monitor user data traffic and report any observed violation of traffic integrity conditions to the manager. It is then up to the manager to take corrective action according to action policies. If we have some metric "error" on error rate and apply the following traffic integrity condition:

error(G_j^k) < threshold   [S4],

a corresponding action policy might be, using sink^E(G_j^k) to denote the sink having made the most retransmission requests:

if (violated(S4)) then { perform forced-leave for sink^E(G_j^k) }   [AS4]

During the establishment phase of a subgroup, it is often advisable to apply a less restrictive set of integrity conditions in order to allow it to build up its membership set. "Tighter" conditions can be added by authorized members later. Further extending the initial example, we assume that U_1 successfully completed the requested leave (thus no corrective action was necessary) and that all users are domestic, so state i+1 fulfills S1 and S3. We now define a set K = {U_2, U_4} and introduce a new condition:

P(G_j^k) ∩ K ≥ 1   [S5]

i.e. we demand that at least one of users U_2 and U_4 be members of the subgroup. During the policy set re-evaluation triggered by adding this new condition, S5 is determined to be met during state i+1, so no action is required by M(G_j^k). However, the immediate question arises what to do if both U_2 and U_4 later, during the same state, request to leave G_j^k. We observe that introducing a new *integrity condition* on *state* may require a new *policy* for state *transitions*, i.e. a procedure stating how to handle requests that would result in violation of this condition in the subsequent state. We call this type of subgroup policies *transition policies*, not to be confused with (descriptive) integrity conditions on state transitions. Transition policies are evaluated in a defined order. A sample transition policy with respect to S5 is, using leave(G_j^k) to denote the set of members having requested, during the current state, to leave G_j^k:

if $K \subseteq$ leave(G_j^k) then

{ deny leave request by $U_l \in K$ having issued the request first }   [TS5]

Unlike action policies, transition policies never require an immediate commit. While transition policies are applied to resolve conflicts among requests received by the group manager, it is obvious that policies themselves might be inconsistent. For the set of integrity conditions on *state*, it is computationally possible to prove their consistency by constructing a sample for which all of them are met. For *state transition* integrity conditions, and in particular for *action* and *transition policies*, it is in the general case computationally impossible to determine whether they are consistent. [17] provides some discussion on policy conflict determination schemes in the context of programmable networks. In our work, we currently rely on manual inspection of policies before they are added to the applicable policy set at any level.

4   Group Policies

Our policy framework introduced for subgroups is imposed on groups accordingly. The set of group policies conceptually includes the policies of all subgroups. In this section, however, we discuss group policies referring to integrity conditions or actions applied *across subgroups*, i.e. defining the inter-relation of a group's subgroups.

We again distinguish between integrity conditions on group *state* and on group *state transitions*. Both are discrete and include *membership and role* related as well as *topology* and, new, *group organization* related conditions. The former define how members may be distributed among the subgroups, with what roles, rights and duties. For example, for group G_j with n subgroups $G_j^0, ..., G_j^{n-1}$, there might be a condition

$P(G_j^h) \cap P(G_j^k) = \varnothing \ \forall \ h \neq k$ with h, k $\in \{0, ..., n-1\}$ [G1]

expressing that no user may be a member of more than one subgroup at a time[3], and, assuming condition S1 is enforced for all subgroups to avoid "zero" member counts:

$| P(G_j^h) | / | P(G_j^k) | \in [0.5, 2] \ \forall \ h \neq k$ with h, k $\in \{0, ..., n-1\}$ [G2]

so that the number of members be somewhat balanced among the subgroups.

Group organization refers to requirements on what subgroups, with what properties, have to exist within the group. A group state integrity condition on both topology and group organization is:

$\exists \ k \in \{0,...,n-1\}$: G_j^k non-partitioned and $\exists \ T(G_j^k, G_j^h) \ \forall h \neq k$, h $\in \{0,...,n-1\}$[G3]

stating that there must be at least one non-partitioned subgroup out of which all other subgroups can be generated by an existing transformer (which implies $G_j^h \rightarrow G_j^k$).

---

[3] We have to relax this condition if transformers are to be deployed.

Integrity conditions on *state transitions* describe how groups may advance from one state to the next, again with regard to *membership and role* as well as *topology* and *group organization*. For example, the condition:

$$\nexists\, l,\, h: U_l \in {}^{i-1}P(G_j^h) \text{ and } U_l \in {}^{i}P(G_j^{k\neq h}) \text{ and } U_l \in {}^{i+1}P(G_j^h) \qquad [G4]$$

would, along with condition G1, prohibit oscillating behavior by a user switching back and forth between the same subgroups.

Even though, by definition, user data traffic is exchanged only in subgroups, continuous integrity conditions on *traffic* have to be evaluated at group level. If continuous media is multicast in different qualities or formats in subgroups of a group G_j that thus mirror each other, the group manager $M(G_j)$ or its *agents* have to monitor if the subgroups remain synchronized. Moreover, a violation of traffic integrity in one subgroup G_j^k can affect traffic integrity in another subgroup G_j^h if G_j^h is fed by a transformer $T(G_j^k, G_j^h)$ and there is no other subgroup G_j^e for which $G_j^h \rightarrow G_j^e$ with operational transformer $T(G_j^e, G_j^h)$.

Action policies on group level specify how the group manager has to re-establish group level integrity. With above condition G2, if the unexpected death (detected by the group manager through regular polling) of a number of members has resulted in unbalanced subgroup membership numbers, $M(G_j)$ might react by forcefully switching remaining members between subgroups. If, however, conflicting requests are received by $M(G_j)$ from members intending to switch subgroups, the manager would decide according to group-level *transition policies*.

Generally, if the integrity of any subgroup is violated, the same is true for the group. The group manager can re-establish integrity for the group by re-establishing integrity for the affected subgroup, or by suspending or terminating it. If the subgroup's integrity cannot be re-established and the non-suspended presence of the subgroup is required by group organization integrity conditions, group action policy may state that the entire group be suspended or terminated. Otherwise, suspended subgroups with violated integrity do not constitute a group level integrity violation.

5   Meta Group Policies

For multimedia multicasting, we now extend the scope of our integrity concept to two or more semantically related media transmitted simultaneously. In this multimedia case, we are dealing with two or more multicast groups, each with the properties introduced above. All these groups together form what we call a *meta group*. In particular, each group has an individual group manager. In order to coordinate and control them, a *meta group manager* is established, denoted MM(G) if, referring to the example in figure 2, G is the meta group formed by groups $G_1, ..., G_4$. We say that groups $G_1, ..., G_4$ are (actively) *associated* with G.

In our concept, the meta group manager controls meta group (i.e. inter-group) integrity by applying meta group integrity conditions set forth in a policy set with *state* and *state transition* integrity conditions, *traffic* integrity conditions, *action policies* and *transition policies* on meta group level.

We discuss meta group integrity along a comprehensive example, a video conference with the following four groups:

- G_1 for video, with subgroups G_1^0 for high quality and G_1^1 for low quality
- G_2 for voice audio, with subgroups G_2^0 for format A and G_2^1 for format B
- G_3 for sign language video[4] generated out of audio by a transformer, with just one subgroup G_3^0
- G_4 for control, with just one subgroup G_4^0

Together, they form meta group G. (Note that there are two separate video groups.)

The meta group manager MM(G) enforces the following meta group level *state* integrity conditions:

$$P(G_4) \supseteq P(G_1) \cup P(G_2) \cup P(G_3) \qquad \text{[M1]}$$

i.e. any member of G_1, G_2 or G_3 must be a member of G_4, too, and

$$source(G_1) \subseteq source(G_2) \qquad \text{[M2]}$$

i.e. any source in G_1 must be a source in G_2, too, and

$$sink(G_2) \cap sink(G_3) = \varnothing \qquad \text{[M3]}$$

i.e. no user may be a sink in both G_2 and G_3 at the same time[5], and (along with M1)

$$\nexists\, U_k \in P(G_1)\text{: InitiateVoting}(G_1, U_k) \wedge \neg\text{InitiateVoting}(G_4, U_k) \qquad \text{[M4]}$$

i.e. it is not permitted to grant members the *InitiateVoting* right in G_1 but not in G_4, and, as an organizational integrity condition:

$$\exists\, j \in \{0, 1\}\text{: } G_3^0 \to G_2^j \text{ and } \exists\, T(G_2^j, G_3^0) \text{ operational} \qquad \text{[M5]}$$

i.e. we need a subgroup in G_2 out of which G_3^0 can be generated by an existing and operational transformer.

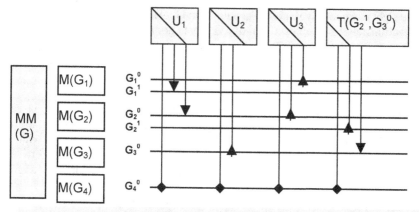

Fig. 2. Sample Meta Group

Assuming proper rights allocation according to M4, these conditions M1-M5 are all met in the state depicted in figure 2 with users U_1, U_2, U_3 and transformer $T(G_2^1, G_3^0)$. (Additional users would, of course, be required to establish a meaningful video conference scenario, but we leave them out in this example.)

The following is a sample integrity condition on *state transition*:

$$^i sink(G_3) \cap {}^{i+1} sink(G_2) = \varnothing \qquad \text{[M6]}$$

i.e. no sink may switch from G_3 to G_2 during a state transition.

A typical *traffic* integrity condition demands that G_1, G_2, and G_3 remain in sync.

---

[4] For users who are hearing impaired
[5] An exception might again be appropriate for a transformer, and for monitoring purposes.

Note that $MM(G)$ does not care how the G_2 members are distributed among subgroups G_2^0 and G_2^1. If we now further assume that $G_3^0 \rightarrow G_2^1$, but *not* $G_3^0 \rightarrow G_2^0$, an organizational integrity condition is imposed on G_2 (and enforced by $M(G_2)$, not $MM(G)$) stating that G_2^1 *super-mirror* G_2^0. It is then up to $M(G_2)$ to decide whether this be best accomplished by deploying a transformer $T(G_2^0, G_2^1)$ or by requiring that all sources in G_2^0 must also be sources in G_2^1.

At meta group level, *action* and *transition policies* state how to re-establish meta group integrity and how to handle *group manager* requests directed towards the meta group manager, respectively. A sample action policy associated with M2 is:

if $U_k \in$ source$(G_1) \setminus$ source(G_2) then { forced join of U_k to G_2; commit} [AM2]

i.e. G_1 members who, for whatever reason, lost their member status in G_2 are, by way of $M(G_2)$, forced to join G_2 (again).

A subgroup G_i^j always non-ambiguously forms part of group G_i, and, in most cases, a group G_i is associated only to a *single* meta group G, as in our example. However, it is sometimes appropriate to allow G_i to be associated to another meta group G' at the same time (e.g. for a general newsfeed that is of interest to several parallel video conferences). If this relaxation was applied, more than one meta group manager would act as the "final authority" on G_i, resulting in potentially conflicting policies being applied to G_i since we do not require any policy alignment *across* meta groups. To overcome this problem, we introduce a *passive association*: If $MM(G')$ accepts G_i to be passively associated to G', it agrees to have no further control on G_i than the right to forcefully remove G_i again from G'. Any G' integrity violation caused by G_i is ultimately resolved by a "remove G_i" meta group action policy.

6   Related Work

So far, group integrity has received little attention in the multicasting research domain. An early approach to formalize integrity is given in [9] proposing a group communication framework: A *group association* (not to be confused with our terminology in section 5) is established, for the purpose of data transfer, between a subset of group members. There are *active* and *passive* participants in a group association, with active participants forming the *active group*. Active group integrity *(AGI)* conditions are imposed on the active group membership of an association, such as a minimum number of participants. A *multicast conversation (MC)* within an association is an instance of communication, e.g. with one sender (*master*) and several receivers. *Association topology integrity (ATI)* conditions include AGI conditions on individual conversations (now referred to as *MC-AGI*) and conditions on the whole group association, such as a maximum number of concurrent conversations. Their concept is employed in [7] in a TINA context, and, on top of XTP, in [15] with separate treatment of group *establishment conditions* and *communication integrity conditions*. Generally, group management in *XTP 4.0* [20] is based on receiver lists and allows reliable multicasting. Hence, if full reliability is required for all group members, failing members are said to destroy the group's integrity. XTP assumes that sufficient knowledge for a proper reaction, as for any decisions on valid group composition, is available at the application layer only and therefore makes no attempt to provide such functionality itself. There is no framework for group integrity in XTP, but XTP had a considerable influence on newer protocols. Further work touching multicast group integrity is found in [10] and [6]; a comprehensive overview of current multicasting research is provided in [16] and, with multimedia focus, in [13].

[19] proposes a distributed generic membership algorithm for cooperative groups and devises mechanisms for synchronzing data exchange with the evolution of group membership over time. A cooperative group is formed by *agents*, organized in a *cooperation graph* expressing their relation. It is decided at the application layer what rules or predicates a graph needs to fulfill in order to be considered valid. Hence *integrity*, though not specifically addressed, refers to synchronizing data exchange with membership changes and to choosing valid subgraphs of the cooperation graph.

A language for specifying policies (Ponder) is suggested in [5]. [8] describes a policy based role object model for individuals performing roles in distributed systems, also allowing for relationships between roles. Policies for specifying the behavior of programmable networks are addressed in [17]. The RM-ODP ISO standard [14] defines *viewpoints* describing distributed processing in heterogeneous environments.

Computer supported collaborative work (CSCW) systems deal with organizing work groups and data flow between group members. There are systems for *asynchronous* collaboration (i.e members do not process group data simultaneously) and systems for *synchronous* collaboration [19], such as video conferences with simultaneous presence and processing by all participants [12] [1] [4]. Floor control and other group management functions in CSCW systems are generally performed at the application layer. As group members are humans, integrity refers to conditions on the composition of the set of human participants and their individual rights and roles.

7   Conclusions and Future Work

Following our observation that current multicast models are not well suited for group integrity management, we have described a novel concept for group management in multimedia multicasting. Groups were subdivided into subgroups, allowing for different formats for transmission of one medium; inter-related groups were said to form a meta group. We employed centralized group management performed by group and meta group managers. Special focus was given to integrity conditions imposed on subgroups, groups and meta groups, with regard to state, state transitions, and traffic. We additionally included action policies and transition policies in our policy set. It was shown in a number of examples that our framework is applicable to common scenarios in monomedia and multimedia multicasting.

Several extensions of this framework are possible and left for future work: *Fault tolerance*, especially in case of group manager failure, is an issue to be resolved. We have, up to this point, considered only centrally managed groups (and sub- and meta groups). However, in future work, we intend to drop this limitation and analyze *decentralized* scenarios, e.g. with peering members who vote in order to reach a group management decision by themselves. Currently, we are evaluating if the Ponder language [5] can be used for policy specification in our context. We have so far not addressed in detail how *inconsistencies among policies* may be determined and resolved; we intend to look into this on a theoretical basis in future work.

References

1. I. Beier, H. Koenig: GCSVA - A Multiparty Videoconferencing System with Distributed Group and QoS Management. Proc. of the 7th International Conference on Computer Communications and Networks ICCCN'98, Lafayette, USA, 1998, pp 594-598
2. S. Bhattacharyya et al: A framework for Source-Specific IP Multicast Deployment. Internet Draft <draft-bhattach-pim-ssm-00.txt>, July 2000
3. B. Cain, S. Deering, B. Fenner, I. Kouvelas, A. Thyagarajan: Internet Group Mana- gement Protocol, Version 3. Internet Draft <draft-ietf-idmr-igmp-v3-07.txt>, March 2001
4. S. T. Chanson, A. Hui, H. König, M Zühlke: Das OCTOPUS-Videokonferenzsystem, PIK 23 (2000) No. 4, pp 189-198 (in German)
5. N. Damianou, N. Dulay, E. Lupu, M. Sloman: The Ponder Policy Specification Language. Proc. Workshop on Policies for Distributed Systems and Networks (Policy 2001), Bristol, UK, Jan. 2001, Springer Verlag LNCS 1995, pp 18-39
6. C. Diot, W. Dabbous, J. Crowcroft: Multipoint Communications: A Survey of Protocols, Functions, and Mechanisms. IEEE Journal on Selected Areas in Communications, Vol. 15 (3), April 1997
7. E. Koerner, A. Danthine: Towards a TINA-based framework for collaborative work. Interoperable Communication Networks, 1 (1998), Baltzer, pp 17-40
8. E. Lupu, M. Sloman: A Policy Based Role Object Model. Proc. First International Enterprise Distributed Object Computing Workshop (EDOC'97), Gold Coast, Queensland, Australia, October 1997, pp 36-47
9. L. Mathy, G. Leduc, O. Bonaventure, A. Danthine: A Group Communication Framework. Broadband Islands '94 Connecting with the End-User, W. Bauerfeld, O. Spaniol and F. Williams, eds., Elsevier North-Holland, 1994, pp 167-178
10. A. Mauthe, D. Hutchison, G. Coulson, S. Namuye: From Requirements to Services: A Study on Group Communictation Support for Distributed Multimedia Systems. Technical Report MPG-95-10, Computing Department, Lancaster University, Lancaster, UK, 1995
11. A. Mauthe, G. Coulson, D. Hutchison, S. Namuye: Group Support in Multimedia Communications Systems. Proceedings of the 2nd COST 237 Workshop on Teleservices and Multimedia Communications, Copenhagen, Denmark, 1995
12. M. Nguyen, M. Schwartz: MCMP: A Transport/Session Level Distributed Protocol for Desktop Conference Setup. IEEE Journal on Selected Areas in Communications, Vol. 14, No. 7, Sept. 1996
13. J. C. Pasquale, G. C. Polyzos, G. Xylomenos: The multimedia multicasting problem. Multimedia Systems (1998) 6, pp 43-59
14. J. Putman: Architecting with RM-ODP, Prentice Hall, 2001, ISBN 0130191167
15. J. F. de Rezende, A. Mauthe, S. Fdida, D. Hutchison: M-Connection Service: A Multicast Service for Distributed Multimedia Applications. Proc. of Multimedia Transport and Teleservices, International COST237 Workshop, (Copenhagen, Denmark), Nov. 1995
16. V. Roca, L. Costa, R. Vida, A. Dracinschi, S. Fdida: A Survey of Multicast Technologies. Technical Report RP-LIP6-2000-20, Université P.&M. Curie LIP6, Paris, Sept. 2000 (WiP)
17. M. Sloman, E. Lupu: Policy Specification for Programmable Networks. Proc. First International Working Conference on Active Networks (IWAN'99), Berlin, June 1999, ed. S. Civaci, Springer Verlag LNCS
18. R. Vida, L. Costa, R. Zara, S. Fdida, S. Deering, B. Fenner, I. Kouvelas, B. Haberman: Multicast Listener Discovery Version 2 (MLDv2) for IPv6. Internet Draft <draft-vida-mld-v2-00.txt>, February 2001
19. T. Villemur, M. Diaz: A collaborative membership service and protocol for structured groups. International Conference on Parallel and Distributed Processing, Techniques and Applications (PDPTA'99), Las Vegas (USA), June-July 1999, Vol. IV, pp 2115-2121
20. The Xpress Transport Protocol, XTP 4.0 Specification, see http://www.ca.sandia.gov/xtp/biblio.html

Constraint-Based Configuration of Proxylets for Programmable Networks

Krish T. Krishnakumar, Morris Sloman

Department of Computing, Imperial College,
London SW7 2BZ, UK
{tkkumar,m.sloman}@doc.ic.ac.uk

Abstract. Applications such as multimedia streaming for mobile users, or video conferencing, require support within the network for transcoding, compression etc. Proxylets running on servers within the network may be used to transform the media flows in order to meet application or QoS requirements. In this paper we examine the feasibility of performing constraint based configuration of the required proxylets. A set of constraints can be defined to select the required proxylets. A second stage is to define constraints relating to the placement of proxylets on nodes in the network. Eventually we will investigate the use of constraints for dynamic re-configuration to accommodate user mobility, or QoS variation. Some preliminary implementations of the architecture are presented and we discuss our approach to incorporate dynamic configuration to cater for load and QoS variations.

1   Introduction

The Alpine project [2] is investigating the use of application-level proxylets which execute on servers within the network to support the rapid provision of new services, such as on-demand multi-point video conferencing or multi-media streaming services for mobile users. A proxylet based system provides many of the advantages of active or programmable network type of services [1], such as transformation of media encodings, to take place within the network but without the security risks of programming at the 'fast-path' level within networks. However there is the need to be able to configure the various proxylets required to support particular applications by selecting suitable proxylets from a database of the those available and deciding on the most appropriate servers on which these proxylets should be loaded. These configuration management decisions can be non-trivial when taking into account the various constraints imposed by the specific application requirements, services which the user may be authorized to use, physical capabilities of mobile computing devices and available quality of service (QoS) provided by a wireless network. Typical users will be non-technical and so will not be capable of making the selections required to support the service they require. Thus, there is a need to automate the configuration of proxylets, taking into consideration all the above constraints. This will avoid the errors which are often introduced, even by technically competent users, when configuring complex systems.

D. Shepherd et al. (Eds.): IDMS 2001, LNCS 2158, pp. 245-256, 2001.

This paper describes initial work on the configuration of required proxylets, from an available collection, in a programmable network infrastructure. We are looking at applying constraint satisfaction techniques to facilitate automated provisioning of resources for a particular user/service in accordance with an application request. This requires integration of constraint based configuration for a dynamically changing network environment. The proposed system would accept user specification of the service required, derive a preliminary set of proxylet configurations, from the proxylets which support the required functionality, check for constraint violations of the above set of configurations and allocate the proxylets to servers, taking into consideration other constraints such as QoS requirements, available bandwidth, server loading, security risks or charging for use of servers.

The configuration of software components can be defined by a set of attributes (or components) whose possible values belong to a finite set and a set of feasibility constraints over these attributes which specify their compatible combinations of values. The problem is to find a feasible product (i.e., to choose a value such as a particular proxylet or server for each attribute which corresponds to a configuration variable) that satisfies not only the feasibility constraints but also some user requirements (such as QoS policy). Real-world problems in computer vision, planning, scheduling, configuration and diagnosing can be viewed as Constraint Satisfaction Problems (CSP) [4]. We are using Daniel Jackson's Alloy/ALCOA [15] to express and analyse the constraints. Eventually we would like to extend this approach to cater for dynamic re-configuration of proxylets in which the proxylets may have to move to new nodes to support user mobility, or variations in actual QoS within the network.

This paper describes the prototype implementation of a simple scenario using constraint based configuration of proxylets and indicates how we intend to extend the work to cater for dynamic reconfiguration of proxylets. Section 2 of the paper outlines the Application Level Active Network (ALAN) proxylet approach being used in the Alpine project. In Section 3, we formally define constraint based satisfaction in terms of configuration spaces, and introduce constraint variables and values for the ALAN mechanism. The derivation of proxylet configuration and constraint checks are also presented in section 3 with the customer service requirements. The overall architecture of our approach and the current progress in the implementation are described in section 4. In Section 5, we provide a discussion of future work followed by a discussion of related work in section 6.

2   ALAN System Overview

The ALAN system [3] assumes clients access remote servers across the internet using the HTTP protocol. Protocol entities called Proxylets can be dynamically loaded onto intermediate Dynamic Proxy Servers (DPS) within the network, to perform application-specific functions such as compression / decompression, protocol transformations, multicast reflecting, etc. The proxylet is dynamic code in a single jar file which is downloaded and run on a DPS. The proxylet can be referenced via a URL, and if not already on the DPS, it is loaded from a proxylet repository. The DPS is an application layer active network node which accepts requests and creates an environment for the execution of proxylets. The DPSs are selected at optimal distance for an end-to-end path between client and end-server (Figure 1). We are also using proxylets to perform the configuration management tasks such as proxylet selection and allocation to optimal DPS servers. The reason is that configuration may be instigated by a mobile user with very limited processing resources, although our architecture does allow for a DPS server to be based on a more powerful mobile device such as a laptop computer.

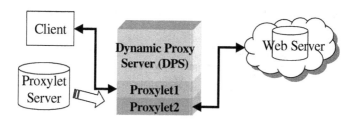

Fig. 1. Application Level Active Networking Architecture

3 A Simple Scenario

3.1 Example Description

Typical real applications involve hundreds of constraints and values for each variable, but we have focused on a very simplified example based on a user accessing remote media streams from a wireless (wl) or wired device to illustrate the approach. There are three different classes of users, Gold, Silver and Economy which relate to the QoS they will receive as well as whether they can use wireless connections etc. We give some constraint variables for the scenario (see Figure 2):

Browsers: Access to multi media streams from either wireless or wired devices.
Mode: Real time mode (to transcode the video/audio stream as it is being downloaded) and download mode (to first download the compressed media stream, decompress it and then start playing the stream using a suitable media tool).
Proxylet: It has been assumed that multiple proxylets are available for modifying the content presentation to be more suitable for the client device. We assume proxylets are available to cater for WAP phones, compression, decompression, real-time trancoding, a RealPlayer and DPS location selection.
DPS Location: This is the location of the DPS in relation to the browser/server. For simplicity, this parameter is assumed to have values as such nearer to the browser, intermediate (within the network), nearer to the server.
Cache: This is to indicate whether data can be cached at a local server.
Payload Type: The multi media payload packets may contain video, audio or data streams.
QoS package: There are 3 classes of users - Gold, Silver or Economy which relate to the class of Qos they will receive.

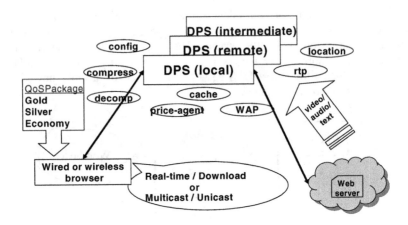

Fig. 2. Simplified ALAN

3.2   Constraint Specification

A constraint is simply a logical relation among several unknowns (or variables), each taking a value in a given domain. For example X+Y > 5 defines a constraint on permitted values of X and Y and (P ∨ Q) ∧ (¬P ∨ ¬S) is a constraint on the permitted values of the booleans P, Q and S. The specification of a configuration in terms of assembling the parts into a required system, involve two distinct phases. One is *domain knowledge* to describe the objects of an application and the relationships among them. The other is a specification of the desired product which defines requirements that must be satisfied by the product and the structure or topology of the product.

A Constraint Satisfaction Problem (CSP) is defined as $P= <V, Dv, Cv>$, where
- A set of variables V representing all the variables that may potentially become active and appear in a configuration. $V = \{V_1,....,V_n\}$.
- D_v is the set of domains, with val_i representing the set of all possible values for variable V_i
- A set of constraints (Cv) to restrict the value assignment of some variables or configure the components according to their behavioral models.

Figure 3a shows some variables and their related values in the example shown in Figure 2. These constraints will be specified via a user interface yielding a text file of constraint specifications. Using these variables and values, we can derive an initial constraint model for the configuration. For this scenario, the domain knowledge is essentially static and it would be possible to find an initial configuration of components, for example to support a mobile browser, that satisfies the constraints.

In Figure 3a, constraint (wl =/= video) states that if the browser is a wireless device then video content delivery is not supported. The (wired = audio) means that the wired browsers are allowed to download audio clips providing that the constraints between the other necessary variables are not violated for this audio clip download. Constraint (wl =/= E) states that a user with Economy QoS Package is prevented from using wireless browsers to access the services provided in our system.

Domains (D$_v$):	Variables (V):
DPSnode : local, remote, intermediate	n : DPSnode
Proxylet : wap, comp, decomp, deployment, config,	pl : Proxylet
rtpRx, rtpTx, realPlayer, handoff	b : Browser
Browser : wired, wl	p : Payload
Payload : text, audio, video	q : QoSPack
QoS Pack : G, S, E	m : Mode
Mode : realTime, download	c : Cache
Cache : true, false	
Constraint (C$_v$):	
b, p : (wired = text), (wired = audio), (wired = video), (wl = text), (wl =/= video)	
n, pl : (local = wap), (local = decomp), (local = rtpTx), (local = realPlayer), ...	
b, q : (wired = G), (wired = S), (wired = E), (wl = G), (wl = S), (wl =/= E)	
p, q : (text = G), (text = S), (video = G), (video =/= S), (video =/= E), (audio =/= E)	
....	

Fig. 3a. Domain Knowledge - Variables, Values and Compatibility Constraints

In Figure 3b, some of the complete set of constraint based configurations (CBC), which have been derived from the domain knowledge shown in Figure 3a, are listed. These configuration setups in XML will be the output of the system presented in section 4 of this paper.

CBC_1(Pack=>Gold, payload=>audio) ={	CBC_2 (Pack=Gold, payload=audio) = {
wired-browser, realtime-listening,	wirelessbrowser, downloadmode,
dps-local => (decompression-Proxylet,	**dps-local** -> (deployment-Proxylet,
realtime-audio-player-applet-	handoffProxylet, wired-wireless-
proxylet, rtpProxylet, deployment-	converter-proxylet,
Proxylet,),	decompression-Proxylet)
dps-remote => (compression-proxylet)	**dps-remote** => (compression-
}	proxylet) }

Fig. 3b. Sample Constraint Based Proxylet Configuration Setups.

The CBC_1 is for the case when the payload is audio and the QoS for the user is Gold which will lead to a real time listening of the audio stream. In this case, the required resources to be configured for a wired-browser are a realtime-audio-player-proxylet, location-proxylet, real-time-protocol (rtp) proxylet to be downloaded on local DPS and Compression proxylet at the DPS which is optimally located close to the server.

4   Implementation Approach

Step 1: Constraint Verification using Alcoa / Alloy

We are using "Alcoa / Alloy" constraint analyzer [15] which can perform a deep semantic analysis of models that incorporate complex textual constraints. Using this tool, we have checked the consistency of our constraints, generated sample configurations, simulated execution of operations, and checked that operations preserve constraints. The Alloy language is used to specify constraints and the Alcoa tool for analysis of the constraints. We used Alcoa to interactively define the configuration scenario, incorporating constraints, in only 65 lines of Alloy code. However it is not possible to generate executable Java code from this. We use the Java Constraint Libraries to program our constraint based configuration of Proxylets similar to the Alcoa approach, as explained in Step 2 below. The main purpose of using Alloy for initial checking is to reduce development cycle time by detecting errors prior to implementation.

We specify the scenario plus relevant constraints relating to the components in Alloy. Alcoa is a compiler which translates the model definition into a very large boolean formula. This formula then gets solved by the SAT solver in the tool and the solution is interpreted back into Alloy language for the model. Next, a paragraph or schema (e.g. a constraint) in the model is selected to be run for verification. Alcoa responds with an instance or with a message if no instance was found. We may then choose to edit the model, recompile or run. So, using this tool, we are able to analyze the constraints more effectively prior to the Java implementation of our constraint based Proxylet configuration framework.

Figure 4 shows the Alloy specification for the scenario. An invariant (denoted by key word **inv**) defines a constraint in the **model** being defined. For example, inv PLC1 indicates that the wireless browsers does not have the feature of downloading a video stream. Condition (**cond**) gives a hint to Alcoa on generating a sample architectural instance over a given scope.

Step 2: Current Implementation

Initially, all the constraint variables, domain values and compatibility constraints, which were analyzed using Alcoa, are manually derived from an Alloy model definition. For example, the wireless browser is constrained by the **PLC1** invariant in Alloy. This invariant is mapped to the format shown in figure 5 for implementation purposes.

The Constraint Solution Mechanism takes in all these parameters and generates partial configuration setups (subset of constraint variables which satisfy all the of the constraints within the subset) for the constraint specified. These subsets are stored in ConstraintDB as initial basic configuration setups (as shown in Figure 6). The ConstraintDB is currently stored in a text file but a relational database or directory would be needed for a large scale system with 100s of DPSs and Proxylets. The Java Constraint Library has been used to implement the mechanism for populating the ConstraintDB. The constraint variables, values and the compatibility constraints can be specified or modified via the ConstraintDB UI. When a modification is made to the constraint specification, the ConstraintDB has to be regenerated to reflect the changes and possibly new proxylets will have to be downloaded to an appropriate DPS and executed when there is a request for a HTTP content delivery.

```
model ALPINE {
  domain {browser, proxylet, payload, DPS}
  state {
    // The following are the subjects or values of the variables and
    // their relationships in accordance to the ALOCA syntax.
    disjoint wireless, wired : browser
    partition text, audio, video: payload
    disjoint E, S, G: QoSPack
    partition local, remote : DPS
    partition wapplet, decompresplet, compresplet, configplet, ...
    requires: browser -> local!
    runs: DPS -> proxylet+
    ......
    supports: browser -> payload
    comp : compresplet -> payload+
    decomp: decompresplet  -> payload+
    ......
  }
  ......
  inv PLC1 { all b:wireless | b.supports != video }
  inv PL1 { sole p:locationplet | p in local.runs }
  ......
  cond con1 {
    some DPS1:local|some DPS2: remote|one b:wireless|(DPS1 != DPS2)
  }
  ......
}
```

Fig. 4. Alloy Sepecification of Scenarion Constraints

Figure 6 shows the interactions involved. A DPS near the user's browser is loaded with the *config proxylet,* if it is not already running. The user-specific constraint variables and values are passed to the *config proxylet* to start selecting a suitable configuration setup (e.g. the parameters required by the config proxylet in the scenario are type of browser, class of service and the content type to be downloaded). In a real system, these parameters could be detected automatically, but in our implementation, they are entered manually via a user interface.

(b) browser (p) payload: (wired = text), (wired = audio), (wired = video), (wl = text), (wl = audio), (wl =/= video)

Fig. 5. Constraints between Browser and Payload

For a given set of constraint variables and their values, the ConstraintDB is queried and searched for a set of suitable configuration subsets to be composed to make a complete parameter list. The configuration process also involves identifying a DPS close to the web server which contains the requested content. During this process, the

Proxylet Store (PIB) is also checked to determine if the required proxylets are available in the network. The PIB is currently an XML file but could be a database or directory for a large scale system. If the *config proxylet* could not find a suitable configuration satisfying the compatibility constraints e.g. because a particular proxylet cannot be found or a suitable server is not available, then an error is flagged.

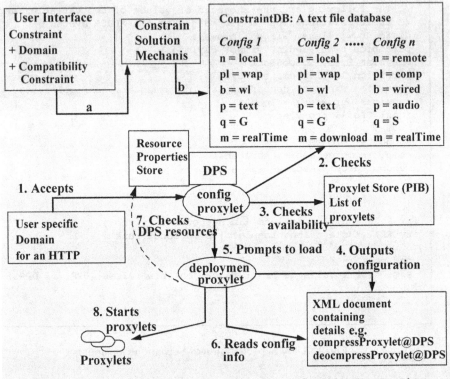

Fig. 6 . Prototype Implementation of Proxylet Configuration Framework

The final configuration is translated into a list of the URLs of the needed proxylets and their corresponding execution environments in a single XML document and submitted to the DPS *deployment proxylet* via the load() method. The *deployment proxylet* is started by the *config proxylet* on the same DPS. The configuration setup is also displayed in the GUI in the form shown in Figure 3b. For demonstration purpose, this GUI also allows the user to select whether the device is wired or wireless; class of user; video, audio, or text service etc. The *config* and *deployment proxylets* can contain multiple threads each of which is working on a different configuration for multiple users.

The *deployment proxylet* running at a local DPS chooses a suitable configuration setup by checking against its resource capability before downloading the computational proxylets or requesting the other DPSs to download the computational proxylets to perform the actual service required by the user. The *deployment proxylet* will also be able to determine whether installing a set of proxylets (on one or more

DPSs) violate constraints relating to available resources by checking against the properties of DPSs. However, this feature is not currently implemented in our experimental model. The availability of the resources for the constraint based configuration can be reserved. We intend to extend the *deployment proxylet* to perform checks on the bandwidth of the links between the DPS-local and DPS-remote to make sure it can handle the bit-rate required by the user. The current Framework also has a User Interfaces (UI) for modifying the configuration and specifying constraints.

5 Further Work

We intend to apply constraint specification to resource management so that allocation of Proxylets to nodes can take into consideration DPS loading, link bandwidth requirements etc. This includes routing decisions for choosing a path from source to destination. Dynamic configuration of an application may take different forms:

- Programs and users may interact with an editable model of the underlying application - adding or removing proxylets, changing intermediate-DPS or modifying the settings of connections. One of the major requirements for a dynamically configurable system is that it should allow the possibility of modifying the provisioning of the components, without requiring an application restart or any changes to the existing code. In order to integrate a new component to the current topology, the system needs to perform a series of checks for constraint compatibility.
- User mobility may result in variations of QoS due to fading or loss of radio signal, which DPS is local to the user etc. Thus the configuration constraints will dynamically change requiring updates to the topology. Connections between DPSs may have to be rerouted, or a proxylet performing a 'local' function may have to be migrated to a different DPS which is now local to the user. This means that the topology which was originally adopted has to be reconfigured using a different CSP.
- We are also looking into using the Ponder policy specification language [6] to define authorization policy in terms of what services a user is permitted to access and QoS policy in terms of what resources such as bandwidth should be allocated for an application or a user. Our approach is to translate these policy statements into constraint specifications for the proxylet deployment.

There are several interesting issues emerging from this work that need further investigation. One of the key issues is *Proxylet Migration*. It is a mechanism to continue the execution of a proxylet on another DPS node and it includes the transport of data stream and execution state of the proxylet. Migration only makes sense under certain network and resource conditions. So, here the basic motivations for proxylet migration are, to support user mobility or re-routing the data stream to maintain required QoS. This may be handled by adopting a constraint based re-routing mechanism.

We are concentrating on the infrastructure support for constraint based configuration, but in order for this to be useful to non-technical users, a very simple user-interface (UI) would be needed. We consider that it will be easier to investigate the UI once we have a clearer idea of the full functionality of the infrastructure support. It may be possible to make much of the functionality completely transparent to the user. For example, the user may not need to select a class of service, but would be allocated one depending on what service they have signed up for.

6   Related Work

The programmable network has been identified in [1] as an important research area from which ALAN has been identified as a key subtopic in [2]. In our current work, we are attempting to address problems in deploying proxylets and solving issues in dynamic routing with proxylets for programmable networks. We are also aware of some of the work done on runtime resource management for advanced network services, similar to that in active networking.

Work on constraint satisfaction problem (CSP) has a long history in the field of Artificial Intelligence (AI) engineering [10]. CSP has been used for a range of applications such as aircraft maintenance scheduling, route planning for setting up the links for virtual private networks and various monitoring and control applications [11], but we are unaware of any other applications of CSP to configuration management in a programmable or active networks.

Programmable networks is a very active research area, but there is not much work on configuration of components. In the early work on ALAN [3], a similar application scenario based on streaming audio was described, but the proxylet configuration was performed manually. BT Colleagues in the ALAN project are using policy-based adaptive control techniques with genetic algorithms to configure proxylets for services [5, 13]. The idea is that the 'useful' proxylets, e.g. those that generate income for a service provider, will be replicated and propagated around the network whereas less useful ones will gradually die out. In our environment this would improve the probability that a required proxylet is already loaded in an appropriate DPS, but it would still have to be configured into a specific application. The paper does not address the issue of how to select a set of distributed proxylets for a particular application or service.

Lancaster University colleagues are working on composing a complete functional proxylet for a service from predefined set of sub-components specified using XML [12]. The selection criteria could be based on the characteristics of the specific DPS platform. Part of our future work activities will be to investigate whether our constraint approach can be used to automate the composition of proxylet sub-components at run-time or whether the funtionality of the proxylet can be adapted by means of invoking management operations with new configuration parameters during runtime.

There is considerable interest in using policies as a means specifying adaptive behaviour in programmable networks. Some initial work on policies for both management and security is described in [7] and work on policy based content delivery in an ALAN environment is described in [14]. However, none of the above have addressed configuration of proxylets in a policy based AN. In ALAN, an enforcement of management or authentication policy means systematically making use of functional proxylets in the system. Some of our work will look at how the constraints can be deduced from, for example, authentication policies.

In our project, we considered a novel approach for the configuration of proxylets in ALAN with two main domains in mind: constraint based configuration and support for dynamic routing. This led to the design of new framework for the configuration management of proxylets. First we targeted the new trend in networking related to "policy based content delivery", then we approached the problem of how the proxylets can be configured without violating any pre-defined constraints. The aim is to produce an interactive real-time display for immediate diagnosis of configuration problems. There is not much work currently being done on interactive configuration management systems for active programmable networks. Our past work on interactive configuration management of distributed systems [8] inspired us to look at whether any of these ideas can be applied to proxylet configuration supporting the mobility of users. The Active Node (DPS) built with our above-mentioned framework can allocate resources to the various virtual end-to-end networks, undertaking configuration and reconfiguration functions with routing decisions and making the network more responsive to users' demands.

7   Summary

In this paper, we described our initial implementation of constraint based configuration of proxylets. We have shown that it is possible to automate the selection and deployment of proxylets while satisfying diverse constraints related to a QoS class, what the users are permitted to do and what types of devices they are using. Although we have focused on configuration of proxylets in a programmable network environment, this approach could be used for deployments of software components in any distributed processing environment.

An ubiquitous computing environment [16] could benefit from our framework. The mobile users will be able to join in the ALAN network without the need touse pre-configured or resource rich mobile browsers. The on-demand services could be dynamically composed and executed on local or intermediate nodes with the help of functional proxylets. For example, the user does not have to figure out which system supports an on-demand service since our framework could deploy the necessary components and protocols along the end-to-end path to enable a service to be reached at an end system.

Acknowledgements

We gratefully acknowledge the support of British Telecom for ALPINE research project as well as comments and suggestions from our colleagues involved in this project.

References

1. D.L. Tennenhouse and D.J. Wetherall, "Towards the Active Network Architecture", ACM Computer Comms. Review, vol. 26, no. 2, pp. 5-18, Apr. 1996.
2. "Alpine: Application Level Programmable Inter-Network Environment", http://www.cs.ucl.ac.uk/research/alpine/
3. M. Fry and A. Ghosh, "Application Layer Active Networking", Computer Networks, 31, 7, pp. 655-667, 1999.
4. Mittal and Falkenhainer, "Dynamic Constraint Satisfaction Problems", In proceedings of the 8th AAAI, pages 25-32, 1990
5. I.W.Marshall and P.Mckee, "A Policy Based Management Architecture for Large Scale Active Communication Systems" in Policies for Distributed Systems and Networks, LNCS 1995, ed. Sloman, Lobo and Lupu, Springer-Verlag 2001
6. N. Damianou, N. Dulay, E. Lupu, and M. Sloman: "The Ponder Specification Language", Proc. Policy 2001: Workshop on Policies for Distributed Systems and Networks, Bristol, UK, 29-31 Jan. 2001, Springer-Verlag LNCS 1995, pp. 18-39.
7. M. Sloman and E. Lupu, "Policy Specification for Programmable Networks", In proc. 1st Int Working Conference, IWAN'99, Berlin, Germany, June/July 1999, LNCS 1653, p. 73 ff.
8. H. Fossa and M. Sloman, "Implementing Interactive Configuration Management for Distributed System", Int Conf on Configurable Distributed Systems (ICCDS' 96), Annapolis, Maryland, May 1996, Proceedings pub by IEEE press.
9. "Java Constraint Library", http://liawww.epfl.ch/~torrens/Project/JCL/.
10. E. Freuder, and A. Mackworth, "Constraint-Based Reasoning", Artificial Intelligence, 1992, 58.
11. C. Lecki, "Experience and Trends in AI for Network Monitoring and Diagnosis", Proceedings IJCAI-95 Workshop on AI in Distributed Information Networks.
12. S. Simpson, P. Smith, M. Banfield, and D. Hutchison, "Component Compatibility for Heterogeneous Active Networking", Presented at IEE Informatics, Nov. 2000, London. http://www.activenet.lancs.ac.uk/papers/ieealan2000.pdf
13. I.W. Marshall and C.M. Roadknight "Adaptive Management of an Active Services Network" BT Technical Journal special issue on "Biologically Inspired Computing", 18, 4, pp78-84 Oct. 2000.
14. G. MacLarty and M. Fry, "Policy-based Content Delivery: an Active Network Approach", 5th Int Web Caching and Content Delivery Workshop. http://www.terena.nl/conf/wcw/Proceedings/S7/S7-2.pdf
15. D. Jackson, I. Schechter and I. Shlyakhter, "Alcoa: the Alloy Constraint Analyzer", Proc. ICSE, Limerick, Ireland, June 2000.
16. D. Milojicic, A. Messer, P. Bernadat, I. Greenberg and W. Schroder-Preikschat, "ψ-Pervasive Services Infrastructure", HP Labs, Palo Alto, USA, http://www.hpl.hp.com/techreports/2001/HPL-2001-87.html.

Author Index

Lecture Notes in Computer Science

For information about Vols. 1–2084
please contact your bookseller or Springer-Verlag

Vol. 2124: W. Skarbek (Ed.). Computer Analysis of Images and Patterns. Proceedings, 2001. XV, 743 pages. 2001.

Vol. 2125: F. Dehne, J.-R. Sack, R. Tamassia (Eds.), Algorithms and Data Structures. Proceedings, 2001. XII, 484 pages. 2001.

Vol. 2126: P. Cousot (Ed.), Static Analysis. Proceedings, 2001. XI, 439 pages. 2001.

Vol. 2127: V. Malyshkin (Ed.), Parallel Computing Technologies. Proceedings, 2001. XII, 516 pages. 2001.

Vol. 2129: M. Goemans, K. Jansen, J.D.P. Rolim, L. Trevisan (Eds.), Approximation, Randomization, and Combinatorial Optimization. Proceedings, 2001. IX, 297 pages. 2001.

Vol. 2130: G. Dorffner, H. Bischof, K. Hornik (Eds.), Artificial Neural Networks – ICANN 2001. Proceedings, 2001. XXII. 1259 pages. 2001.

Vol. 2132: S.-T. Yuan, M. Yokoo (Eds.), Intelligent Agents. Specification, Modeling, and Application. Proceedings, 2001. X, 237 pages. 2001. (Subseries LNAI).

Vol. 2136: J. Sgall, A. Pultr, P. Kolman (Eds.), Mathematical Foundations of Computer Science 2001. Proceedings, 2001. XII, 716 pages. 2001.

Vol. 2138: R. Freivalds (Ed.), Fundamentals of Computation Theory. Proceedings, 2001. XIII, 542 pages. 2001.

Vol. 2139: J. Kilian (Ed.), Advances in Cryptology – CRYPTO 2001. Proceedings, 2001. XI, 599 pages. 2001.

Vol. 2141: G.S. Brodal, D. Frigioni, A. Marchetti-Spaccamela (Eds.), Algorithm Engineering. Proceedings, 2001. X, 199 pages. 2001.

Vol. 2142: L. Fribourg (Ed.), Computer Science Logic. Proceedings, 2001. XII, 615 pages. 2001.

Vol. 2143: S. Benferhat, P. Besnard (Eds.), Symbolic and Quantitative Approaches to Reasoning with Uncertainty. Proceedings, 2001. XIV, 818 pages. 2001. (Subseries LNAI).

Vol. 2146: J.H. Silverman (Eds.), Cryptography and Lattices. Proceedings, 2001. VII, 219 pages. 2001.

Vol. 2147: G. Brebner, R. Woods (Eds.), Field-Programmable Logic and Applications. Proceedings, 2001. XV, 665 pages. 2001.

Vol. 2149: O. Gascuel, B.M.E. Moret (Eds.). Algorithms in Bioinformatics. Proceedings, 2001. X, 307 pages. 2001.

Vol. 2150: R. Sakellariou, J. Keane, J. Gurd, L. Freeman (Eds.), Euro-Par 2001 Parallel Processing. Proceedings. 2001. XXX, 943 pages. 2001.

Vol. 2151: A. Caplinskas, J. Eder (Eds.), Advances in Databases and Information Systems. Proceedings, 2001. XIII, 381 pages. 2001.

Vol. 2152: R.J. Boulton, P.B. Jackson (Eds.), Theorem Proving in Higher Order Logics. Proceedings, 2001. X, 395 pages. 2001.

Vol. 2153: A.L. Buchsbaum, J. Snoeyink (Eds.), Algorithm Engineering and Experimentation. Proceedings. 2001. VIII, 231 pages. 2001.

Vol. 2154: K.G. Larsen, M. Nielsen (Eds.), CONCUR 2001 – Concurrency Theory. Proceedings, 2001. XI, 583 pages. 2001.

Vol. 2157: C. Rouveirol, M. Sebag (Eds.), Inductive Logic Programming. Proceedings, 2001. X, 261 pages. 2001. (Subseries LNAI).

Vol. 2158: D. Shepherd, J. Finney, L. Mathy, N. Race (Eds.), Interactive Distributed Multimedia Systems. Proceedings, 2001. XIII, 258 pages. 2001.

Vol. 2159: J. Kelemen, P. Sosík (Eds.), Advances in Artificial Life. Proceedings, 2001. XIX, 724 pages. 2001. (Subseries LNAI).

Vol. 2161: F. Meyer auf der Heide (Ed.), Algorithms – ESA 2001. Proceedings, 2001. XII. 538 pages. 2001.

Vol. 2162: Ç. K. Koç, D. Naccache, C. Paar (Eds.), Cryptographic Hardware and Embedded Systems – CHES 2001. Proceedings, 2001. XIV. 411 pages. 2001.

Vol. 2164: S. Pierre, R. Glitho (Eds.), Mobile Agents for Telecommunication Applications. Proceedings, 2001. XI. 292 pages. 2001.

Vol. 2165: L. de Alfaro, S. Gilmore (Eds.), Process Algebra and Probabilistic Methods. Proceedings, 2001. XII. 217 pages. 2001.

Vol. 2166: V. Matoušek, P. Mautner, R. Mouček, K. Taušer (Eds.), Text, Speech and Dialogue. Proceedings. 2001. XIII, 452 pages. 2001. (Subseries LNAI).

Vol. 2170: S. Palazzo (Ed.), Evolutionary Trends of the Internet. Proceedings, 2001. XIII. 722 pages. 2001.

Vol. 2172: C. Batini, F. Giunchiglia, P. Giorgini, M. Mecella (Eds.), Cooperative Information Systems. Proceedings, 2001. XI, 450 pages. 2001.

Vol. 2176: K.-D. Althoff, R.L. Feldmann, W. Müller (Eds.), Advances in Learning Software Organizations. Proceedings, 2001. XI, 241 pages. 2001.

Vol. 2177: G. Butler, S. Jarzabek (Eds.), Generative and Component-Based Software Engineering. Proceedings. 2001. X, 203 pages. 2001.

Vol. 2181: C. Y. Westort (Eds.), Digital Earth Moving. Proceedings. 2001. XII, 117 pages. 2001.

Vol. 2184: M. Tucci (Ed.), Multimedia Databases and Image Communication. Proceedings, 2001. X, 225 pages. 2001.

Vol. 2186: J. Bosch (Ed.), Generative and Component-Based Software Engineering. Proceedings, 2001. VIII, 17 pages. 2001.

Vol. 2188: F. Bomarius, S. Komi-Sirviö (Eds.), Product Focused Software Process Improvement. Proceedings 2001. XI, 382 pages. 2001.

Vol. 2189: F. Hoffmann, D.J. Hand, N. Adams, D. Fisher, G. Guimaraes (Eds.), Advances in Intelligent Data Analysis. Proceedings, 2001. XII, 384 pages. 2001.

Vol. 2190: A. de Antonio, R. Aylett, D. Ballin (Eds.), Intelligent Virtual Agents. Proceedings, 2001. VIII. 24 pages. 2001. (Subseries LNAI).

Vol. 2191: B. Radig, S. Florczyk (Eds.), Pattern Recognition. Proceedings, 2001. XVI, 452 pages. 2001.

Vol. 2193: F. Casati, D. Georgakopoulos, M.-C. Shan (Eds.), Technologies for E-Services. Proceedings, 2001. X, 213 pages. 2001.